W9-BOB-749

And to Think
I GOT IN FREE!

And to Think
I GOT IN FREE!

Highlights from Fifty Years on the Sports Beat

Jim Taylor

HARBOUR PUBLISHING

Copyright © 2010 Jim Taylor

1 2 3 4 5 — 14 13 12 11 10

All rights reserved. No part of this publication may be reproduced, stored in a retrieval system or transmitted, in any form or by any means, without prior permission of the publisher or, in the case of photocopying or other reprographic copying, a licence from Access Copyright, www.accesscopyright.ca, 1-800-893-5777, info@accesscopyright.ca.

Harbour Publishing Co. Ltd.
P.O. Box 219, Madeira Park, BC, V0N 2H0
www.harbourpublishing.com

Edited by Ian Whitelaw
Cover illustration by Bob Krieger
Printed and bound in Canada

Harbour Publishing acknowledges financial support from the Government of Canada through the Canada Book Fund and the Canada Council for the Arts, and from the Province of British Columbia through the BC Arts Council and the Book Publishing Tax Credit.

Canada Council   Conseil des Arts
for the Arts   du Canada

BRITISH COLUMBIA
ARTS COUNCIL
An agency of the Province of British Columbia

Library and Archives Canada Cataloguing in Publication

Taylor, Jim, 1937–
    And to think I got in free! : highlights from fifty years on the sports beat / Jim Taylor.

Includes index.
ISBN 978-1-55017-499-1

    1. Sports. 2. Sports—Canada. I. Title.

GV707.T385 2010   796   C2010-903881-9

For Victoria's *Daily Colonist,* for my first job and first byline; the Vancouver *Times,* for big-city exposure and impossible do-everything deadlines; and most of all to *The Vancouver Sun, The Province* and the *Calgary Sun,* for allowing me to do it my way, and now to relive the best parts on these pages. I can't thank you enough.

Contents

Foreword . . .   9

1   Just For Laughs   13

2   To Absent Friends   37

3   Time Out for Romance   62

4   The Puck Stops Here   80

5   History Lessons   106

6   When in Doubt, Punt   117

7   "You Wanna Write About *What*???"   150

8   Okay, Sometimes I Got Mad   175

9   Life with Fred and Martha   208

10 The Sweet Science   224

11 Sex and the (Semi-) Single Jock   242

12 Some Folks Along the Way   258

Index   285

Foreword . . .

THE FIRST THING I EVER WROTE FOR PUBLICATION was a pack of lies. Come to think of it, that's a lie, too, because it wasn't actually published—it was pinned to the wall above the blackboard in second grade by Miss Guysler, a dark-eyed first year teacher for whom I had the hots, or would have had if I'd known what they were.

She had just written "The sun is setting in the west" on the blackboard. When she asked us to add a second line that would make it a poem, a kid named Johnny Lukoni shot his hand up and said, "The birds are singing in their nest."

"Suck-hole," I whispered.

It never worried me saying things like that, not even to the tough kids. Sure, there was recess and noon hour to get through afterward, but who was going to beat up on a chicken-boned little kid with sticky tape on his glasses—two weeks covering one lens, two weeks covering the other and, later on, the top half of both lenses all the time? ("Lazy eye," the doctor called it. "This will strengthen it." It never did.)

They could tease, and they did. But they couldn't hit me. Not a four-eyed, half-blind wimp. And a sharp-tongued little brat could always get his own back in class. So I needled Johnny Lukoni—until I noticed that Miss Guysler, my fantasy love, was applauding and all the other kids were looking at him as though he'd just invented jawbreakers.

Jeez, all that for one lousy two-line poem when she gives him the first line?

When she asked us all to try to write our *own* two-line poem, I pulled out a sheet of that lined foolscap paper they used to give us that was so rough it still had pieces of pulp sticking out, and wrote one that ran *eight* lines. Eat this, Lukoni!

I can still remember every word:

> I have the cutest little pup,
> On his hind legs he stands up.
> He never, ever runs away,
> For he is very happy and gay.

Second verse:

> My pup can do a lot of tricks.
> He brings me the paper, he picks up sticks.
> And you may be sure that he walks with me,
> And brings me home in time for tea.

Of course, I didn't drink tea. I was seven years old, for God's sake. And I didn't have a pup. In Nipawin, Sask. (pop. 2,300), the paper only came once a week, and I was the kid who delivered it to all 12 subscribers. But Miss Guysler patted my head and said: "Look, class, Jimmy has written an *eight*-line poem! Let's all give him a big clap!"

She pinned it on the blackboard. People read it, and nobody thumped me at recess. Maybe I was on to something here . . .

Okay, maybe Miss Guysler wasn't really the one who gave me the first nudge into the profession that would become my life. Maybe I was fated to be in the writing game from the beginning. If I've proven one thing over the years it was that I had no other marketable talent, although I can't really prove that either, because the media—newspapers, radio, even some television—is the only employment field I've ever played in since I got shoved unwillingly into the sports department of Victoria's *Daily Colonist* as a high school reporter at 17 by an English teacher named Stan Murphy who accepted the job for me before he told me about it and said he'd kick my ass if I didn't take it. Maybe the Good Lord decided a typewriter was my only hope.

The columns assembled here, scribbled and typed and telephoned and laptopped in too many press boxes to remember, are mostly funny, or meant to be. When sport makes instant millionaires out of kids who can hit a ball or a puck with a stick or stuff a leather balloon through a fishnet, what's not to laugh at? Sometimes they are sad. More than once the screen or paper blurred in the writing.

They are tales of good guys and jerks, strivers and fakers, journeymen and giants playing games for a living with the world peering into the fishbowl and bigger, stronger, faster challengers coming at them every year.

Following them has been mostly a joy and sometimes a pain. But staring at blank paper or empty screen with deadline looming, trying to make the words assemble and march and sing—ah, that's been magical.

Enjoy. I did.

—JIM TAYLOR

Just For Laughs

ONCE IN A WHILE I speak to high school journalism or English classes. When you're convinced that the spoken word is sinking into the rap lyric swamp and the written word into cutesie-poo text-message shorthand that, a generation or so down the road, will produce teenagers with extra-long, pointy texting thumbs whose vocal communication is done in primordial grunts when they bother to speak at all— well, you set whatever back fires you can and hope to save a tree or two as the forest turns to ashes around them.

(Oops! The old fart's off again. That guy who called him a dinosaur was right: How does he type with those tiny arms?)

But here's the thing: I like words. I like the way they can paint pictures, the way they can make you laugh and cry and think and react. Words last. Properly assembled, they can march like armies and change the world. If Shakespeare had Twittered, could he have written *Hamlet*? ("2 B or not 2 B. That's the ?")

With the kids, I usually concentrate on humour, trying to convince them that the dreaded 1,000-word essay can actually be an adventure if you're not afraid to go off the wall once in a while to harpoon the ridiculous, make a point with satire or sarcasm, or stick a pin in pomposity and watch it fly all over the room before landing in a deflated heap.

Writing humour isn't easy. When it doesn't work, it just lies there, and sometimes the people you're poking fun at don't see it that way at all. Poke fun at someone else's sport, fine. Just don't be poking fun at theirs.

What they don't understand is that every sport is wide open to mockery. Take baseball. We've all heard about the pinch of garlic, the dose of salt, the ounce of prevention and the pound of cure. The big one is missing: a doze of baseball. To be properly appreciated, baseball requires a great sofa. In an era when hyper-pituitarial giraffes forego their senior year of collegiate basket weaving, square dancing and Parking Lot Supervision 101 to accept millions of dollars to play a game originally invented as a church basement recreation for days when it was raining outside, when 18-year-olds who think high school is a classroom with more than two floors and matriculate on the bus between Melfort and Yorkton are suddenly pulling on NHL caps and deciding whether to buy the Mercedes or the Hummer, I found it increasingly difficult to keep a straight face. So, I didn't . . .

Dear Izaak: No Thanks
Calgary Sun, June 21, 2001

THE INVITATION WAS GRACIOUS: Would I like to take part in a fishing derby?

Translation: Would you like to spend a day on the ocean with your stomach heaving, dropping a barbed hook over the side on the off chance that some fish will bite it so you can haul him into the boat and hit him with a club?

No.

My past is dotted with too many fishing derbies and endless columns about them, written under threat of keel-hauling by the publisher of the paper that sponsored them and signed my cheques.

It ended with the column where the aliens in the UFO were human-fishing, dropping hot-dog-baited lines into elementary school yards and hauling small children into the mother ship for sport and lunch. "You just put the knife here in this thing called the belly button, slit it up and down, wash out the insides and pan-fry 'em in butter," the alien guide explains. "Delicious.

"Oh, and don't worry about the hook hurting them. Humans don't feel pain. All our scientists say so."

The publisher, perhaps suspecting that fisherpeople might not appreciate the subtle humour, demanded to know what was wrong with fishing derbies.

"They're backward," I explained. "People catch fish, bring them in and pour water over them to slow dehydration until the weigh-in. So they're lying there with their mouths open and their eyes glazed—and these are the *winners*? Show me another sport where the winner gets his picture taken hanging from a hook and the losers swim home to the kids."

It was, he agreed, a thought to ponder. But, in the meantime, interview some of the winners—oh, and stop calling them fish-killers.

So I interviewed two: a guy named Karl who said he'd been fishing for 25 years, swore by the Solunar Tables and kept a lifetime chart of every fish he'd caught and where he'd caught it; and a little kid who borrowed a 10-foot boat, rowed 150 yards from the dock, and had one of the big winners landed before the hotshots in the big boats had finished stowing their six-packs.

Three hundred years ago, Izaak Walton, the patron saint of piscine assassination, observed in *The Compleat Angler* that "Angling may be said to be so like the Mathematics, that it can never be fully learnt."

What he didn't mention is that your most dedicated angler might be a few scales short.

Take the guy who took first place in one of the newspaper derbies, had his picture taken and all the stories written, only to be undone by a call from a taxi driver saying that, in the early-morning hours, he'd driven someone who looked just like the guy in the picture to the marina. And he was carrying this honking big fish.

We checked it out.

Strangely enough, there was only the one report of a guy climbing into a cab carrying a huge fish and being dropped off at a marina where they were about to hold a big derby. Faced with the evidence, he 'fessed up. He'd bought the fish, tied it to the end of his boat and hauled it in later.

Between that and the derby where the ferry that had just left came back early to unload a guy who'd attempted to commit suicide, another guy had a heart attack pulling the rope on his outboard and the ambulances roared down the dock while the mariachi band played and the publisher urged us to "keep things upbeat," and the fact that my newspaper career began with typing out lists of derby winners so long I was developing an urge to go upriver and spawn, my interest in pursuing the killer salmon is pretty much nil.

Thanks anyway. But if you do get lucky, I'll bring the pan and the butter.

Who Gives a Spit?
Calgary Sun, March 6, 2001

THERE'S A DRINK ON THE MARKET whose main ingredient is wasp spit. It smells like they misspelled spit.

I'd been wondering about it since that Japanese marathoner, Naoko Takahashi, won the Olympic gold medal in Sydney and called it a crucial factor in her victory.

Key questions flashed through my head:

How do they teach the little suckers to spit? Or do they just take the rude ones who don't know any better?

What if the wasp—which is actually a Japanese killer hornet—doesn't *want* to spit? Three times as big as your average wasp, lethal enough to kill 40 people a year—*you* wanna tell him he has to?

After a hard day flapping their wings 1,000 times a minute and flying miles in search of food, do the guys kick back at night seeing who can hit teensy little wasp spittoons?

If there's a wasp drink, is there also one for Roman Catholics?

But according to one of Vancouver's morning papers, this is serious business. Because among those who've been trying the stuff are . . . sssh!—the BC Lions.

All perfectly legal. The drink, whose name escapes me, has been passed by the Canadian Food Inspection Agency, with a rider that it's a no-no for people allergic to wasps. It's been on the North American market for three years.

But the BC Lions won the Grey Cup last year.

What if we were all wrong, giving the credit to Damon Allen? What if the real MVP was some boorish wasp in Osaka?

Do the Stampeders rush out and buy cases of the stuff? Can Wally Buono really afford to let his troops get caught in the wasp-spit gap?

Will the next Grey Cup MVP interview begin with: "First, I'd like to thank those nameless wasps in Tokyo. I'm comin' to visit y'all, and I'm bringin' honey!"

Or maybe not Tokyo. Apparently the Japanese wasps aren't spitting fast enough to meet the saliva demand, forcing manufacturers to import the extract from the Philippines.

Makes you wonder, doesn't it? How long before we're reading exposés about the exploitation of underage Philippine wasps forced to sit there spitting into bottles, working for a pittance in badly heated, substandard nests?

"But what is this stuff, anyway?" you ask.

Skipping the scientific stuff—which we all know from school is boring so who cares?—the hornet larvae pass the stuff to the hornet through what is called a "kiss." (In school, this was called "swapping spit" and we were told if we did it we'd go blind or something, which shows how much teachers know.)

Apparently it allows the body to burn fat instead of glycogen stored in muscle cells. And—great news!—it works really well on mice!

Scientific tests apparently show that mice given the drink and thrown into the water swam a whole lot longer than mice who went in with nothing more than little red pants and white gloves. Or something. Which, you have to admit, will be really important the day mouse swimming becomes an Olympic event.

Okay, enough science. Time to return to the really important competitive sports like contractual whining, substance abuse, free agency and jock paternity suits. But remember this: The company selling this stuff (what *is* that brand name?) might not be Coca-Cola yet—but it has great expectorations.

Uproar in Deadmonton
Calgary Sun, August 9, 2001

SO, THE BRITS ARE TAKING SHOTS AT EDMONTON. Big deal. What can you expect from a country so small that if you dropped it in the middle of British Columbia you might forget where you left it? And it would be a good idea.

Yessir, boy, there's nothing quite like kicking back in the fog with a warm, flat beer recalling the day Cedric's horse stepped on the polo ball during the big match at Pimple-on-Thigh, or reading great-grand-papa's diaries about the days when he was stationed in Inja and the sun never set on the British Empire. (See: Lost Civilizations.)

Edmonton should be amused—you know, like Queen Victoria said she wasn't? Because the shooting was so deucedly, well, *amateurish*.

"A visually unappealing corner of Canada"?

"Deadmonton"?

What's next—"Nya-nya-nya, your mother boffed Lord Nelson"?

These guys should be forced to read from the works of Jim Murray, one-two with Red Smith, the best sporting journalist who ever pounded an Underwood.

Murray was a self-described "serial killer of cities" who once visited Edmonton, watched the locals curling, and fired off a column exposing The Great Overshoe Conspiracy.

The city took it well, knowing it had merely been swatted in passing by the man who once wrote that if the Russians ever attacked they would bypass Cincinnati, as it looked as if it had already been taken and destroyed. And, on seeing a year later that the freeway was still unfinished, noted that it must have been Kentucky's turn to use the cement mixer.

He wasn't just a city-slagger. His column's opening line the day of the Indianapolis 500 auto race was "Gentlemen, start your coffins." Quarterback John Brodie, he wrote, was "slower than fourth-class mail." But as the seasons passed with one town or another it was the city shots that caught the most attention—so deftly done that it reached the point where cities felt slighted if he visited and *didn't* slag them.

Minneapolis and St. Paul "don't like each other, and from what I can see I don't blame either one of them." Lexington was the place where "they roll up the sidewalks at 11 . . . a.m." Cleveland was "like two Newarks."

If you go to St. Louis, he wrote, "take off your shoes so as not to wake it up." New York's principal purpose was "to catch all the chewing gum chewed in the world and line all the subway platforms with it"

Un-awed by the Kentucky Derby, he snarled that Louisville "smelled like an old bar rag." New Jersey was "a great state if you were a ball-bearing," and if you didn't have a tattoo they knew you were a tourist.

When a track meet was held in Warsaw he wondered how anyone

would get there "since nobody ever went to Warsaw except on the back of a tank or the front of a bayonet."

And Edmontonians are upset about "Deadmonton"? Why? The self-styled "Fleet Street gunners" have fired naught but spitballs.

Mind you, in the lovely city of Edmonton there seems to be, from mayor to media, a frantic preoccupation with being *liked*, a stamp-their-foot determination that it is so a big, world-class city, so there, and is prepared to hold its breath till it dies if you don't admit it.

That's why it keeps bidding for, and so often winning, world-stage sporting events that, in the manner of all the smaller Canadian cities, it stages in a world-class manner. It's going to be on the map, boy, just you wait.

Hindsight says staging the world track and field championships there probably was a mistake. This isn't a track and field nation any more than Great Britain is gaga over hockey. Nor should we feel any obligation to be.

Associations don't rule on what's popular, people do. The IAAF can huff all it wants about the need to show the world a full stadium. It's their need, not ours. Would Wembley fill for the Stamps vs. the Esks?

As for the Brits, worry not, Edmonton. They'll soon be gone, back to that lovely land where, on a clear day . . . oh, sorry.

Hoot, Mon
Calgary Sun, December 17, 2000

IN SCOTLAND TODAY they'll be throwing themselves on their brooms, commiserating with the sheep or, worse yet, eating the haggis.

The country where curling was born will not be competing in the world championships in Switzerland next year. Not the men, anyway, although what with the kilts and all it would be difficult to tell the difference. They can't. They were beaten out for seventh place in the European championships.

By the French.

That's right: France 8, Scotland 2, in a tie-breaker to see which rink back-doored it into the worlds. It's like the US losing a war with Monaco. The Scots haven't been that shaken since somebody raised the price of porridge.

This is their game, damnit.

They invented it, developed it from the simple roots of picking rocks from the hillsides (because they were free) and rolling them down on unsuspecting Englishmen. (See: Rock and Roll.)

They nursed it from the frozen lochs to the drafty rinks with the pot-bellied stove surrounded by pot-bellied curlers and into winter clubs so posh that when curlers discuss ice quality they mean the cubes in the scotch.

They invented the lounge, where people whose rinks have already been eliminated can pick up a drink or a companion while staring down at the ice and second-guessing the ones who beat them.

Without the Scots there might never have been the push-broom, developed because curlers who'd done too much second-guessing the night before (See: Lounge) found them easier to lean on while pretending to sweep.

Name one other nation that's invented a game where a fat man can be narrow and a skinny man wide.

Show me another game where a team member's duties are so clearly defined by name: the Lead, who's first to the bar; the Second, who's just behind him; the Third, who's often required to clean up after both of them; and the Skip, so named because he's never there to pick up the tab.

Oh, they made a few mistakes.

It's pretty hard to claim the game takes intelligence when you'll never have to count higher than eight.

It might have been smarter not to call both the teams and the places they play in "rinks" and have their kids growing up believing that the best place to throw rocks is in the house.

They might have done a better job explaining about sweeping, and how, when the dirty rocks go down the ice, there's a reason you clean in front of them where they'll only get it dirty again, instead of behind them where they've just dirtied it up.

The "end" thing probably hurt the game's development. Prospective curlers tend to glaze over when you explain how the game is played.

"You play the first end by throwing all the rocks to the other end. Then you go to that end and play the second end by throwing them back to this end."

"Wouldn't it be easier just to leave them here in the first place?"

"No, because after the second end you end up having to throw them back to the other end."

"That would be the end we just left?"

"Right. That end. As opposed to this end, which would, of course, be that end if you happened to be standing down there and throwing down here. You do that 10 times, and that's the end."

"It's over?"

"Unless they're tied after the last end, in which case it isn't."

"Isn't what?"

"The end."

The confusion may be part of the reason the game hasn't been developing good young male curlers. The Scots had the same problem developing good female golfers. They didn't understand about the ball-washer.

Low Bridge
Calgary Sun, March 4, 2000

MARC HODLER WANTS BRIDGE to be recognized as an Olympic sport, which pretty much clears up the question of who'd be dummy.

"I'm a firm believer that the human brain is at least as important as muscles," says the man who opened the worm can on Olympic bribery and left IOC members scrambling to cover their blazered butts.

Possibly because the IOC isn't sure how many other rocks Hodler might be prepared to overturn, it has given him his way and agreed to recognize bridge as a sport.

But that's not good enough for Hodler, himself a bridge fanatic. (Is there no end to coincidence?) He now wants it accepted as a demonstration sport at the 2002 Winter Games in Salt Lake City, the traditional first step toward eventual full-medal acceptance.

Bridge, an Olympic sport. From the wonderful folks who've brought you ballroom dancing: Shuffling! Dealing! Bidding! Coming soon to an Olympiad near you!

"To hell with the Canada-Russia hockey, Mabel, let's get over to the bridge tournament or we'll miss the breaking-the-deck-seal ceremony. I hear they're using Bicycle cards!"

Personally, I blame the ballroom dancers. Once they talked their way into the Olympics, sport as we knew it was over.

But at least the dancers are athletes. A decathloner thinks he's in shape, let's see him make it to the jitterbug finals. But bridge as a spectator sport? Bridge on live TV?

"Well, Fred, it looks as though Canada has won the deal against the Americans. How do you read that as this great field of masters embarks on the historic first Olympian rubber?"

"Bob, I just don't know. On one hand, you get to shuffle, and we all know what sort of edge that could give a team like, say, the Americans, recruited from Las Vegas, and what they might have up their well-starched sleeves. But on the other hand—you should excuse the pun, ha-ha—the other team gets to cut, which could negate any shuffle ploy the dealer might attempt."

"That's right, Fred. And already we have a controversy reminiscent of the America's Cup keel wars: Just which shuffling technique will the Canadians use?"

"Exactly right, Bob. Security has been watertight around their training table. There's been speculation that they'll go for the traditional split-deck, both-halves-on-the-table, interlace-the-corners. Others insist it will be the cup-the-palms-and-riffle technique made popular in the James Bond movies."

"Well, we'll know in a matter of seconds, and let me tell the millions watching, you could cut the electricity with a knife."

"Although we wouldn't advise it. Ha-ha."

"And here's the shuffle—IT'S THE SPLIT-DECK! They went for the split-deck, Bob! And it seems to have the Las Vegas pair in total confusion! Let's go live now to the table and listen to the Canadian dealer via lapel mike as he attempts to press the advantage!"

("One for you, one for you, one for you, one for me. Two for you, two for you, two for you, and two for me. Three for . . .")

"The Americans are screaming, Fred! 'Table talk! Table talk!' They're pounding the table with their slippers! Now they've knocked it over! They're throwing the card boxes at each other!"

"I tell you, Bob, in all the years this veteran reporter has covered the no-quarter world of top-level bridge, I've never seen anything like it. Good Lord! I think— pan that camera over section 2!—Yes! They've *awakened the spectators!*"

Stay tuned. There's a report out of Spain that Juan Antonio Samaranch likes Parcheesi.

Go, Slobbies, Go!
The Province, June 18, 1985

OUR PAPER IS FULL OF TRENDY ORGANIZATIONS these days—Yuppies, Puppies, Yubbies—a classic example of journalism at its shoddiest.

I have nothing against Young Urban Professionals, Young Urban Breadwinners or any of those other groups who seem to feel it's not what you do, it's how you dress, eat, think and drive while you're doing it. But *The Province* has overlooked the biggest, most dedicated group of all, and frankly I think it's a damned shame.

I refer, of course, to the Slobbies.

Slobbies are the athletic counter-culture, Nature's attempt to achieve some sort of balance before the jock-minded take over the earth and turn it into one big Vic Tanny's. We started out, most of us, as charter members of SLOBS, the Society to Let Our Bodies Stagnate. Maturity and evolution have brought us to where we stand—actually, sit—today: Slobbies—the Society to Let Our Bodies Indulge to Excess.

Slobbies are neither trendy nor social minded. Not for us the gay, mad whirl. (Remember when you could say "gay, mad whirl" without getting queer looks? Remember when you could say "queer"?) It's all too tiring. But, like the Yuppies, Yubbies and the rest, we have our standards and our code:

- Slobbies think softball is a physical condition.
- Slobbies never drink mineral water, and think diet soft drinks and lite beer are Commie plots.
- Slobbies believe golf would be a great game if they eliminated clubs, balls, tees and the first 18 holes and proceeded immediately to the 19th for the drinking and lying.
- Slobbies are in love with the fat little blonde tap dancer in the Molson Golden commercials.
- Slobbies' lone concession to exercise is to watch *The 60-Second Workout* on TV. Watching the girls in tight leotards increases their pulse rate.
- Slobbies don't care what kind of car they drive, as long as they don't have to walk.
- Slobbies know that when one of their members shows up the

day after his birthday in matching joggers and track suit, his wife is after the insurance money.
- Slobbies know that joggers are people too stupid to figure out why they're sweating.
- Devout Slobbies believe that if God had meant man to cover ground at anything faster than a walk, he'd have an exhaust pipe sticking out his fanny.
- Slobbies' heaven is a condo with a TV set, a sofa, a chocolate layer cake and a six-pack.
- Fashion-conscious Slobbies believe a real track suit should have a pocket for the Racing Form.
- Slobbies feel that anyone stupid enough to go looking for a wall of pain deserves to find it.
- Slobbies know Rosie Ruiz had the right idea.
- Slobbies believe the Charter of Human Rights is an all-male fishing trip with a stocked cooler and at least one tourist who believes you can draw to an inside straight.
- Slobbies are constantly recruiting new members for the women's auxiliary (the lovely Slobbettes) as part of their poignant, never-ending search for Ms. Right—a curvaceous and pliable lady, strong of wrist for the removal of twist-off caps and willing to do wonderful things with lasagne.

We are not Yuppies or Yubbies any more than in the old days we were Yippies or Hippies. We are Slobbies, and proud of it. We'll even drink a toast to ourselves. If you're buying.

Greenhorn at Wembley
The Vancouver Sun, March 23, 1978

HE WAS A LITTLE MAN in a blue trench coat who looked like he might pick your pocket or cop your watch. He spoke like a man wearing novocaine lipstick.

"Yrlookinfrtickets?"

"I beg your pardon?"

"Tickets," he muttered, peering fearfully around the mob. "Yrlookinfrticketsornot?"

Well, you know how I feel about ticket scalpers. Bloodsuckers, they are. Jockstrap vampires. Should be folded, stapled, spindled and mutilated. Two little holes punched in their lower orchestra.

You know that business about the guy who paid $50 for two tickets to the Canucks-Canadiens game, then got escorted out of Pacific Coliseum by the police because the tickets were stolen? I read that and laughed. Serves him right, boy. Anybody who'd deal with a scalper . . .

But this was different. I was on the concourse outside Wembley Stadium—*Wembley!*—an hour before the Liverpool–Notts Forest League Cup game. We'd flown over specially, just to see it. *And I didn't have a ticket!*

That's how I met my first tout.

We were standing among a couple of thousand semi-sober, late-teens/early-20s soccer fans, many of whom were looking for tickets themselves. I don't know how he picked us out. Maybe it was because none of us was carrying anything red and white. Then again, maybe it was because none of us was carrying a beer bottle.

But there he was, materializing as though just beamed down from the *Enterprise.*

"Yrlookinfrtickets?"

Well, I was pretty excited.

"Hey," I yelled to my friends, "there's a guy here with . . ."

"Shuddup!" he hissed. "You tryin' to get me killed?"

He pivoted away from us and stared fixedly at the twin towers of Wembley. With his back turned, he gave me the facts of life.

"Don't show nuthin'," he whispered. "No money—nuthin'! These people sees me with tickets or takin' money, they'll beat me up and take it all—the tickets *and* the money."

"How come?" I whispered back.

"They don't like the way I makes me livin'."

We got down to the negotiations—five tourists trying desperately to look casual and one little man in a trench coat who'd fade into the crowd at every passing bobby.

"Y'want five seats, right? No standin'. Y'don't wanna stand, y'know. Cheaper, but uncomfortable in there with all them drunks wavin' flags and singin'. Tell ya what—I got five good ones you can have for £25."

Well, that seemed fair.

"Each," he added.

"Fifty bucks a ticket?"

Instantly he was ten feet away, staring in another direction.

"Talk it over wiv yr friends," the word floated back. "If you want 'em, gimme a nod. *But don't flash no money, and don't say tickets!*"

We talked it over. All but my wife, who didn't want to see the game and thought ten cents would be exorbitant. She just stood there, her mouth working but no sound coming out.

For five of us, we needed £125. We didn't have it.

I myself was ten pounds short due to an earlier sage investment—the purchase of 15 Liverpool hats for a kids' soccer team at home. (I wanted the winners' hats, but they had to be bought before the game because the trailers with the souvenirs were always taken away before it ended, lest they be turned over by the more fun-loving members of the departing mob. But I wasn't worried. Everybody knew Liverpool would win.)

"No way I can work it," I said sadly. "Not unless he'd take a traveller's cheque."

Like that, there he was.

"Sure, I takes 'em," he said.

We made the deal and reached for the tickets. He didn't have them.

"Can't carry 'em on me," he explained, pointing over his shoulder at the mob. "They'd take 'em and break me legs. You come with me. I'll take you down where you can get a cuppa while I go get the tickets. You don't want the ladies stayin' up here. These people turn ugly."

"You want tea?" I asked my wife.

"Fift . . . fift . . . fift . . ."

"Speech impediment," I explained. He nodded sympathetically and escorted us to the Wembley Squash Club coffee bar, ignoring a sign that said Members Only. "Wait here," he said.

It took him 30 minutes. When he came back he was clutching five tickets.

"Best in the 'ouse," he assured us. "They oughta be. They go for five pounds each."

"Five pounds," my wife said faintly. "And for two we're paying fift . . . fift . . ."

He looked at me questioningly.

"She's overcome," I said.

So, for only five times face value, we sat in historic Wembley and watched a two-hour scoreless draw. But at least I had the hats. Liverpool would certainly win the replay. The kids would love me. Imagine—hats of the League Cup champions.

Wednesday afternoon the score came over the wire: Notts Forest 1, Liverpool nil.

I phoned my wife.

"The hats are no good," I said.

"Fift . . . fift . . . fift . . ."

The Big Basho
Calgary Sun, June 6, 1998

IN CASE YOU WERE WONDERING, if a sumo wrestler loses his loincloth, he's disqualified. For a 300–500-pound man standing on a mound of dirt before thousands of people, suddenly wearing nothing but an industrial-strength jockstrap, disqualification would seem the least of his worries. But it's right there in the rules, along with the sport's Eight Forbidden Actions:

- Punch with the closed fist.
- Deliberately pull hair.
- Poke in the eyes.
- Slap both ears at same time.
- Grab genitals.
- Choke opponent.
- Kick stomach or chest.
- Bend back one or two opponent's fingers.

That last one is a bit ambiguous—is it okay to bend three or four at once? Does the thumb count as a finger?—but it's there, and the sumo wrestlers (rikishi) are in Vancouver this weekend, and if you don't know the rules, how can you know when to boo?

It is called the Sumo Canada Basho, this show that's been a year in the making with the tab set at $5 million, an opportunity for the hockey-basketball-football west to see the sport that has been part of Japanese culture, religion and sporting zeal for thousands of years. But the locals are incidental.

The master plan is not to have Vancouver fall in love with sumo, but to have Japanese people come to sumo and fall in love with Vancouver. Or so says the May edition of Tokyo's *Sumo World* magazine in a glowing tribute to promoter Parmesh Bhatt written, or so says the byline, by Parmesh Bhatt. Hey, you want something done right . . .

I ha'e ma doots.

This is the fast-food continent, the land where history is yesterday and ancient history is last week, the home of instant franchises, carpetbag owners who change cities like they change underwear, and games that last longer than World War I. We may be looking at two sporting cultures that defy mixing.

Consider . . .

SUMO: Only special soil (it took a year to find the right stuff for Vancouver) will do to build the ring—which, strangely enough, is a circle, some six metres in circumference and 60 cm high. Torreya nuts, washed rice, chestnuts, kelp, dried cuttlefish and salt must be buried in it for luck and the whole thing is purified with salt.

NHL: Gas up the Zamboni.

SUMO: Two rikishi, hospital clean, hair carefully combed and knotted, crouch inches apart, then lunge forward trying to push each other out of the circle. The last time there was a collision that hard, Secretariat was conceived.

NHL: Two stubble-bearded, sweat-stained guys spit on the ice, grab each other's sweaters and yap until the linesmen separate them.

SUMO: Average length of bout—70 seconds.

NHL: Average length of game—Forever.

SUMO: Referee carries knife, symbolic of willingness to commit hara-kiri in the event of a bad call.

NHL: Referee carries whistle, symbolic of willingness to admit that even when he's wrong, he's right.

As a cultural mix, it just doesn't seem in the cards.

Sumo fans look at near-naked rikishi and see centuries of tradition. North Americans look at the same guy and see advertising space. ("Jeez! The decals we could slap on that guy . . .")

The twain, I fear, will never meet. For which the rikishi should perhaps be thankful.

The Fun League
The Province, July 30, 1982

A CHAP IN OUR OFFICE has a twisted knee. "Stretching a single into a double," he says, leaning proudly on his crutches.

Down at the radio station a sports reporter is learning to type one-handed until the sling comes off his separated shoulder. "I was dribbling through the box just ready to shoot," he says, "and POW! Two guys sandwiched me." His boss is sympathetic, and should be. He did the same thing diving for a line drive.

I tell you, it's a disease. Participaction Backlash, the new madness of the masses.

In offices and supermarkets and factories all over the country, eager-beaver ex-jocks or wannabe jocks run around with clipboards or hang signs on the wall:

> FUN! FUN! FUN!
> SUPERMARKET SOFTBALL LEAGUE!
> NO SKILL NECESSARY!
> SEE GLADYS IN FROZEN FOODS!

Pretty soon Gladys is hanging over the checkout counter checking out the muscles on the bag boy.

"Hey, kid, you comin' out for the Canadian Kippers practice tonight? We got a big game Sunday against those Prime Cutters turkeys from Meats."

"Uh, sorry, but I've already signed up with the Green Bayleaf Packers over in Condiments. They outbid the Tony Tigers from Cereals. Offered me parsley, sage and thyme, but I held out for Rosemary. You know, the one with the . . ."

"The Packers! Listen, kid, you wanna go through life sniffing cinnamon, that's your business, but at least hear our offer. And don't you believe that stuff they say about Frozen Foods. We're not all frigid. Let's drive over to my place and discuss it, okay? Your cart or mine?"

There are two great flaws in the Participaction Theory. The first is the assumption that the average person is physically equipped to handle it. The second is the idea that pick-up team sport is based on fun. It's not. It just starts out that way.

Someone decides to form, say, an inter-departmental softball league. They scrounge around for a few bats, a couple of balls, throw some jackets around the field for bases, and start. The wives or husbands join in, and the kids, and it doesn't matter if the score is 146–2, because who's counting?

Then the rot sets in. You can almost graph it.

Someone calls a practice—and shows up with a team list and league standings. The kids don't play anymore because the other team will come loaded, right, and they're not gonna pull that crap on us. The wife with the good swing can play but the one who can't see her shoes, let alone first base—"Uh, honey? Why don't you be in charge of watching the cooler?"

Then someone gets an idea:

"Hey, why don't we get *hats?* You know, so we'd all look like the same team!" After the hats come the T-shirts with the name on the front. But these things cost money, so why don't we get a sponsor? Maybe the supermarket would do it—employee relations and all that.

One day the wife in charge of the cooler notices a stranger. The pitcher, maybe, or a guy who stands 6'5" and holds a bat like he's done it before.

"Who's that?" she asks. "He doesn't work at the store."

"SSHHHH! Fred from Canned Goods brought him in. It's his cousin. Used to play senior 'A.' Hit .500 and has a sinker they'll never see. This is the big one, honey. We're playing the Stock Room Reds for all the marbles. This is no time to take chances!"

They trot out on to the field and Fred's cousin hits three home runs. The only batter to touch his sinker is a guy nobody knows who hits four homers and says his job in the stock room is to feed the cattle.

Meanwhile, the ones still playing for fun are throwing their out-of-shape bodies in front of line drives they can't catch, swinging at pitches they can't see, and wearing their bandages like medals of honour.

"Okay, so we lost this time," says the guy with the clipboard. "But next year, boy, I'm bringing in five guys from the House of David. Next year, we're gonna have *fun . . ."*

Belly to Belly
The Province, August 7, 1985

No, ADMITS TOM BUTLER, there has never been a major league belly-floppers' strike, nor does he anticipate one. "I hold all the cards," he says. "I've got all the tickets to the beer tent."

Speculation has been semi-rife that the bellyfloppers might follow the lead of major league players and force high-level contract negotiations as zero hour approaches for Superflop XI, the World Bellyflop and Cannonball Diving Championships on August 31 at the campground in Otter Springs, Florida. (For those requiring more detailed directions, Otter Springs is to Gainesville what Green Bay is to Milwaukee.)

Commissioner Butler merely smiles. He knows that for true floppers the risks are far too great: potential loss of the magnificent three-and-a-half-foot World Championship Trophy (simulated gold plate, $49.95 Canadian plus tax and engraving), the $1,000 first prize and, worst of all, the missed opportunity to don the Coveted Green Bathrobe, the Masters blazer of the wet set.

"There will be no strike," he says. "In fact, I have cabled my counterpart, Mr. Ueberroth, offering our assistance in filling the gap left by the absence of baseball during their strike. We stand ready to place one world-calibre flopper in each of the 14 major league cities, each man ready to perform the full Superflop program for each of the remaining home dates. One show only, doubleheaders extra."

Does he feel Mr. Ueberroth will accept?

"It's debatable," he concedes. "After all, if we once get established he may never get his crowds back. Once they've seen a Butch Hilterson, a Rickey Henderson ain't all that much."

To aficionados of the flop, Butch Hilterson is legend. In 1980, the 325-pound plumber from Denver, Colorado, competed in the championships wearing a snowy-white tutu in tulle with chic scalloped bodice. Although he didn't win, he was named Ms. Congeniality and got to help take down the decorations.

Hilterson thus earned his place in flopdom's Hall of Fame next to the immortal Butts Giraud, the three-time champion who knew it was time to retire the day he went into his bathroom and blew himself up.

Strong men weep at the memory.

Giraud was getting ready for his final dive of the 1978 championships, riding a string of two perfect sixes. He knew he could collect enough points to win just by concentrating on height-of-splash and water displacement, two of the three elements of the flop. But inside that bulbous body lurked the heart of a Barnum. He would risk everything and pin his all on the third element: showmanship.

He had imported a Hollywood stunt man to design a body pack that would fit under his shirt, with a detonator wire running down the sleeve to his hand. At the peak of his dive he'd push the button and burst into flames as the shirt burned off his back, but hit the water and extinguish before he got hurt.

He was standing in the bathroom when he decided on an instrument check.

"I just push this button like this, right?" he asked—and exploded.

He was too big to stuff in the john, so they rolled him in a blanket until he went out, then reloaded him. Giraud strode to the board, ignited on schedule, and scored another six. Big deal, Reggie Jackson.

Butler, who owns the franchise rights to floppery, feels this month's show will prove that flopping is a sport whose time has come—the only sport where a guy goes into the tank and it doesn't matter. "If baseball strikes for three weeks," he warns, "it's history."

Giraud, now a mere shadow of his former selves, will not make it to Otter Springs, but old-timers are hoping for a guest appearance by Christie Wilson, the 450-pound former Miss WBFCDC.

"She wasn't just our queen," Butler remembers fondly. "She was also first and second runner-up."

Hoist the Martini: A Tale of the Sea
The Province, May 3, 1991

As you all know, yachting is my life.

There's nothing like the thrill of climbing up the stairs to the main floor of one of those big shippy things, strolling from the pointy end to the back, then popping downstairs for a spot of grog (or, as we yachtsmen call it, Perrier).

It's a humbling thing, standing alone out there with nothing between you and the briny deep but a solid teak floor and a basement full of about $60,000 worth of navigational and sonar gear to track the fish you may want to kill later, gazing up at the stars you'll soon be counting on to guide you the 30 or 40 yards down the dock to the yacht club.

For years I've been enthralled by the sheer beauty of these vessels as they sit parked by the dock, listening to the colourful language of the sailors who yearn to go down to the sea in ships and will if they can ever get everything working at the same time.

"Aw, Dad, I polished the teak last time! Can't I go play football?"

"Polish the goddamn teak! This is a family outing! Have fun or I'll kill you!"

"Harry, don't you yell at him like that! It isn't enough that we mortgaged the house to buy this thing, which we never get to sail because it's always broken and we spend every waking hour trying to fix it. No! You've gotta strut around like some kinda Captain Bligh! You know what you are, Harry? You're nothing but a big . . . what's the name of that white whale?"

"You mean Moby Dick?"

"Well, I dunno about the Moby part, but you're definitely a . . ."

But that's the beauty of being a yachting fan: *You never have to go out on the water!*

Face it, there's nothing to do out there anyway but drink and get seasick. Veteran fans sit in restaurants overlooking the dock, sipping something cool and gazing at the boats of their dreams, because *they never actually go out to sea, either!*

Think about it: Have you ever passed a boat-parking place that isn't jammed? Never! They're never ready (or, as we say, shipshape). They just sit there, supported by the lapping waters and overlapping mortgages.

Not all of them. It is a little-known fact, but some yachts actually get out to sea and race. That's when the excitement really gets out of hand.

Take the weekend Swiftsure Classic race in Juan de Fuca Strait, a body of water so cold a person would have to be terminally dumb to sail on it in anything smaller than the *Queen Mary.*

On Sunday, John Buchan of Seattle was declared the winner in his sloop (a nautical term meaning "really expensive") which he named

Heather, perhaps because *Hang On Sloopy* sounded common. Rookie yacht-watchers were not surprised, since Buchan crossed the finish line first, one hour and 44 minutes ahead of his brother, Bill, on board his sloop *Sachem*, named after the late, great New Orleans skipper, Sir Louis of Armstrong.

But wait! The margin of victory was then lowered to eight minutes after figuring in the "ratings," a complex procedure in which factors such as weight, length, height and the number of crew sailing three sheets to the wind are fed into a computer which spews out figures about as simple to read as the Dead Sea Scrolls.

However, John was still the winner.

But wait again! With computers rolling at flank speed it took officials only until Wednesday to discover that the machine had fouled up and *Bill* was the real winner by 11 minutes and 59 seconds. Pending appeal, which can happen any time in the next three weeks.

How fortunate we are that Columbus was a simple sailor. If he'd been a yachtsman, we'd all still be living in Genoa.

Bulk Beefcake Meets the Steroid Challenge
The Province, July 17, 1991

> *World Wrestling Federation announces crackdown on use of anabolic steroids.*
>
> —News item

BULK BEEFCAKE, WORLD WRESTLING CHAMPION, cracked a walnut between his eyelashes and glared around the shell fragments at his accusers.

"I never took no stereos," he said. "An album here, a single there, sure. But I was just a kid. Besides, I already had a stereo."

"Mr. Beefcake, we are not here to discuss your musical preferences. We would like you to explain how you grew from a 98-pound weakling to a 287-pound wrestler."

"Exercise! Sure, I remember those days when I weighed 98 pounds . . ."

"You should. It was three weeks ago."

"Well, I'm a quick study. Once I risked that stamp and Charlie Atlas sent me the course, I put on muscle so fast I changed jock size overnight."

"And what about the injections?"

"The what?"

"The needles, Mr. Beefcake. The injections given you by that South African witch doctor you saw once a week."

"Psoriasis, your honour. I was sufferin' from the heartbreak of psoriasis. The itchy, dry-scalp feeling, not to mention the embarrassment of all those flakes on your shoulder just as you're about to put a move on some chick. Well, I figure you never get a second chance to make a first impression, so . . ."

"You expect us to believe that, Mr. Beefcake?"

"Hey, you guys run pro rasslin' and you're hassling *me* about credibility? You wanna stomp on the steroid freaks, why don'tcha go after that Turtle mob?"

"Turtle mob?"

"Yeah, those turtle kids with all the muscles and the street-gang names: Lennie, Ralphie, Mikie and Nevertello."

"You mean the Teenage Mutant Ninja Turtles? You're saying the Turtles are on steroids?"

"Hey, they were two inches tall and just like that they're 5'10", wearing masks, carrying weapons and showing tendencies toward random violence. I rest my case."

"Mr. Beefcake, the Turtles are not on trial here, you are. And speaking of random violence, only last night did you not pin your opponent, Cpl. Punishment, to the canvas?"

"I'm a wrestler, for Pete's sake! That's what wrestlers do!"

"With industrial staples?"

"Okay, so I got a little excited. But what I want to say, your honour, is that I ain't takin' my psoriasis stuff any more and I've joined the fight against stereo abuse."

"In what way?"

"I'm workin' with the kids. My company, Bulk-Up Productions, is coming out with a whole new line of Bulk Beefcake action dolls. Only instead of selling add-on accessories, the kid starts with the complete doll with removable muscles.

"See, now that you guys are policing . . . uh, now that I've seen the light and aren't taking my medicine no more, I'll start to get skinny. Every time a kid watches me on TV and sees where I've lost weight, he removes the corresponding muscle. The objective is to be the first kid on the block to get me down to human-being size."

"Commendable, Mr. Beefcake. And what happens then?"

"That's the whole point, your honour: I wrestle, and I *lose.*"

"And then?"

"Well, the kid starts buying new replacement muscle parts. He can keep watching me fight to regain my title, and put them back one by one."

"And what will you accomplish by all this?"

"Well, for one thing, your honour, I'll sell a hell of a lot of dolls."

To Absent Friends

WHEN I ARRIVED IN VANCOUVER IN 1964 to see if I could write in a major market, Canada's newspaper firmament was ablaze with more stars than I could count. Most of them are gone now, along with many of the Runyon-esque oddballs they immortalized.

I worshipped Jim Coleman, the country's first nationally syndicated sports columnist, who spread the racetrack gospel of Johnny Needle-Nose, the Blow-Back Kid and so many other fictional winners and losers and still found time to befriend and encourage grass-green wannabes like me. Dick Beddoes, Jim Kearney and Denny Boyd held sway in Vancouver. Haunting the exchange table with its stacks of week-old eastern papers introduced me to Milt Dunnell, Scott Young, Jim Proudfoot and Trent Frayne—maybe the most lyrical writer of them all—in Toronto, Jack Matheson in Winnipeg, and the ever-hilarious John Robertson in Regina, whose columns taught me that it wasn't merely *okay* to be irreverent, that sometimes it was the best way—and the most fun—to make a point.

They're all gone now—or retired, which to most writers is another form of falling off the planet—replaced by eager young talents finding their way in the new-media world of internet blogs, cell phones, talk shows and, God help us, Twitter. So are most of the sports radio and TV icons of the day, people like Bill Good Sr., Don Chevrier, Don Wittman, Ted Reynolds and Tiger Al Davidson, who painted pictures with the spoken word as I tried to do with the written and, unlike we ink-stained wretches, often did it live without benefit of eraser or oops.

I miss them, and the people of whom we all wrote and broadcast. When you've lived in the best of all possible working worlds, as I have for so many decades now, you're caught between mourning the passing of friends and wondering when it will be your turn.

Years ago, Jim Kearney, Ted Reynolds and I made the ferry trip to Victoria, where we'd all begun our careers, to attend the funeral of Bill "Sunny" Walker, sports editor of the Victoria *Times*. We were almost there when Kearney had a thought.

"I wonder," he said, "how many people from over there will make this trip the other way to come to ours?"

We all used the line, of course. In the media, no line is ever wasted. But sometimes saying goodbye, however sincere or heartfelt, is more than another day's work done. Sometimes, you just want to cry . . .

Crichton Was a Fan
The Vancouver Sun, January 19, 1972

R. CRICHTON HAWKSHAW died Tuesday morning, and somehow that doesn't seem right. If he had to go, just two months short of his 60th birthday, there should have been football players there, and cameramen and newspaper types, and Crichton handing out those funny little business cards, the letters twisted to form a picture of Sherlock Holmes, so we'd be sure to get the name right. No one could handle a Hawkshaw story like Hawkshaw, and no one would have loved it more.

I guess you could call him a character. He said he was BC Lions' No. 1 fan, and worked at it with an unabashed enthusiasm that often drew the ire of the less dedicated majority. But he was a nice character.

Some guys collect stamps. Crichton collected football. Players, coaches, trainers, directors, reporters—anyone connected, however remotely, with the football team that was his passion. He thrived unashamedly on the associations, the limelight, and the sense of belonging. The laughter could be with him or at him. It was enough that it was there. "I like to see my name in the paper," he told me once. "Everybody does. And I like football. You tell me, where's the harm?"

There never was any harm, of course, but there were some great stories.

Once Jim Kearney met him at some football function in the ballroom of the Georgia and scoffed at suggestions that Crichton wore undershorts in Lions' black and orange. Crichton dropped his trousers and proved it.

Legend has it that he and his wife, Ivy, were in Calgary watching a game when she tripped and broke an ankle. Ivy went to hospital by ambulance. Crichton watched the rest of the game before following. I asked him about it once and he had a logical explanation. "We were behind," he said.

Being a man of modest means, Crichton couldn't make many road trips. Occasionally, though, he'd get one as part of his duties running the Touchdown Club. Win or lose, he liked to keep everybody loose.

In 1966, the Lions were in Calgary airport. It was midnight, and they had lost. At such times you say nothing, it being neither polite nor safe to antagonize a 250-pound football player who might shave you with a propeller.

Crichton had an air horn. A large, loud, ear-splitting air horn, and he was standing right behind Wayne Foster, who'd played a stinker and knew it.

Yes, he did.

Foster leaped, pivoted, and took one step forward. Somebody asked him where he was going. "I think," Foster said thoughtfully, "yes . . . I think I am going to kill him."

Crichton wasn't being smart. He just preferred happy groups to sad ones, and maybe a blast on the horn . . .

But Hawkshaw's all-time greatest road trip escapade was not in the stands or on the plane or in the dressing room he so loved to crash. It was in a cocktail lounge in Regina. We called it the Swizzle Stick Caper.

A bunch of press guys were building the world's tallest swizzle stick tower, melting the ends together with matches. It was a noble purpose. Unfortunately, to get swizzle sticks, one had to buy drinks. Some of us could barely lift the matches.

Crichton, supervising, decided we needed a stick of purest white to top our edifice. And lo, there at a nearby table, was such a stick. It lay next to the empty glass of a faultlessly groomed, attractive lady in her late 30s, dining elegantly and alone.

Crichton walked over, excused himself, and picked up the stick.

The lovely lady, this vision of good breeding and proper schools, picked up her steak knife, reached out, and placed the point approximately two inches from Hawkshaw's throat.

"Give me back my swizzle stick," she said pleasantly.

Crichton dropped the stick like a hot rock, stared dumbfounded, and walked back to our table. "Fellas," he said, "I think we can skip the white one."

He was a good guy, and I hope he knew the Lions' corrected their membership list. He was in the office the other day, and they'd misspelled his name. It would have been the ultimate indignity.

"You Only Have So Many Years . . ."
The Vancouver Sun, June 25, 1974

I KEEP SEEING HIM with that cigarette dangling from the corner of his mouth and remembering that he would have been 26 next Wednesday.

Cancer took Ken Phillips Monday as it has taken so many and will take so many more. And the guys who played and laughed with him in his three-plus years as a BC Lion will be remembering today and maybe butting out a cigarette unfinished, because they used to kid him that that was the way he'd go.

There is no provable connection between the way he lived and the way he died. There seldom is. The question just hangs there, because almost every Ken Phillips story involves cigarettes. Porky Punter, they called him, but not at first. When he came to the Lions in 1969 the players named him after the brand he favoured. No one ever knew how many he smoked. How could we? He was so rarely without one. It became, God help us, a joke.

Denny Veitch found him, a chubby kid of 20 he hauled away from the Vancouver Meralomas because the Lions were desperate for a punter. Coach Jim Champion took one look at him and almost laughed. Then he took a second look, and signed him. The kid did everything wrong. He was left-footed. He dropped the ball awkwardly when he took the snap. He took an extra step, and the stride was ridiculous. But when he hit it, sometimes you had to look for it. They signed him as a prospect and he stayed three full seasons. Twice he led the Western Conference and the other year he was second.

When they cut him after six games in 1972 it was only because they had too many specialists and a reserve quarterback named Eric Guthrie who could also punt. The day the players knew in their minds he was going they prepared a surprise. Phillips reached into his equipment bag at that final practice and pulled out a dead pigeon. "Tough," he grinned, and that was Ken Phillips, too.

I don't think he ever was a rookie. His approach to the game wouldn't allow it. He was absolutely devoid of the awe that is the rookie's trademark. You kick the ball for fun; you kick it for pay. You still kick it. He was totally nerveless, so the heat could never get to him. He was there to kick, so he kicked. Why sweat? It wasn't that he cared or competed any less. He just knew that while winning meant a lot, it didn't mean everything. He had his priorities straight, and living was first.

It was in 1971, I think, that Ted Gerela was battling the devils that periodically ride his placement kicking. I looked for Phillips, figuring that maybe a fellow kicker could give some insight. He was located at a McDonald's having a pre-practice meal—two cheeseburgers and a milkshake. How did he view the problem?

"I don't know what the fuss is about," he munched. "I'll kick the (bleeping) thing."

Football for Porky Punter could never be anything but fun for which he happened to get paid. The traditions were not for him. On a road trip to Winnipeg in 1970, he proved it. The team stayed on the second floor of the hotel, the coaching staff on the first. The night the game was played, Jackie Parker and the press were holding a post-mortem well past curfew. The door was slightly open. Things might have grown a little bit loud.

Suddenly, it opened all the way. Porky strode in and confronted Parker. "Would you mind keeping it down, coach?" he demanded. "Some of us are trying to sleep."

Before Parker could react, he was gone.

Other players might put an extra piece of foam in the top of their helmets. Not Porky. That was where he kept his cigarettes. In practice he'd sneak a smoke and when the time came to punt he'd put it carefully on the edge of the bench, run out, punt, and come back to pick it up. Somebody asked Parker once why he was allowed to get away with it.

"You don't mess around," he said fondly, "with an athlete that finely tuned."

Phillips was proud of being in football and loved the notoriety of being Porky Punter. It made everything more fun. It was going into his second full season, I think, that he showed up at practice in a T-shirt he'd had made up in Gastown. On the front there was the head of a pig, a cigarette dangling from the snout. "Porky Punter," the caption read.

"You know," he told me, "if I have another good season, I might market these. You only have so many years."

Letter from Tap City
The Vancouver Sun, August 25, 1977

THIS TIME NOTHING CAN GO WRONG. No more ankle express. No more gaspipe. It's champagne in the fridge, opera on the stereo and an elderly-type broad reclining on the bed. This time The Matchmaker has it made.

I have this on the authority of none other than The Matchmaker himself, who has found another hotel that runs a tab and has used its stationery to fire off another of his State of the Wallet reports:

Friend Taylor,
This could be a double large deal, just like winning Lotto Canada ticket, this deal will launch my nudest [*sic*] camp its either brick-house or bleep-house because there are plans of printing ten million calendars in 20 languages.

Happy New Year.
Zube

The letter arrives in a big cardboard tube, and you know right away Nick is serious because it does not come postage due. Also in the tube are four copies of a large poster, one copy of a letter of intent between Nick and W. James Mills Communications Ltd. of Toronto, a document showing that Nick has the posters copyrighted so nobody should muscle his action, and a press release The Matchmaker must have written himself because it says the first posters have already gone to Moscow and Pravda.

Nick Zubray, 56 years on the make, has finally pulled it off.

He told me three years ago it would happen. "I got a collection of pictures of every heavyweight champ who ever was," he said. "Some day I'm gonna find me a kind stranger with a roll, put them all together on one big poster, and him and me are gonna get seriously rich."

I didn't believe him.

After all, it was Nick who booked closed-circuit TV of the Mac Foster–Muhammad Ali fight into the Coliseum at seven dollars a pop, then found out the night before the fight that it was live on home television out of Seattle. He had a simple explanation: "What happened was, somebody made a mistake."

It was Nick who talked Murray Pezim—his bankroll on the closed-circuit caper—into backing an Ali–George Chuvalo heavyweight title fight here. Pezim took a $180,000 bath, Nick said $42,000 of it was his, and thereafter took a lot of interest in Murray's health.

"He gets sick there a while ago, I even go to church a couple times to light candles," he says virtuously. "Because if he croaks, where am I? I got an investment in the guy."

It was Nick whose plan to start a nudist colony outside Edmonton died of the financial shorts. "Couple of lakes and the rest we was gonna leave in bushes so the kids could fool around," he said then. "Sure, the nudist season in Edmonton is kinda short, but how can it miss? You show me a kid in today's younger generation don't wanna run around naked."

It's been Nick who bounced all over western Canada with closed-circuit promotions, sometimes hitting semi-big, sometimes crapping out, sometimes letting his enthusiasm trap him. He once gave away 350 tickets, beamed at the full house, then noticed that the paid gate was 18.

For Nick, defeat is a temporary inconvenience. There is always a stranger around the corner waiting with a roll and an itch to invest it. It's just a matter of staying alive until you find him. "You go by limousine, you go by boxcar, you're still movin'," he shrugs. "And if you can't ride there's always the Ankle Express. The action, that's what counts."

I have known The Matchmaker for years and sometimes suspect that we are friends. He is an old-school hustler who talks like Harry the Horse, runs up enormous hotel tabs when down with the shorts, but stuffs the fridge with champagne, puts pictures of his latest lady on the dresser—"a nice, elderly-type broad," he'll say affectionately—and fills the room with opera from the record collection that travels with him even when he goes by ankle.

If you have some money he'll come for it. If you lose it he'll weep, because his plan was always to make you both rich. The tabs get paid when he hits his next score. Sometimes it takes a while, but I would put his handshake in the bank.

His record hotel bill to date is $10,400, but when he settled the manager knocked off the $400. Until then he tended to stay in a lot because once he was out they might change the locks.

Now Nick has maybe hit one that will stick. The poster, with every heavyweight champ from John L. Sullivan to Ali, is a first-class, beautifully-conceived little number that could be very big in rec room, bar and gym.

Naturally, Nick is optimistic. He has found his bread man. "We make 100, maybe even 600 big ones out of this," he chortles, "and that ain't even countin' the ash trays and the glasses and stuff. They come later."

His partners no doubt take a more cautious view. But caution is not Nick's bag.

"Listen," he says, "I figure over the years I promoted maybe three million dollars in deals and ended up getting screwed on a lot. But this time I hit big.

"I'll tell ya," says The Matchmaker, "It'll be like shootin' fish wit a axe."

I have one of Zube's posters on my wall, beautifully framed in copper, covered with that arm-and-a-leg double-glaze, no-glare glass. He gave it to me one night on the corner of Georgia and Granville when he didn't have two nickels to rub together and there wasn't a mark in sight.

He'd phoned to say he was in town and could I meet him. Now it was 10 p.m. and he was standing there in his cracked-but-shiny patent leather shoes and the black suit with the white tie, sausage-sized knuckles bent from too many fights, the ears curled over from slipping too many headlocks in the bad old wrestling days.

Word had come down that Nick had hit hard times. The posters hadn't sold. A couple of other things had gone sour. "He sold his record collection," a guy said, "so you know he's gotta be in tough." But he didn't say anything about it that night on the street corner. For Nick, he didn't say much at all.

"This is for you," he said. "We know each other a long time."

Then he turned and walked into the darkness. It was the last time I saw him.

I was on a road trip when word came that Nick had died. I phoned a friend in Edmonton and asked how the funeral had gone.

"Nick would have loved it," the guy said. "It out-drew his last three promotions."

One Last Round for Byron
The Province, September 16, 1981

WE SAID GOODBYE TO BYRON SCOTT Tuesday morning at the church, the cemetery and the Piccadilly Hotel pub.

He'd have liked the funeral. Mind you, the morning air at the cemetery might have gotten to him because, as Pam Glass said in opening the eulogy, "It's a little early for Byron to be up." But he would have loved the wake.

When Byron Scott died last week his body was 70, his heart was 21, and his liver was 306. He was a drinker, was Byron—not a mean drinker or a slobbery drinker or a trouble-making drinker, just a drinker—a guy who'd done it for a long time and always enjoyed the laughter and the stories as much if not more than the booze. And they were telling Byron stories at The Pic.

No one knew him, really—not his drinking buddies or the newspaper and radio and race track and street people who gathered to see him off. He was just a stocky, brash little guy who materialized one day in the 1950s and stayed forever. He claimed a newspaper and radio background and straddled the poverty line by cadging freelance assignments. He had an ex-wife somewhere and a son somewhere else. Until he died, that's about all anyone knew.

Byron didn't help. When he spoke of himself it was usually a put-down. He brushed off his army career by reporting that when he came home "that's when we started to win the war." Until yesterday, we didn't know about the Distinguished Service Medal he had won in 1943.

He lived in the cheapest quarters he could find. For years that meant the Kingston Hotel—"Where the celebs meet the debs," he'd explain. When he moved into the Sunset Towers, a subsidized senior citizens' complex, Byron called it "going uptown."

He'd keep track of the sports press conferences and crash as many as he could because the sandwiches and companionship were free. But he'd also keep track of the birthdays and the expectant mothers, and there was money for flowers or candies when there was barely money for food.

He was just . . . Byron. The phone would ring and a voice would say "Byron Patrick Scott!" and you knew he was there with curling results or basketball results or word that he was going on the wagon for two weeks because he'd be covering the horse show. He was always on the wagon for that one. When he fell off, the crash was awe-inspiring.

He claimed he got his clothes from the coroner. "Great coat, eh?" he'd say. "Just this one little spot of blood on the sleeve."

One day after a press conference, none of the guys he usually rode with was going his way. "No problem," he said, "I'll call an ambulance." He made the call, told a reporter to clear a spot on the floor, and lay down to wait. "He'll be here soon," he said. "The service is really quick."

He could drive you crazy.

A few years ago we were sitting at the press table in the Pacific Coliseum for an exhibition basketball game. The legendary Bill Russell was coaching the Seattle Supersonics. Suddenly, during the warm-up, Byron leaned over and waved frantically. "Bill! Bill!" he yelled.

Russell thought we were part of the scorer's table. He unfolded and ambled over.

"Yes?" he asked.

"If you need any help," Byron said, "just call."

He used to phone Bud Poile, the Canucks' then-general manager, getting past his private secretary by announcing himself as "Byron Patrick Scott, representing the provincial government." When Poile rapped him for it he was indignant.

"I am with the provincial government," he said. "I'm on welfare."

He drifted in and out of our lives, and the harsh fact is we didn't care as much as we should have. If we had, we'd have kept better track. It shouldn't have taken four days to confirm rumours that his heart had given out and he was in the morgue. His drinking buddies knew right away.

They flocked to The Pic yesterday, maybe 100 of them, scoffing sandwiches and booze and remembering Byron in the way he'd have liked best. They figured there'd be more at 4:30, when the second shift came in. He couldn't have asked for a better goodbye.

Goodbye, Joe
The Province, June 3, 1988

THE SOCCER BOOTS are around somewhere, the keepsake-sized pair on a chain that Joe Johnson gave my son 16 summers ago. "For working hardest, Dad," he said. "I wasn't the best, but Joe says I worked the hardest." You could have read by the glow in his eyes.

He was eight years old, a quiet, introverted little cuss trying to come to terms with the fact that he was small enough to pass for six. Enrolling him in soccer school had been our idea, not his. He was well co-ordinated, bubbling with an energy that had to be channelled before it exploded. Soccer, we thought, was worth a shot.

It was more than that. We dropped him into a sea of boys at the UBC campus and he bobbed up a different kid. He'd found a game where size didn't matter, a team game requiring individual skills based not on strength but on co-ordination and agility, and it was love at first sight.

The love never died. It took us through house league—two years with shirts that hung skirt-length, playing for Nightingale Pharmacy, 11 kids converging on the ball as though the earth had tilted in its direction, and seven more years working up through the juvenile ranks.

I say "we" because I was fortunate enough to be there, leaning against the fence with the other parents at first, bringing the half-time oranges when my turn arrived, later as manager—a term meaning you fill out the forms, clean the noses, take the injured to the emergency ward and drive the forgotten kids home. And later, as the boy turned 17, a chance to start over with another group of ten-year-olds, him coaching, me still playing manager. Golden times . . .

We talked about them yesterday, when word came that Joe Johnson had died Tuesday night.

We remembered the little soccer boots, and the sea of kids out on the UBC fields, and how, no matter how many age groups were

47

involved, Joe always managed to wind up the sessions playing with the littlest kids, running along barefoot and laughing, cheering them on, dropping deft little passes or doodling through them in outrageous games of keep-away. He'd had a great professional career with the Glasgow Rangers, but he never had more fun than in the summer romps with the kids.

When the camp wasn't in operation, Joe coached juvenile teams—sticking again to the little guys he loved most of all. He held strong opinions about how kids should be coached, how parents should be involved if they can enjoy and encourage without pressuring, and how, if they can't "they should bloody stay at home!" He knew his kids, knew their problems and their needs. "Sometimes they need more than coaching," he told me once. "Sometimes they just need a hug, and someone telling them they're doing fine."

Sitting here writing this, I found myself wondering if there'd ever be a statue of Joe out at the UBC soccer pitch. Then, as my son packed the car full of soccer balls and plastic triangles and headed off for another practice with another group of ten-year-olds, I realized how foolish that was. Joe doesn't need a monument. He's got thousands of them.

Grannie Goalie
The Province, December 14, 1988

PAUL REINHART would have been 11 years old when Mary Gretzky leaned over the boards at the Brantford Arena and smacked him over the head with her purse.

He was playing defence for an Atom League team called the Kitchener Krauts and pinning her grandson against the boards in a manner that everyone in the rink deemed legal except Mary. She didn't hesitate. "Let him go!" she yelled, and began flailing away at Reinhart with her purse.

"Grandma," Wayne Gretzky says fondly, "was a competitor."

She was also a friend, a confidante, and the first goalie Gretzky ever faced, bouncing rubber balls off her legs as she sat in the big chair in the farmhouse by the Nith River where, two months shy of his third birthday, he took his first, hesitant step on skates. When she died Saturday at 85, No. 99 lost his No. 1 fan.

I met her first in 1983, out on the farm near Canning, Ontario, where her five children were born and raised and where Wayne and his sister and brothers did much of their growing up. We'd driven the 12 miles out from Brantford after lunch, but she insisted we sit down and have a little something, which turned out to be a huge bowl of homemade soup so thick with vegetables the spoon all but stood on its own.

"I don't think I can . . ."

"Eat," she said.

We ate, and watched the pickup game in the yard—tennis ball, tennis racquet, over the trailer is out, and into her vegetable garden, you deal with Grandma. The Gretzky kids played, along with guests in town for the Celebrity Tennis Tournament, and Mary shook her head and told me stories about the way it was.

She always knew Wayne would be rich. "Hairy arms," she said, with a finality steeped in Polish folklore. "I told him, 'Hairy arms mean you be rich someday.' And in the mornings he would come and ask me if he had any more hair."

The farm was where Gretzky built the high jump pit after practising by jumping over the wire fence to feed her chickens. It was the place he first learned to fish and, in later years, the sanctuary that was always there when the pressure of being Wayne Gretzky grew too severe.

It had been a working farm, and Mary kept her part of it that way to the end. Walter would bring her home from a hospital session she'd spent battling a heart problem or stroke, full of doctor's warnings to take it easy. She'd nod yes, and the next day she'd be in the garden harvesting potatoes. "This is my life," she said. "What else would I do?"

The other part of her life was watching Wayne. Once Frank Mahovlich had been her hero. Now it was the WHL, the Wayne Hockey League, and there was only one player in it.

For years she squirreled money away, bit by bit, against the day she'd be able to buy him a car. When he turned pro at 17 and bought one of his own, her first reaction was, "Now what will I do with the $4,000?"

She was in Edmonton when Wayne married Janet Jones, making the trip with a nurse by her side. "Nice," she said, looking around the hotel ballroom. Then she looked at Wayne and Janet. "*Very* nice," she beamed.

A couple of years ago technology came to the farmhouse on

the Nith: a satellite dish so she and her daughter, Ellen—a Down's Syndrome victim—could watch more of Wayne's games, there in the room where he'd crouched on the floor beside her, watching Toronto Maple Leafs. "So many games," she mused. "So many things . . ."

Today the Gretzkys say goodbye to Grandma. Then Wayne jumps a plane for Pittsburgh to join the LA Kings for another showdown with Mario Lemieux. Maybe, somewhere, she'll be watching. It's one she'd have hated to miss.

The Other Babe

The Province, December 18, 1988

DAMNIT, BABE, YOU WEREN'T SUPPOSED TO GO YET. Six of us had tickets for *Cabaret!* You know how hard those things were to get?

We were supposed to go together—you and Floss and Greg and Diane Douglas and Deb and I—and at those prices you were our insurance policy: Joel Grey could fall flat on *his* pratt, but we knew ours would be strictly Tony Award. When it came to revivals and memories and stories of the times and games that were, nobody did it better than you.

Did you know that, Babe? Did you have any idea, standing up at those hundreds of head tables at everything from black tie bashes in posh hotels to minor hockey fundraisers in drafty rinks all over the province, just how well you did it, or the respect in which you were held?

"These jokes are old," you told me once, "but what the hell—so am I." Then you'd kind of wander up to the mike and start in with the "At my age I don't buy long-playing records (pause, two-three) I don't even buy green bananas" shtick, and the big shooters who had to follow you would start looking at each other and wondering why the hell they were there.

I'm a little ticked off at you, Babe. *Cabaret* was going to be the first night we'd ever be together on a purely social basis—no banquets, no press conferences, no post-game shows, no hockey games. At some point in the evening I wanted to tell you how much I enjoyed your work and the way you never alibi-ed for the Canucks in the mostly bad years; how you could absolutely trash them when you felt they deserved it, yet do it in a way that never disguised the fact that this was and would remain your team, playing the best it could in the game you loved.

And there were some stories I wanted to check.

That time in July 1956, when the Mounties caught you speeding on the Barnett Highway, did you really beat the rap by telling the judge that radar was unreliable because the *Andrea Doria* and the *Stockholm* had collided in the North Sea the day before and what good did their radar do *them?*

Did you mean it, that night you watched one of the Western League Canucks shy away from a corner and sniffed "How'd you like to have a heart transplant and get his?"

Or how about the night Hugh Watson, the old Canucks' PR man, borrowed a microphone and did a phoney between-periods interview with the head of a Seattle Totems' Fan Club? When the guy (who thought you were really on the air) was finished offering his opinions of the first period and Watson put the microphone in front of you as the local colour man, did you really look at the guy and say "Sir, you're full of shit!"?

In the old days, when Lester Patrick was running the Rangers on the cheap and kept the team on the trains overnight rather than pay for hotel rooms, did he really stay up all night huddled under a blanket, waiting for you to sneak in from a party? And did he fine you $1,000—mammoth in those days—and say the only way you could get the money back was if you promised to quit drinking?

And is it true that you tried, and by Christmas you were playing so badly that the rest of the team took up a collection, gave you back the $1,000 and told you to go back to doing it your way?

There were a lot of things I wanted to ask you, Babe, and now you've ducked out. And you know what gets me about that? Of all the things that could have gone wrong, the heart was the last I'd have bet on. I always figured yours was big enough to survive anything.

The Crazy Canuck's Last Run
The Province, October 25, 1990

THE VIDEOTAPE WAS MADE IN 1987 when only his closest friends knew how severely Dave Murray was already gripped by the cancer that claimed him yesterday at 37.

It begins with various clips of Murray in flight—yellow suit and red helmet, body tucked into that projectile package, the elder statesman of the Crazy Canucks playing bullet down the ski hills of the world.

Then comes the parade to the microphone: former national team coach John Ritchie and the other three Crazy Canuck originals, Ken Read, Dave Irwin and Steve Podborski, poking fun at their old teammate, telling stories of the days when no course was too steep, no party too long, and life was going to go on forever.

Periodically, the camera switches to Murray, longish hair neatly trimmed, slimmer by far than the slab-shouldered old man of the mountain who led them in the 1970s, but looking good in his tux with the red tie. And laughing. Laughing a lot.

Officially, it was a dinner to launch the Dave Murray Ski Foundation. As such it was an overwhelming success, raising $80,000. If the central figures knew it was also a bit of a goodbye they hid it well under the laughter and the obvious love.

Read claims Murray "set a new standard for longest hair and straggliest beard in the World Cup '74." Ritchie discusses a world class haemorrhoid and the novelty of giving coaching instructions that included "cheeks well spread." Irwin recalls the first time they looked down the hill at Kitzbuhl, convinced that no one in their right mind would ever design a course like that, and how much time Murray spent after they first tried it, going from bed to bathroom at each remembered fright.

Podborski praises Murray's ability to read while lying stark naked with the book flopped down on his chest, and the day he found the maids taking turns vacuuming in front of their room "because the door was open and Dave was in there, chest-reading."

The version of the tape photographer Pat Bell gave me ends with more scenes of Murray flashing down the mountain, sometimes falling, sometimes finishing, but always going full bore. The music is upbeat, the snow is flying, and every line of his body shows a man having the time of his life.

That's how we should remember him. I met him only once or twice in passing, but from what his friends have told me I suspect he'd want it that way. The battle with cancer was a private fight by a private man who didn't want it getting in other people's way or changing their approach to him.

"He didn't want people seeing him sick," Bell says. "The last time

I saw him he was pretty bad, but he kept asking me how I felt and how things were going with me. 'Don't slow down,' he said. 'Keep your speed.''

There is another, longer version of the banquet tape. Bell put it together on his own hook as a gift. Murray didn't want it shown around because it might look as though he was blowing his own horn. Instead, he put it away so that, someday, it could be shown to his then-unborn daughter, to give her a memory of her father who might not be there.

It will be a beautiful memory. And when she sees him flashing down the mountain, she'll know her father was a good man who led a good life, and lived it every inch of the way.

The Tiger Named Big Al
The Province, August 9, 1991

WE SHOULD HAVE KNOWN SOMETHING WAS WRONG. Tiger Al Davidson had missed all three BC Lions home games. Healthy, he'd never have let that happen.

Healthy, he'd have been there in the media lounge holding court, needling the current crop of broadcasters, mixing today's stories with yesterday's, recalling the days when he was The Tiger and football was football and to miss his *Spotlight on Sport* was to miss the wildest, most-listened-to sportscast in town.

It never mattered that he wasn't on the air any more, that his years with CKNW had ended in a bitter wrongful dismissal suit where his victory is currently under appeal, that the CJOR experiment had failed, that for all the help he'd given to so many people over the years there wasn't anyone around to give him the things he needed more than oxygen: a microphone and a platform from which to use it.

Sometimes, when he didn't know you were looking, the shoulders would droop and the eyes would take on the look of the lost. Sometimes the phone would ring in the morning and a friend from one of the radio or TV stations or newspaper sports departments would hear that down-in-the-valley baritone:

"Skull? Al. What's happening?"

It wasn't the money he missed as much as the action. This man who'd been the storm centre of local sport for so long was on the outside with his nose pressed against the glass, wanting nothing more than to get back into the warmth with his friends.

Mostly, though, he was Big Al, smiling, telling the old jokes, diving into the bull sessions, assuring all and sundry that he'd be back. The bad times piled up—the two court cases, repeated eye surgery, a medical sheet that led one physician to call him "a walking time bomb"— but he was there with his head up.

So why didn't we pick it up? Three football games, and he misses all of them? We wondered, but we didn't check. If he could, Big Al would be needling us about that this morning. "Skull," he'd say. "You missed the big one." Yesterday, his wife, Pat, gave us that story, the one no one wanted to hear.

"Al has a brain tumour," she said. "He's had trouble with his co-ordination on the left side, difficulty moving his leg. They've done a biopsy. It doesn't look good."

Last night, the reports from VGH had worsened. Al was haemorrhaging. He was not responding. They knew that if there was any way, he'd be in there fighting it. But the doctors offered little hope. Al had been given last rites.

I'm sitting here now wondering what to say about The Tiger, how to paint the real picture of this fire plug who could be so abrasive on the air and such a softie off; this walking contradiction who could carve you a new rear one minute and shake your hand the next and be utterly sincere on both occasions; this ranting, feuding, gentle, arrogant, caring, kind and loving family man who sometimes let his heart and tongue rule his common sense but seldom met an adversary he couldn't melt with two words: "Nothing personal."

All I know for sure is that if you needed a friend he was there, and that even those who didn't agree with his opinions would rather skip lunch than miss his shows. When they took his microphone away they forgot one thing: They forgot that they'd never find a replacement. Love him or laugh at him, rave with him or at him, there was only one Big Al.

Cactus Jack
Calgary Sun, July 13, 2001

THIS IS MOSTLY ABOUT DEAD PEOPLE—not seen, but remembered—and how the memories inter-connect.

On Grey Cup day, 1953, I lay on a bed in Winnipeg listening to the Winnipeg–Hamilton game as described by the Bomber play-by-play team of Cactus Jack Wells and Mo Simovitch.

My Bombers were trailing, 12–6, but marching. On the game's final play, Indian Jack Jacobs dropped back and threw to Tom "Citation" Casey on the goal line.

Casey would catch it, fall over the line for the five-point touchdown (three years later they were upped to six), the Bombers would convert for the tie, and Indian Jack would kick Ticat ass in overtime.

I knew this. I was 16. I knew everything.

Except that Casey didn't catch the ball. A Hamilton guy named Lou Kusserow hit him before it got there. The referee, clearly blind, did not call pass interference. Incomplete pass. Game over. Hamilton wins.

It was bare-faced robbery. We knew that, because Cactus Jack said so and Mo backed him up.

Maybe others saw it differently on TV. Three Canadian TV stations were carrying the game live (for which the league received the princely sum of $20,500), but who needed television, which was mostly grey dots and clear as a crypt at midnight? We had Cactus and Mo, painting word pictures on the screen inside our heads.

Kusserow robbed us.

Years passed, and suddenly I was a beat reporter covering the BC Lions, doing half-time radio on the Winnipeg station and answering questions from—Migawd! Jack Wells! I was being interviewed live on the radio by Cactus Jack Wells!

I froze. No problem. Cactus did a monologue.

We became friends, because friends were the only people he knew. Before life got in the way, there was a plan to write a book where he'd tell all the stories like the time Indian Jack punched him in the eye, or the one where he and his buddies went to New York and got on TV passing themselves off as the Canadian curling champions. "It seemed like a good idea at the time," he said.

He's gone now, and Mo, taking their classic CFL lines with them.

"Sure is coming down, Mo," Cactus said on a stormy night at Osborne Stadium.

"Sure would look funny goin' up, Jack."

Simpler times.

But the Kusserow hit would never go away. Nor would it, as it turned out, for Cactus.

The Palm Springs *Sun* carried a story the other day about a Lou Kusserow, who'd played for the New York Yankees 1950–62 and the Hamilton Tiger-Cats from '52–56, who'd died at 72. And a long-time CFL and Stampeder fan named Les Inkster wrote from Palm Desert with a story.

Mr. Inkster is one of those never-met connections that tie the CFL together. Has Stamps' season tickets dating back to 1947, mostly used by his kids and grandkids now, although he gets up for an occasional game. Played junior football and remembers sneaking into Mewata Stadium when the Stamps were the Bronks "and should have gone to the Grey Cup a couple of times."

Cactus wintered down there, he said, and one post-golf night he heard someone in the bar mention the CFL.

One thing led to another, and soon the guy said if Cactus knew so damned much about the CFL, who won the Grey Cup in '53?

"Hamilton," snorts Cactus, tells the Kusserow story, and sticks out his hand. "Jack Wells," he booms.

"Glad to meet you," the guy replies. "I'm Lou Kusserow."

Exit, Full Throttle

My Shattered Nerves, October 17, 1995

> *(This one never made the newspaper. Ken "the Dobber"*
> *Dobson died in 1995, a brash, bull-throated broadcaster*
> *much loved by everyone in Victoria and damned near*
> *everyone else he ever met wherever he happened to be.*
> *His biography* My Shattered Nerves, *written by friend*
> *and co-worker Drew Snider, came out that same year.*
> *Drew asked me to write the foreword . . .)*

I DON'T KNOW WHY HE EVER BOTHERED phoning me in Vancouver. He could have just stuck his head out an east window and yelled.

But he'd call, usually before his morning show, to say he'd liked something I'd written, or disagreed with it, or to tell me he'd found a book in a second-hand store he thought I'd like to read so he was mailing it over. And he always did.

We were friends in a curious way, the Dobber and I, because we hardly ever met. Mostly we collided annually during Grey Cup week, when he and Johnny Zee would set up shop in a hotel lobby in Toronto or Vancouver or Winnipeg or wherever for some of the zaniest hours in sports radio.

Here is the Dobber in action, live and in full throttle from the Royal York in Toronto:

"We're speaking now with Jim Taylor of the Vancouver . . . Wait! There's Alan Eagleson! Al! Get your butt over here!"

And Alan Eagleson, the power of international hockey at the time, the man who built the Canada Cup series, stopped dead, hesitated for a second, then came obediently to the microphone. I'm still not sure he even knew the Dobber at the time. He just couldn't disobey that drill-sergeant bark.

The Dobber . . .

How good do you have to be—how loved?—to become a one-word name? This wasn't a broadcast gimmick, a DJ thing where some guy named Joe Smith becomes Bobby McGee or Dow Jones or the Big Bopper. He was the Dobber not just because it was a natural offshoot of his name but because . . . well, because he *was*. It came as naturally as breathing, as natural as the man himself.

When he died, people phoned to ask for Dobber stories. I remember two.

Dobber was MC-ing Victoria's Athlete of the Year banquet. Sitting next to him was former BC Lions head coach Jim Champion. As a hedge against potential chill, they had stashed extra bottles of wine under the table at their feet. It was a long, long evening. The final speaker droned on and on. Heads were nodding when he said "I'll close with one more story . . ."

Dobber leaped to his feet.

"Well, for God's sake," he said, "keep it short!"

The last time I spoke to him, the Dobber was on the phone,

apologizing and asking a favour. We both knew he was dying, that he might not come back from the European cruise he and his wife, Maisie, were taking, the one where he'd promised to do a live report from the men's room at the Leaning Tower of Pisa to see if the list would make him pee on his shoes.

"Your Gretzky book!" he barked. "Can't buy as many as I did of the last one. Too damned expensive! But, listen . . . if I buy one and send it to you, could you sign it specially to some friends of mine? It's a Christmas present. I need to get it wrapped before I go, just in case . . ."

He'll be ticked off at me telling that story. The best exits, he knew, are when you leave 'em laughing. If he is, he'll probably find a way to let me know. As I write this, the rain is pouring down to the roar of thunder. Or maybe not. Maybe it's just the Dobber, clearing his throat.

Schmirler the Curler

Calgary Sun, March 3, 2000

YOU KNEW SHE WAS IN TOUGH when you saw her in the hat, for they are too often the badge of the cancer fighter—the hats and scarves and caps and tams, some defiantly outlandish, some splashes of colour, all carrying the unspoken message: "I'm still here, and I'm fighting. Don't you *dare* pity me!"

But you hoped and maybe even prayed that she would be one who bucked the odds.

People beat cancer, you told yourself. Lots of them. And if it came down to last rock against the unspeakable, who better to throw it than Sandra Schmirler, the woman you'd never met but who was somehow your friend.

The chemotherapy could work, you assured each other. One day soon the hair could be grown back and she could send that hateful hat skying into the wind.

The voice, so painfully scratchy and low in that last TV appearance, could regain the old glass-rattling intensity, and Schmirler the Curler could be back where she belonged, with Jan Betker and Joan McCusker and Marcia Gudereit, playing the game they dominated with the old, unfettered joy.

Then the word came down on Thursday that Sandra Schmirler was gone, and it was like a cold wind whistling through your heart.

You thought about the husband and two little girls, two-year-old Sara and Jenna, just eight months, and railed against the fates that would rob them of a wife and mother just turned 36.

You remembered how, in the middle of the fight when she knew she might be in trouble, she told you how she planned to sneak back into the rink when things were better, and just quietly throw a few rocks.

You remembered that she'd laughed and said the one good thing about missing a curling season was that, finally, there could be a winter vacation to some summery clime where she would stretch out, dig her bare toes into the sand, and soak up the sunshine.

She didn't tell you personally, of course. You saw her on television during that press conference from Moncton, when she sat there under the hat, face so frighteningly gaunt, somehow mustering a semblance of that trademark grin as she dared to speak of a future that might not be.

But that was the thing about her and about her rink. They could shoot the eyes out, they were arguably the best women's rink ever assembled, but they looked and acted like they could be in your kitchen knocking back coffee and swapping gossip. Next-door people.

Sure, they built a huge following among curlers. But they also built another, full of people who may never have played the game but loved the way they played it, loved the "Schmirler the Curler" tag, loved the way she'd scream from the moment the rock left the hand as though she could guide it home on strength of will.

And, maybe most of all, the way the good shots were met with a grin and the bad ones with a never-mind, get-'em-next-time shrug.

A friend of mine watched them in a Tournament of Hearts, her two small children there on the couch with her.

"I wanted them to see what sport really meant," she said. "About trying hard and doing your best, but remembering that it's a game and you're out there having fun."

She'd never seen Sandra Schmirler anywhere but on television. But watching, she knew that was the way it was for the four ordinary folk from Saskatchewan who climbed to the top of the mountain but never forgot their prairie roots.

Yesterday she lost a friend she'd never met. She cried a little, then smiled and said she hoped, wherever Heaven was, that it had great ice, and a warm spot for lying down, soaking up sunshine, and digging your toes in the sand.

The Bish
Calgary Sun, April 6, 2000

HE WAS A THROWBACK to a better, funnier time, and it's a good thing. Starting out today, he'd get his irreverent ass fired.

The morning after his first Stampeders' play-by-play, somebody with horn-rims and a sincere suit would have him on the carpet explaining that in future, kick-offs were not to be described as "And it's hi-diddle-diddle, right up the middle!"

They might not be ready, the suits, for a guy doing play-by-play for a junior hockey team he owned, let alone for having him leave the broadcast booth in mid-game—tossing the mike to a green newspaper kid with a "Here's your chance to be famous"—to go down and coach the team when the guy he'd hired got tossed.

Chances are they wouldn't appreciate his response to reports that the malcontents on his team were revolting.

"Revolting?" he screamed into the phone to a reporter. "You're bleeping right they're revolting!"

In today's PC world of saying nothing that any human being, dog or cat in the known universe might possibly find offensive, they'd be into cardiac arrest at his sportscast description of the women's curling championships:

"Same old broads," he said, "only broader."

They'd never hire him. And they'd never understand that it would be their loss.

We said goodbye to Eric Bishop on Wednesday, sending him off to a bigger, better press box where Gordie Hunter, Hal Walker, Bill Good, Al Davidson, Henry Viney and so many others of his newspaper and broadcast cronies are waiting and the air is blue with cigar smoke and salted rhetoric.

There'll be no heat, of course. In the press section, the boys will be using windshield scrapers to chip away the frost so they can see the game, but over in the broadcast booth the window will be thrown open to the elements lest the Bish miss a block or a clip or another screw-up by the zebras.

There'll be portable typewriters, not computers, and no one will know how to type. The microphone will be a stand-up model with a lead base the size of a bowling ball, and there'll be the sound of gloved hands pounding their ballpoints into dampened notepads, trying to make the ink flow.

And Bish will be in his element, the only place this side of a hot deck or hotter dice that he ever wanted to be.

Simpler times, of course. We'd talk about them, this last couple of years, as he sat in his wheelchair in the corner of the Stampeders' box, cheerfully dissing Kelvin Anderson, the resident fullback.

In his heart, Bish knew Kelvin was a good'un. His crime was that he wasn't Earl Lunsford, Earthquake Earl, from the old Stamps the Bish loved best.

"Seven yards!" he'd snort. "Lunsford would still be running!"

He always liked the old guys best, did Bish. He could do 10 minutes on Larry Robinson, or Thumper Harris, or the way Herm Harrison could swallow a football in one massive hand and squeeze it until the commissioner's signature cried Uncle.

He wasn't putting down the new. Nobody had to tell Bish that today's athletes were bigger, stronger and better. He just couldn't come to terms with the money, the contracts, and the fact that so many were unapproachable or had nothing to say when you got there.

He was a pistol, was Bish.

He lost a leg to diabetes, but at a Flames game he razzed me for waiting the prescribed 15 minutes after an insulin shot to have the pre-game meal.

"I take the damned stuff whenever I feel like it," he scoffed.

"Bish," I said, "I'm getting diabetes advice from a one-legged man."

"Well," he conceded, "there is that."

We were supposed to have dinner the next time I was in town. Now he's gone. Somehow, you never get a chance to say the things you want to. But we all tried yesterday.

Bish would have liked the service, but he would have loved the reception. There was food and drink and fellowship, and the stories flowed like wine. For the Bish, that's all it ever took.

Time Out for Romance

BEHIND EVERY GOOD MAN there's a good woman, and I have the very best. The former Deborah Easton does not yet understand my passion for sports, writing, old western movies, big band music or Mel Tormé over Rod Stewart, but we've only been married 50 years and I refuse to give up hope.

I tell people she knows I was a sports writer because a half-century ago I told her. Could she prove it by quoting something from a column I'd written? Probably not. But then, back in the '70s when she worked in a microbiology lab and was part of a team that did the first successful cloning experiment at University of BC, replicating some genes of the drosophila fruit fly, I hadn't a clue about her job either.

Deb's a do-er, not a watcher. She's gone on an African safari where late-night bathroom trips required a Masai warrior on the other side of the bush to scare off predators, cruised on a Russian trawler damn near to the North Pole and swum in a tributary of the Amazon river when the guide assured her that it wasn't the time of year when the piranha were hungry. But the thought that millions of people would pay money to watch other people don skates to hit a piece of rubber with a stick remains beyond her comprehension.

Which, for a five-a-week sports columnist, made her a godsend . . .

Communication Gap
The Province, December 31, 1979

"YOU'RE GOING TO DO IT AGAIN, aren't you?" snarled the former Deborah Easton. "You're going to watch football all day."

She was staring at me. Ice slowly formed on my considerable forehead. Instinctively, I knew her game plan: Hit him with the old You Never Talk to Me Anymore. But for every play there's a defence. George Allen says so. I opted for the full blitz.

"What's your beef?" I snarled right back. "I distinctly remember speaking to you Saturday afternoon between 4:15 and 5. Vernon Perry had just intercepted his fourth pass for Houston and it wasn't time for *Hockey Night in Canada*. I even remember what I said: 'When's dinner?'"

"Do you remember what I said?" she asked sweetly.

"Of course, but that's stupid. You can't take a football and eat it."

"I didn't say eat it," she said.

There are wives who like football. *National Geographic* occasionally finds little pockets of them, usually in tiny villages so primitive the sets are black and white. Mostly, though, they hate it. Worse, they demand equal time, which can be rough. Take Sunday.

"When are you going to phone about the New Year's Eve reservations?" she asked.

"Look at that Steel Curtain!" I replied. "Three shots from the two-yard line and Miami can't get in."

"The furnace has stopped," she said. "The water in the aquarium is freezing the guppies."

"You ever see a guy as tough as that Franco Harris?" I asked. "Three guys just hit him—beat the *crap* out of him—and he gets up smiling. Super Bowl City! Nobody's gonna stop those guys. Nobody!"

"The neighbours' kids have just set fire to the cat."

That stopped me. "This could be serious," I said. "Cat fur smells when it burns. Tell them not to do it in the house. And when the cat's done, tell them not to forget we've got another one."

"What are you *saying?*"

"I dunno," I said wearily. "I've got a lot of things on my mind. Lynn Swan hasn't been in since the first half. The Steelers are starting to crack. They've already missed a convert and . . ."

I could see she was upset. So I made one of those considerate, tactful moves that help make a marriage work during playoffs.

"Let's forget football and talk," I suggested.

She looked at me, eyes shining. "Really?" she said.

"Sure. It's the two-minute warning. We've got 60 seconds."

She was silent. Obviously overcome.

"Let's use it constructively," I rushed on, one eye on the set. "Let's figure out when we're going to have some time to ourselves—you know, just the two of us. After all, it's almost a new decade."

The old soft soap. Gets 'em every time.

"Tomorrow, then," she relented. "I know you like watching the NFL, but it won't be on tomorrow and it's New Year's Eve. We can sit at home by the fire and . . ."

"Right," I said, flipping the remote to pick up the Rams and Cowboys while the Dolphins and Steelers were into commercial. "That's it, then. Home by the fire until 11:30. Then we'll eat lunch right there. Just you and me and the fire and the Peach Bowl."

"Peach Bowl? You know I don't make dessert."

"Uh, no," I explained. "The Peach Bowl *game*. Baylor vs. Clemson."

Something told me she was disturbed. Nineteen years married, you learn to detect the signs. Maybe it was the way she picked up the poker.

"Not to worry," I added hastily. "It'll be over by 2:30. After that, no more football. Promise. I'll even skip the Blue Bonnet Bowl."

"No more football?" she asked doubtfully.

"Not a down," I said. "It's up against the hockey. Montreal vs. Red Army. Oh, I could probably catch the fourth quarter when the hockey's over, but no way. This is your night."

"My night," she repeated. "We do what *I* want."

"Absolutely."

"Good," she gushed. "I've got it all planned. We go out for dinner at about eight. Then dancing. It's time you learned. The last time we went to a dance they stamped the back of our hands and made us take off our penny loafers. Then we come home and put another log on the fire. I'll have the champagne chilled. We'll drink in the 1980s. Maybe even have some friends in. We'll party through the night. We'll drink and laugh and talk until . . ."

"Twelve-oh-five," I interrupted. "Twelve-thirty tops."

She eyed the poker. "Why?" she said dangerously.

"Training," I explained. "The old eyeballs aren't what they used to be. Got to get my sleep. Sugar and Cotton Bowl games start at 11. I figure with the remote I can get the best of both. Then the Rose Bowl's from two to five and the Orange Bowl from five to eight . . ."

"Let me understand this," she said slowly. "You plan to usher in the '80s by lying flat on your butt on that couch watching football *from 11 a.m. to 8 p.m.?*"

Her voice sounded funny.

"Well, sure," I said. "Oh, I was gonna watch the Rose Parade first, but that starts at 8:30 in the morning and I wasn't sure you'd want to be up that early."

"*Up?*" she screamed. "*Up?* Give me one good reason I should be up at 8:30 on New Year's Day when you're going to spend it all watching *football!*"

"To make my coffee," I said reasonably.

She's a nice girl, but kind of slow.

The Dish Meets the Dish

The Province, December 5, 1982

THE DISH IN THE LIVING ROOM is not impressed with the dish on the roof. "Your legs will atrophy," sniffs the former Deborah Easton. "You'll be nothing but bald head and belly."

The dish in the living room does not like spectator sports. She doesn't read sports pages. She knows I'm a sports writer because 22 years ago when I married her, I told her. The idea of putting a 300-pound bird bath on the roof to reach into space and grab other games was not greeted with huzzahs. But it's there and it hasn't changed a thing. I'm pigging out on sports. She's still in the living room. I think.

If anything, I'm better organized. When you jump from 13 channels to roughly 140 and one of them is a 24-hour sports channel, you've got to be, or you'll miss something. Take the other night. I got so interested in watching Kentucky play UCLA in college basketball that I missed an entire period of Oilers–Flyers hockey. And last night I fell asleep with a minute or so left in the UCLA–Notre Dame game and blew the final of the Wendy's Classic tournament.

But not to worry: ESPN will give it to me again. And again, and once more after that. Showing sports 24 hours a day forces some repetition. Still, if you don't know the score, watching Herschel Walker and Georgia beat Georgia Tech at 1 a.m. is just as much fun as watching it live.

Whatshername just called me. "When do you want dinner?" she asked.

"Half time," I said. "Here."

"You want to eat it," she asked sweetly, "or wear it?"

A hard loser, old Della . . . er, Deborah. Take the night we had a dish brought over for a demonstration.

The guy backed it into the driveway on a flatbed truck, made some adjustments, turned on a set in the van—and suddenly, while my neighbours were getting ready to battle traffic to watch the mighty Canucks play Hartford, I was standing in my driveway watching the Sabres and Canadiens play to a 7–7 tie.

"Where's the movie channel?" Dolores asked.

The guy started flipping channels as I went in to get a coat. When I came out, Daphne had a message.

"The Playboy channel works," she said.

"You mean the one with the X-rated movies and live nude centrefolds?"

"That's the one."

"I better check it out, just in case," I suggested.

"Trust me on this," she said. "It works."

"But, this thing is EXPENSIVE! It's gonna cost me a lot of money."

"Not as much as it's gonna cost you if I catch you watching that channel," she replied. You can take the girl out of Victoria, but . . .

We did not rush into the dish purchase. First the man had to do a site check. There were problems: there was no room in the back yard for the dish; the neighbours, a nice, quiet lot, might not want a ten-foot circular birdbath decorating the front.

"On the roof," the man said. "We'll put it on the roof."

Our house has slanty roofs in all but one area about 15 feet square. "Amazing," the man said. "That's exactly where the dish would have to go."

"You see?" I said, pivoting triumphantly. "That proves it!"

"Proves what?" Denise asked.

"God wants me to have a dish!"

So we bought it. I had to agree to buy a VCR so we could tape movies, and run outlets to a set in another room so she could watch them "while you watch those idiots sweat," but it's in. I can watch NBA and college basketball, all the New York Islanders' games and most of the Oilers', NFL football till it comes out of my ears—if you wear a jock to play it, I can watch it.

And it's wonderful. There are, however, minor drawbacks. The December issue of the monthly satellite TV listings (magazine-sized, 133 crammed pages per month) hasn't arrived yet, forcing me to spend as much time searching as watching. I even phoned the publisher in Haley, Idaho, to question the delay.

"Canada?" she asked. "What providence [sic] are you in?"

"Divine," I snarled.

"That's our worst one for delivery," she cooed.

But I'll get by. After all, I've got a family, and there's nothing nicer than meaningful family dialogue. Just the other night my 18-year-old son said, "Dad, I can't find the Playboy channel."

"Gosh, son," I replied, "let old Dad help you."

I pushed a few buttons—and suddenly we were looking at a man with a microphone doing a Howard Cosell while several nude couples cavorted on cots. "Welcome," he said, "to the Heterosexual Olympics!"

"UUHHH!" said the young lady who lives with us.

"Migawd!" said Whatshername.

"Dad," my son said, "I think you found it."

Kitty Litter

The Province, July 23, 1987

THIS WEEK I WENT to see *Cats*. Not Katz the bookie, *Cats* the musical.

The lighting was brilliant, the staging magnificent, the costumes out of this world. So why didn't I like it?

Possibly because I hate cats. In my humble opinion, God put cats on earth to make tennis racquets, and the decline of civilization began with the development of the nylon string.

Admittedly, the relationship between cats and sport is tenuous at best. There is no real justification for writing this on a sports page, except possibly that some species of cat are hunted (although not nearly enough) and hunting is considered a sport by those too young to have seen *Bambi*. That will have to do, because I'm going to write it anyway.

Cats the musical has the same problem as cats the animals. Once you get over the golly gee, isn't that (she, he) beautiful, nothing happens. On stage, a bunch of cats dance and sing or recite poems by T.S. Eliot. We are told that one cat has to die (I'd heard that—it was the only reason I went) and sure enough, about two hours later, one does.

"One down," I muttered. The cat person next to me sank an elbow into my rib cage. I love her, but she irks easily.

Even then, the cat comes back. That's another thing about cats: They always come back. Every day you read about some cat that was lost two years ago on a family vacation and found her way across three states and six provinces to get back home to little Marvin or Janie. Nobody ever interviews Marvin or Janie's father, who'd wasted a lot of time accidentally tying the cat to a tree.

Other than "Memory"—maybe the most beautiful piece of music written in a decade—that's about it, although I did note a couple of striking similarities between the stage cats and those that infest the human home. The stage cats had stupid names like Tum Tugger and Skimbleshanks (our two are named Nosey and Pookie—I rest my case) and according to the program notes it costs the touring company $50,000 per year just to replace light bulbs, which is about average for any home with teenage kids.

I watched, and found myself thinking: Why did they choose *Cats*? Why not *Dogs*? Why not *Lassie: the Musical*?

Dogs are far more intelligent than cats who—when they're not sneaking into the bedroom at night to lie on your face and smother you, or going out to mug some bird—basically just lie around waiting to be fed.

Put Lassie up there. She could at least fetch, or roll over, or bury a bone. Or Rin-Tin-Tin. Now there was a dog! The kid would say "Okay, Rinty, go to the colonel and tell them the Indians are gonna hit the fort at dawn and this time they must be serious, 'cause they're bringin' the Braves with 'em. Oh, yeah, and they've got nuclear weapons. Got that, Rinty?" And the dog would arf once and run off to save the regiment.

Or what about Sandy, Little Orphan Annie's dog? Guided Annie out of many a fix, he did, which was a hell of a trick for a dog whose eyes had no pupils.

Could a cat do that? Of course not. Worse yet, a cat wouldn't even try. So, kids, listen carefully:

If you don't want to wake up with a cat on your face or get lost in the woods with no one around to save you but some smarmy little Siamese with a rhinestone collar and a voice like Streisand on steroids, go stand in front of Mommy and Daddy and cry until they trade the cat in on a dog.

If they won't, just write to me. I'll send you instructions on how to make yourself a nice new tennis racquet.

The Duck Stops Here
The Province, April 10, 1990

Mr. Tony Eberts,
Outdoors Editor,
The Province

Tony,

There are ducks in my swimming pool. Three, counting the decoy.

We discovered them Monday morning. My wife looked through the sliding glass doors and made a funny sound. "Ooh!" she cooed. I was immediately suspicious. The last time she cooed like that we wound up owning a cat.

"No more cats," I snarled.

"Not cats, ducks," she said.

"Don't call me ducks. Call me disturbingly handsome, call me sexy, call me . . ."

"Real ducks," she said. "Two of them. In the swimming pool."

I looked. She was right. There was the wooden one and two others that looked even stupider. One with a green head, the other looking fat, smug and know-it-all.

"That's the female, right?" I asked. "So how come she's so fat?"

"I think she's getting ready to . . ."

"She already has," I said, peering into the pool. "See, there's some over there, some by the drain, some by the skimmer . . . Jeez! All the ducks in the world and we have to get two with the trots."

"Idiot! I mean, I think she's looking for a place to nest."

"You mean, like . . . ?"

"That's right. Little ducklings."

"Ducklings, hell," I said. "I took biology. Before you get ducks you get eggs, right? And then, you get . . ."

"Cute little ducklings," she nodded.

" . . . breakfast," I concluded.

"Breakfast???"

"Yeah, breakfast. Fried duck-egg sandwiches. Duck omelette. Scrambled, maybe, with a little salt. Or maybe over easy on toast. I know they aren't exactly Grade A large, but if we get lucky and she lays a lot of them . . ."

"But they're so *cute!* I bet if we gave them some bread and stayed very quiet, they'd come right up to the door. Wouldn't that be nice?"

"Go ahead, coddle them," I said.

"You mean, maybe cake instead of bread? I'm not sure ducks like . . ."

"Ducks, hell. I mean the eggs. We find 'em, we put them in the hot tub, and bingo: coddled eggs. I'd say poach 'em, but that would make the tub too hot for the rest of us."

"You have no soul," she complained. "Eggs become baby ducks. Baby ducks become adult ducks. Adult ducks . . ."

"Become dinner. You're right. Eating the eggs would be crazy. We let the eggs grow into big ducks, and then we eat *them*. It's just like hunting, only with home delivery. And you don't have to get up at obscene hours and freeze to death in a duck blind hoping some other hunter doesn't think you're a mallard."

We stopped talking about then, which is why I'm writing.

Is it unusual to have ducks land in your swimming pool?

Why can't I shoot them or eat them or boil their eggs? If I do, will Greenpeace picket my house?

Am I really expected to feel sorry for birds who fly south every winter—which, by the way, I can't afford to do myself?

Please hurry. My wife already wants to name them.

I suggested Poopsie and Poopsie.

"Why the same name for both ducks?" she asked.

"Look in the pool," I said.

Stay Calm And Pass The V-8
The Province, August 9, 1990

THE FURTHER ADVENTURES of Macho Jim, Outdoorsy-Type Guy . . .

Okay, so I'm actually a City-Type Guy. So maybe macho is stretching it and I don't pound my whiskers in with the back of the axe and bite them off from the inside. But it is still possible to have outdoorsy-type adventures right here in the city. I myself have them all the time.

Did I not tell you of how the two ducks landed in my swimming pool and how we all sat enraptured for hours watching them use it as a poopeteria? Well, this one is even more exciting.

Yesterday, 2:30 a.m., we are awakened by the overpowering stench of burning rubber, or possibly smouldering wiring and insulation. It is so powerful we pull on dressing gowns, run out of the room, then out of the house. There is no escaping it.

"The house is on fire," my wife says.

"Omigod! My autographed picture of Cheryl Tiegs is in there! My complete set of Wayne Gretzky trading cards! My *Sports Illustrated* collection!"

"Your son," she reminds me, "and your 92-year-old mother."

"Them, too!"

She runs into the house and calls the fire department. (Well, somebody had to.)

Three minutes, several awaken-the-dead sirens and enough flashing lights for a movie première later, two fire trucks are parked outside the house and one of several firemen is asking my wife whether she'd like some oxygen. Nobody asks me anything.

I wait. They do not rush in to haul my mother and son from their beds. They do not pull down ladders, unroll hoses, chop a hole in my roof or do any of those other firemen things.

"Skunk," says one.

Hey, I know it's late, but there's no call to get insulting.

"Skunk," he repeats. "You can smell it clear over to the school yard."

Our dog wanders by, a purebred Highland collie who makes Lassie look like Roseanne Barr. She smells of burning rubber, or possibly smouldering wiring or insulation.

"Looks like your dog had a fight with a skunk," the fireman says.

The firemen look at one another, then at me. They pack up their oxygen tanks and leave. The dog runs into the house in case there are any rooms left that don't stink. There are. She remedies that.

"The dog," says my wife, "has to be cleaned. I read somewhere that tomato juice cuts skunk odour. Take her out back and bring me some tomato juice."

Crisis. We don't have any tomato juice. Fortunately, we Outdoorsy-Type Guys know how to improvise.

"Clamato or V-8?" I shout.

We settle on the V-8. I hold the dog. She empties this huge tin of V-8 all over it and begins to scrub. In seconds, the dog looks like a Rambo casualty.

"Her white ruff looks all bloody," I protest.

"It's three o'clock in the morning, my house smells of skunk and I'm pouring V-8 juice over a dog," my wife says sweetly. "Do you really want to continue this conversation?"

Not me. I'm camping out at the Pan Pacific until this thing blows over.

Trick Question
The Province, September 27, 1990

"How would *you* like it," my wife asked, "if you were covering a women's team and you went into the locker room and some naked girls came over and stood really close and dared *you* to touch their private parts?"

Inside my headbone, alarm bells sounded.

"This is a trick question, right? One of those where if I say I wouldn't like it you say 'Oh, sure!' and if I say I'd like it just fine, you smack me upside my head."

"It is *not* a trick question. It says right here on your sports pages that some players for the New England Patriots did that to a Boston *Herald* sports writer named Lisa Olson when she was in the dressing room getting an interview and they were coming out of the shower.

"And one of them said 'Is this what you want?', which she says was one of his tamer comments, and the team owner, that Victor Kiam electric shaver person, called her 'A classic bitch!', and her paper was considering a sexual-harassment lawsuit but Kiam and the team have apologized and some players have been fined, and I was just wondering how you'd feel if the shoe was on the other foot."

Dance, Jim. Dance!

"You mean, I've just finished covering the women's professional tennis tour, and I'm in the dressing room interviewing, say, Martina Navratilova, and Gabriela Sabatini is coming out of the shower, and she walks over to me wearing only soapsuds and a smile and says . . . Naah!"

"What do you mean, naah? You're saying Gabriela Sabatini, whom you've only been slobbering all over the TV screen about since she was 17, is standing there starkers, making suggestive suggestions, and you don't even react? Oh, sure!"

"No, I mean . . ."

"*No?* What do you mean, no? Thirty years I give you, and the first time some little 20-year-old comes swishing by mother naked, you go chasing after her offering to towel her down?"

"Wait! I don't mean no, I don't react. I mean, no, it would never be a problem because the offer would never be made! What does Gabriela Sabatini need with a 53-year-old, out-of-shape bald guy? She's gorgeous and stinking rich."

"Then why doesn't she have her own shower room? Why does she need to come parading around after you?"

"Hey, don't blame me! I'm just standing here interviewing Martina Navratilova!"

She paused to regroup.

"All I want to know," she said, dangerously quiet, "is how you would feel as a reporter if you were treated that way in a women's team dressing room."

Bob and weave. Bob and weave . . .

"What happened in New England is that Ms. Olson—a qualified reporter who deserved equal treatment—made a rookie mistake in the way she used her assets. What she should have done when the guy made that crack was show a little leg."

"A little *leg!* Why, you . . ."

"Yeah, a little leg—right up to the knee, just before she brought it up into the guy's crotch. Then she could have said 'No, it's not what I want. And for the next few days you're not gonna want it, either.'

"See, football players are always telling male media guys to stick this and stuff that and perform those physical impossibilities upon themselves, and there's nothing much we can do about it because one swing and we'd wind up in traction. But if a female reporter hauls off and belts some guy who insults her, what's he gonna do—hit her back?"

"All right, but you still haven't told me how you'd handle Gabriela Sabatini."

"I don't know, dear. And you know the sad part? I'll never get the chance to find out."

Sewerperson

The Province, May 20, 1992

My wife is crewing in the Swiftsure yacht race. Training-wheels division.

"I'm navigator," she explained. "And sewerman. I get to haul in the sail and fold it."

This from a woman who hates to fold my shirts. A woman whose unerring sense of where she is and how to get where she wants to go is sometimes nullified by instructions along the lines of:

"Go left right here."

"Left?"

"Right."

But she has a cousin and he has a boat and Swiftsure has a lot of classes. Besides, their three-race record is 1–1–1: one win, one motor-in and one "We didn't race, actually, we spent all day getting the boat ready for next weekend." That's how I know she's ready. Sailors jump in their little sailboats and sail. Yachtspeople stay on the dock fixing their boats for next weekend.

"You want to crew for us?" she asked hopefully.

She knows I can't swim, hate water, and failed miserably in my only attempt to navigate a canoe. I was headed for Shawnigan Lake. It was on top of my car and fell off. At 5 p.m. In the middle of the Oak Street bridge. Onto the hood of another car. I think she's after the life insurance.

But I'm behind her in this Swiftsure thing. Yessir, boy, there's nothing like the feel of a pitching deck as you run from the front end of the boat to the back end, upstairs and downstairs, looking for a place you can toss your cookies without getting it all over the hardy crewperson below. (See: Sewerman.) Those of us staying behind to lie down on the couch and watch the Stanley Cup are as green with envy as they'll be with *mal de mer.*

There were, however, a couple of questions.

"Does your Sophia work?" I asked.

"My what?"

"Your Sophia. That navigational thing that picks up from a chain of stations all over the place that tell you whether you're approaching Race Rocks or the lobby of the Pan-Pacific."

"It's not a Sophia," she said. "It's a Loran. With an 'a.'"

"Whatever. Does it work, or do I have to ruin my weekend in some bumpy Air-Sea Rescue helicopter staring down at the water hoping to find you before the sharks do?"

"It works perfectly," she said in that skipper-to-landlubber tone that says you should kill yourself because neither your jeans nor your genes have salt in them. "Except when we were installing it and pushed an extra button and it thought it was somewhere off Tokyo."

"Kind of the long way around to get back to Victoria."

"Stow it," she said nautically.

But I'm supportive, especially since I found out amateurs can actually win. Bill Koch, who'd never entered before, won the America's Cup on the weekend off San Diego. Cost him only $64,000,000 compared to $100,000,000 for second-place Italy, which only goes to show what kind of bargains there are out there in Yachtland if you really shop around.

A wonderful thing, technology. In Long John Silver's day you loaded a wooden boat full of swabs and went looking for treasure. Today you spend a treasure on the boat and go looking for a trophy that would make a hell of a hubcap if you could figure a way to flatten it.

Which reminded me.

"How much is this gonna cost us?" I asked.

"Ferry fare over and back with the car," she said. "And I've got to pack a lunch."

"Hey, no problem. I read *Treasure Island.* Barrel of water, barrel of flour, easy on the weevils. A tot of rum for the swabs. What can it cost?"

"Man overboard!" she screamed.

"Huh? Where?"

"Come out back," she said sweetly. "I think we should check out the pool."

The Mighty Marys

The Province, April 13, 1995

AS YOU MAY KNOW, yachting is my life.

Not riding in them. A guy could get wet. My specialty is watching them, preferably from a seat in a good restaurant.

There's nothing quite like the thrill of cutting into a good steak while gazing out the window at happy families toiling like galley slaves to get their boat ready for that mythical Next Weekend when it will be ready to sail and they are actually going to get it out in the open water and Have Fun. Meanwhile, they are doing dockside fun things like scraping off barnacles and digging out rot.

But this year, yachting has an appeal that transcends the mere consumption of calories, drinking in the beauty of all those forever-parked boats, and hooting at the people on the dock. It's America's Cup time, and for the first time ever there is an all-female crew in the running to defend against the New Zealanders or Aussies or whoever.

Well, it's not actually ALL female. One male was taken on late in the game to add a pinch of experience in the quest for America's version of the Holy Grail: the right to kick the stuffings out of Dennis Connor. Anyone who has watched Connor or listened to his fund-raising pitch to convince corporate America to shell out millions so he can go boat-racing knows this is a cause at least as noble as the Crusades, more than worthy of support by those of us on the other side of NAFTA.

The female invasion is of particular interest to me, since most of what I know about yachting has been learned from my wife, a weekend sailorette who once served as sewerperson in the Swiftsure race.

The sewerperson's job is to stay in the boat's basement folding the sails so they won't tangle when the Skipper decides to haul them up rather than just saying to hell with it and using the perfectly good motor they keep around for times when the wind dies or it's time for the grog break. She loves it, which says a lot about the effect of salt water on brain cells.

Together we have followed the exploits of the women of America 3 and their new boat, the *Mighty Mary*, in their bid to upset *Young America* and Connor's boat, *Stars and Stripes*, which wouldn't even be in the finals had not the people who run the defence noticed that he was going to finish third in the elimination round and would therefore be out of the semi-finals.

"Here, here, we can't have that," they cried, and changed the rules in midstream, so to speak, to make the final a three-boat competition.

It was not unlike the National Hockey League discovering that the Montreal Canadiens might not make the playoffs, and passing a rule that gives teams whose home ice is the Montreal Forum an automatic berth in the Stanley Cup final. But Connor is in and, given his vast experience, might even sail *Stars and Stripes* into the defender's role.

Still, there is reason to hope that the *Mighty Mary*s may yet prevail.

They've already done better than the French entry on the challengers' side. French skipper Marc Pajot spent $33,000,000—$14,000,000 of it public funds—and lost *France 2* when a crane dropped it on a dock, smashing the keel strut through the deck. *France 3*'s mast broke in half in one race, two sailors fell overboard, and the French contingent went home knowing that, in the words of Ricky Ricardo, they've got a lot of 'splainin' to do.

Mighty Mary, on the other hand, upset *Young America* in the first race of the final. Connor also beat the favoured *Young America* crew in Race 2. Thus we were glued to our TV sets, awaiting the result of the scheduled meeting of the *Mary*s and Connor.

Things did not start out well. *Stars and Stripes* had a big lead and apparently was set to pull away. Then, miracle of miracles, the wind died. The race had to be scrapped and run again from scratch.

My sewerperson cheered. "God is in *Mighty Mary*'s corner," she crowed. "I knew She'd help."

Her Cup Runneth Over

Calgary Sun, June 11, 1998

SO HERE I SIT, feet on the coffee table, coffee at hand, family and visiting relatives warned that should one of them come through the door, the house had better be on fire.

It is 7:30 a.m. PDT and already my wife is suitably unimpressed.

"You're going to watch the whole thing, aren't you?" she snarls becomingly.

Well, see, that's where misunderstandings start. Marriage is about sharing, about a willingness to bend. There are 64 games in the World Cup soccer tournament. To even suggest I'd watch every one of them is ridiculous.

"Fifty," I respond. "Fifty-five, tops."

"Bu ... but that's ... 50 games times 90 minutes ... that's 75 hours in front of a TV set!"

"And your parents said that six months of college before I yanked you out to get married was wasted," I enthuse. "Mind you, you didn't factor in the pre-game shows and the half time and the possibility of extra time and shootouts once they get past the first round, but ..."

"Fifty games!" she hisses. "What about time for *us?*"

Fortunately, I had that figured.

"Friday I'll skip Paraguay and Bulgaria," I promise. "And Saturday, well, Spain and Nigeria could be a big one, but for you ..."

"Two games you skip," she says doubtfully. "On successive days. Just for me."

"Absolutely. It'll be just the two of us, breathing in the fresh air, watching the sun come up while you cook breakfast."

"Wait a minute. What time do the games start?"

"Well, actually, 5:30 a.m. both days," I admit. "But look on the bright side: Until 8:30, when the second game starts, I'm all yours."

She puts her arms around me, always a bad sign.

"It isn't that I've got anything against the World Cup," she coos. "I *loved* the one in Italy when you went to the games and I went to Amsterdam. And the one in the United States was even better. I stayed home, and you were gone.

"But this one ... I mean, you're so ... so ... *here!* And that damned six-by-eight-foot projector TV will be blaring for days, and—wait a minute! How long does this go on?"

"Well, see, there's the good part. After a couple of weeks, when the first round is over, they won't ever play more than two games a day in the second from 7:30 a.m. to 2:30 p.m. After that, a couple of weeks for the sudden-death games—hey, July 13 will be here before you know it."

"But today," she says carefully, "is only June 10."

"There is that," I concede. That's another marriage tip: Never be afraid to concede the obvious.

She pivots and leaves me to Ronaldo and the Brazilians, the class of the field and the most fun to watch because they think defence is de thing that de other teams play because they can't dance. They need luck and an own-goal by Scotland for a 2–1 win, but boy, are they good.

Then it's Morocco with the pony-tailed Mustapha Hadji and Taher El Lakhlej, who can drop a 30-yard pass on a teammate's forehead and offer choice of eyebrow. Twice they blow leads and settle for a 2–2 draw with Norway.

There is a noise outside. My wife is yanking furiously at the TV cable.

Not to worry. If the cable goes, I switch to satellite. Being in love means always having a back-up plan.

The Puck Stops Here

In 1066, William the Conqueror took on the Saxons in a best-of-one series and won England. Nine centuries later, in exactly 1,066 games, 26 National Hockey League teams reduced their number by 10 and won for the rest the right to start all over again.

Obviously, Willie and the Normans had a better system than Gary and the Governors.

Suppose, after that first battle, King Harold the Saxon had told the local scribes, "Okay, that's one. But this is a best-of-seven war, and when the going gets tough, the tough get going. There's a lot of pride in our tent, and once we get our guys playing to a defensive system where they duck those arrows instead of throwing their chests in front of them . . ."

Would England have been any better for a best-of-seven? Before the first battle horn blew, the smart money was on the Normans. Everybody knew they had better equipment, more size and a deeper bench. If there'd been a Vegas, the Saxons would have been 200–1.

And there were no prelims. William and Harold didn't have to stop off at every Pimple-on-Thigh and Water-on-Knee hamlet to squash the local tough guys on the way to Hastings for the final. This was pre-expansion. They weren't just the best, they were the only. So they had the fight, got it over, and the peasants went back to the villages muttering as villagers always have and always will:

"Normans, Saxons, big deal. We all know who's gonna get pillaged in the end. Us—the bloomin' spectators!"

"Too right! You see that Saxon doin' the barterin', floggin' those flippin' white towels? Wanted my cow, 'e did, and I was savin' 'er for an ale."

"You call that a battle? I tell you, they've gotta do something about the violence. There ain't nearly enough of it."

Nine centuries-plus later, we haven't learned a thing. Now it's 30 teams and 1,148 games, and 16 in the playoffs. Why has all this happened? Because the NHL has discovered to its delight that come playoff time the pigeons have short memories and deep pockets. Despite everything, they still do.

We Owe It All To Eaton's
Calgary Sun, March 5, 1997

MR. GARY BETTMAN,
President,
National Hockey League

Sir,

Throughout its long and glorious history, the National Hockey League has always stood up for the little guy and paid homage to its roots.

Well, okay, that's a lie. But you could always start. And I can think of no better way than by making a move that would save a Canadian institution and show that you do, indeed, honour those gallant pioneers without whom your league could never have survived its formative years:

Buy Eaton's.

Now, I realize that as an American you probably think Eaton is what you do when you're not drinkin', thinkin', sleepin' or procreatin'. But no: Eaton's is a department store chain almost as old as this country itself. Before there was a Gimbels or a Macy's, long before Walmart, K-Mart or even Mart Kenny, Eaton's stores dotted the prairies like buffalo chips.

And why, you ask, should the NHL step in to save a bunch of department stores teetering on bankruptcy?

Because, sir, without Eaton's there might not BE a National Hockey League.

Let me explain:

One of the things Eaton's did best was produce a thick catalogue so that people miles from their stores could order everything from argyle socks to zoot suits.

Almost instantly, the Eaton's catalogue was a multi-purpose chunk of Canadiana.

Small boys felt the first stirring of sexual fantasies poring through the pages of women modelling bras, nighties and other unmentionables. Kids thumbed its corners dog-eared doing their Christmas dreaming. Late at night, their parents whispered as they slept, balancing meagre savings against one toy from Santa Claus.

And when Mom and Dad had filled in the order blanks with what little they could afford, the Eaton's catalogue served them one last time—in the outhouse, where you learned early that the newsprint pages were fine, but the thicker coloured ones left pointy corners when you scrunched them that could play hell with a bare and already frozen backside.

But, most important of all, the Eaton's catalogue allowed generations of kids to play hockey.

Stuffed inside socks or under breeks, it provided both warmth and protection from the pain of frozen horse turds propelled at whatever speed could be attained. (Fortunately there was no television then, or FOX would have put them in a white circle.)

Without Eaton's and the warmth of those catalogues, the Bentleys might have gone indoors. Gordie Howe might have turned to baseball. Generations of kids wouldn't have been out there shovelling the snow off the rivers and the prairie ponds where they stayed and played until dinner or darkness forced them to quit.

You made do in those days, Mr. Bettman. There were no equipment giants flogging over-priced, signatured gear. Gordie's first skates fell on his kitchen floor from a gunnysack of used goods handed to his mother by a lady to whom she'd given a few pennies for food. Ask the old-timers. They'll tell you how it was, and every one of them will tell you how they stuffed that catalogue under their pants.

Cold days, hot horses and the Eaton's catalogue, Mr. Bettman. Without them, you'd have no league. If you can't buy the stores, at least put Timothy Eaton in the Hall of Fame.

Everybody Out of the Pool

Calgary Sun, October 1, 2001

THESE ARE THE DAYS I HATE: the hockey pool days, the days of the mad scramble by people who know nothing about the game and call me because they think I do.

Bulletin: I don't.

Not, at least, in the statistical sense. And there is a good reason for this, the reason that is also my answer to every question in the Trivial Pursuit sports edition: I don't care.

If my life depended on it, I could not sit down today and place all 30 NHL teams (there are 30, aren't there?) in their proper divisions, sub-divisions, conferences, cul-de-sacs or whatever they're calling them these days.

Why? See: Trivial Pursuit (above).

Once, I was an ace. My dad used to stand me up on the counter at our coffee shop and bet customers that I could name the stars on all the NHL teams.

It was a snap: There were six teams, one for each year I'd been alive. My dad, who used to stretch out on the couch with me to listen to Foster Hewitt, would never have believed there'd be a 30-team NHL, let alone teams named after birds, fish, animals and oil rigs. A guy who hated the Boston Bruins could never adjust to the Atlanta Thrashers.

Hockey pools hadn't been invented, or my dad would have used me to make out like a bandit. He never took a drink in his life, but show him a deck of cards and you could be in for an interesting evening. A bet would not be out of the question.

Pools, over-and-under, giving a puck or half a puck would have driven him nuts. You took the Leafs or the Habs to win. If they tied, the bet rolled to next time. Guy asked for half a puck, he might be wearing his coffee. Simpler times.

Today, everything is pools. Guys show up at "draft" parties armed with computer print-outs from NHL.com listing everything about a player but his booze and sexual preferences.

Books are published—books!!!—on how to win your office pool. "Up-to-date info!" they scream. Sure, except printing deadlines leave them weeks and trades behind.

Poolies gather around water coolers or over post-work brewskies to discuss their picks, make trades, and snicker at the guy who drafted somebody with a broken leg and a minor leaguer named Fred Howe because at the race track where he hangs out they're always talking about bloodlines.

That's the other thing about pools: They've become such a cultural phenomenon that if your office has one and you're not in, you're an outcast.

So what if you've got the inside scoop about the corporate take-over, or what Freddie and Marge really mean when they discuss a possible mailroom merger. Is Trevor Linden gonna have a big year, or not? (Pool tip: When asked, do not say "Who's Trevor Linden?")

Biggest tip of all: Don't ask me.

Stats are not my thing. I'm a people writer. Some of the people happen to play hockey, which makes some of them interesting and others duller than a rusted Gillette. Just like the rest of the world.

Still, people phone. The only fun is to drive them crazy.

"How are the Canucks gonna do?"

"Well, they're definitely committed to an 81-game season."

"How do the Sedin twins look?"

"Similar."

"Who's gonna spell Cloutier?"

"It's not that difficult, really: Capital C-l-o-u-t-i-e-r. A lot of people forget the 'u', but . . ."

"What's Brian Burke really like?"

"He's a lot like Brian Burke. Hard to tell them apart sometimes."

"What about their record this season?"

"Well, they seem to like 'O Canada' a lot. Not big in the dressing room, but they play it before every game."

"Who's good in the room?"

"At what?"

About there, they start to crack.

"You don't know nuthin' about hockey stats, do you?"

"Absolutely nothing. My dad would be proud."

The Dream Game
The Province, March 29, 1992

TWENTY-ONE THINGS TO DO on game night if the strike means they have to call off the Stanley Cup playoffs:

1. Turn on TV set in den. Lower sound, colour and picture levels until all you have is a blank screen.

2. Close door. Warn wife and children that if that door opens other than to admit bearer of beer and junk food, house had better be on fire.

3. Three minutes after what would have been telecast opening, place hand over heart, rise, and sing "O Canada."

3(b) If this would have been a road game in an American city, invite a couple of insufferably cute little kids over to sing "The Star Spangled Banner." Badly.

4. Yell at wife to get move on with the beer before they drop the puck.

5. Make up imaginary forward lines. Second-guess them.

6. Announce that the opening faceoff is brought to you by a brewery.

7. If you have false teeth, remove them.

8. Spit.

9. Five minutes into what would have been first period, run full-tilt into wall. Jump up, pull off sweater, and beat the stuffings out of chesterfield pillow.

10. Sit in chair in corner for five minutes.

11. Spit.

12. Commercial break. When wife brings in beer, pretend she is voluptuous 22-year-old blonde with brow never furrowed by a single cogent thought. Hold bottle in air. Tilt head back. Smack lips. Do not, under any circumstances, drink the beer. (No one in beer commercials ever tastes the beer. They've all got bottle and mug fetishes.)

13. Spit.

14. Yell "Heshootshescores!"

14(a) For Canuck goal, say "The Russian Rocket! Isn't he something, Jim? He went around that defenceman so fast the guy didn't have a prayer. Is he something, or is he something?"

14(b) For opposition goal, blame defence.

15. Spit.

16. Intermission. Call youngest boy into room, tell him his name is now Ron McLean and his job is to sit down and look bored. You be Don Cherry.

    Say "Yeah, Pavel Bure. Not bad for a Red. Reds are better'n Swedes, y'know. Like I was sayin' to Cam Neeley—great kid, Cam, know him well—the trouble with this league is that it's bringin' in too many foreigners to steal jobs from good Canadian kids like Gretzky, who is pretty good even if his grandfather did come from Russia and . . .

    "Tonight's game? Shuddup, I'm talkin' . . . You think *Hockey Night In Canada* pays me all this money to talk about tonight's game? They pay me to act like a redneck, beer-swilling know-it-all . . . Now, you take that Ulf Samuelsson, when is somebody gonna GET that guy . . ."

17. Pretend to turn off sound.

18. Repeat items (9) through (15), making sure that the great goals by Is-he-something-or-what? outnumber the soft goals caused by defensive lapses.

19. Two minutes before you figure game should end, start singing "Na-na-na-na! Na-na-na-na! Say he-ey! Goodbye!" Then jump up and down screaming "Yessssss!"

20. Turn off set. Return to living room. Do not spit.

21. Warning: As you sit there alone staring at the blank screen recreating the game, DO NOT under any circumstances attempt the Wave. People will think you're crazy.

Just Trying to Get By
Calgary Sun, November 12, 1999

THIS IS A CHAIN LETTER. Do not break the chain or the National Hockey League will send Bob Probert to your house to break your face . . .

Hello. My name is Gary Bettman and I am commissioner of a struggling hockey empire based in the village of New York in a remote nation called The United States of America (and, for now, in some parts of a border country called Canada, although we are trying to fix that).

Survival is not easy in my empire. Often it gets very cold outside, forcing its officers to flee to warmer places like Hawaii or Southern Florida to hold their winter survival meetings. Soon they will run out of such places in their own country and be forced to migrate to foreign places like the Costa del Sol where the champagne is even more expensive and if you buy California wine it's got an "Imported" sticker.

Our plight grows more desperate by the day.

Just this week, for instance, during a caviar break following my report that our empire's revenues have trebled in the '90s to about $14 billion because of expansion fees and several other forms of highway robbery that do not actually involve the use of a gun, it was noted that the governments of our teams in the Canadian colonies are still refusing to grant their teams tax privileges and other pork barrel sustenance not available to the common folk.

Frankly, we are halfway to our wits end trying to convince them to open their hearts and wallets so that our empire can continue to grow and prosper without forcing us to open our own.

How can we make them understand our plight? Why can they not understand that while revenues do range from $60–70 million US for the wealthier outposts, the poorer are getting by on $30–40 million?

How do we get the message across that not all of our tillers in the hockey ice fields earn millions, and that some of our children—18 to 20 years old, some of them—labour for seven months of the year, three hours a day, four or five days a week, for a paltry few hundred thousand dollars?

Desperate, we turn to you for help.

Please send this letter to five of your friends and ask each of them to send us $10 (US funds, no coins or stamps), then send copies to five of *their* friends with instructions to do the same thing.

Or, if you really want to help, place a chess board on your web page and invite them to play a game. First person puts a drawing of a $1 bill on the first square, then sends the actual money to us. Then each person in turn doubles the number of dollars in the previous square.

Won't that be fun? And before you know it, we'll have all the money in the world and be able to bring little Alexei Yashin home from the gulag and pay him whatever he wants.

We beg you not to turn your back on our people—not because it will hurt us, but because dreadful things could happen to you.

Only a few years ago, someone broke one of our earlier chains in Winnipeg, which we understand is in Canada. Within months, their outpost was blown clear to Arizona, leaving their people huddled against an October blizzard on the corner of Portage and Main uttering piteous cries—"TEEE-MU! TEE-MU!"—and lamenting the way they'd ignored the warnings from another Canadian place called Ke-Bec. Or something.

That legend is retold each year as our people gather round the liqueur table at our annual gatherings: the way Quebec people watched one team disappear into Colorado, and for their sins have seen their other team of Flying Frenchmen populated by foreigners and doomed to Finnish in the cellar.

Do not let this happen to you. Do not break the chain. Pick five of your richest friends and add links to our survival fund, named after one of our patron saints. Send all contributions to Fund Our Scam To Expand Revenue (FOSTER), NHL, New York.

No receipts will be issued so that we can save pennies otherwise wasted on stamps.

Hurry. We're running out of pâté.

Stay as Cool as You Are
Calgary Sun, January 25, 1998

CALGARY—HER NAME IS VICTORIA. She is eight years old. If you could bottle her smile you'd be capturing sunshine.

She is standing quietly with her father outside a dressing room at Norma Bush Arena, clutching a Team Canada hockey jersey and a black marking pen. It is 11:30 on a crisp, clear morning ripe with the promise of snowmen or sledding or flopping to make a snow angel just for the joy of it.

Maybe later. Today, Victoria has other plans.

She has been here since 8 a.m., slowly and politely gathering the signatures of Canada's women's Olympic hockey team on the jersey she will wear tomorrow night at the Saddledome when Canada plays the US, then hang it up in her room and never, ever wash it, because the ink might run.

One more autograph to go. Practice is over and there are a million commitments, places to be and things to do. And here comes Hayley Wickenheiser out of the dressing room in sweats, making sure the really important stuff gets done.

She signs her name. She counts all the other names to make sure that Victoria hasn't missed anyone. She chats to this saucer-eyed little girl while they have their picture taken.

"Thank you," says Victoria.

"Thank *you*," says Hayley Wickenheiser.

And it occurs to me that maybe we are missing the point of this Olympic trail-blazing. Maybe there is something here that transcends even gold. Maybe these women who've basically put their lives on hold for four years are doing more than living dreams. Maybe they're planting them.

Not that long ago, a little girl's definition of sport was something her brother did.

The barriers that fell toppled grudgingly. On too many occasions, her right to play or try out for soccer or hockey or baseball or volley-ball along with the boys was won in courts of law—hollow victories by battling parents while the little girl took such school and playground flak that the desire to play spilled away with her tears.

It's infinitely better today. There are girls' hockey teams, and mixed teams and recreational teams for women in most of the once male-only sports. But too often, little girls who try just as hard hear that hateful, condescending addendum: "And the girls play, too! Isn't that *nice*?" Too often, a little voice inside responds with a silent "Why bother?"

Now, suddenly, there is this women's hockey team, going to Nagano just like the NHL players.

Their faces are on cereal boxes. They have their own TV commercials, their own sponsors. They aren't just girls playing hockey in a forgotten corner. Suddenly, they are COOL.

Heady stuff, that, and they handle it well.

Interviews are opportunities, not things to be tolerated. Autograph seekers are fans, not irritants. The million thin slices trimmed from their leisure time by media and well-wishers are part of the accomplishment, not part of the price.

Do not change, ladies. Do not develop the hard-shell indifference of so many of your NHL counterparts. Not now, not ever. Down the road, perhaps just over the horizon past Winter Olympiad 2002, a women's professional league may well be waiting. Do not let it rob you of the joy you feel today. You, or Victoria, to whom you've given the freedom to dream.

Go (Snore) Senators, Go!
The Province, December 7, 1990

NHL EXPANSION INTELLIGENCE TEST. Select the best answer from the following multiple-choice questions:

1. The Ottawa entry in 1992–93 will be called the Senators because:
   (a) Ottawa was one of the original NHL members in 1917–18 with a team called the Senators.
   (b) The way the current NHL clubs will rig the expansion draft,

the only players left for Ottawa will be aged, doddering and basically useless.

(c) What else would you call a team that's elected today but doesn't have to attend a game for two years?

2. Phil Esposito, backed by Japanese money, is front man for Ottawa's new traditional rival, Tampa Bay. He won't last because:
   (a) He thinks Domo Arigato is a head waiter.
   (b) He'll try to trade Tampa for Sault Ste. Marie.
   (c) At his first press conference with his Japanese backers he'll sit down at the piano and attempt to play Chopsticks.

3. The best way to get a spot on the Senators' roster is to:
   (a) Know Brian Mulroney personally.
   (b) Do a Conservative a big favour.
   (c) Catch a Conservative doing someone else a big favour.

4. If you answered (c) to the above, you can best secure your position as a Senator by:
   (a) Developing your skating.
   (b) Developing your shooting.
   (c) Developing your negatives.

5. NHL franchises traditionally attract big tourist dollars from visitors who come to see the game and stay to spend money. From the following list, name Ottawa's No. 1 tourist attraction:
   (a) The House of Commons.
   (b) The house of Russ Jackson.
   (c) The bridge to Hull, Quebec.

6. Plans to build a new rink in Ottawa have been delayed because the site is part of the agricultural land bank. Select the most likely ending to the impasse:
   (a) Franchise owners come to BC and take land re-zoning lessons.
   (b) Conservatives designate land as Senatorial burial ground and arena as crypt to hold 18,000.
   (c) Disgruntled Hamiltonians plant two nests full of baby birds on property and phone the animal rights people.

7. Hamilton has a rink and commitments for a minimum 10,000 season tickets. Ottawa has no rink, no land and no commitment. Ottawa gets franchise because:
   (a) When Tim Hortons backed the Hamilton bid, NHL president John Ziegler said "DUH! Donuts have holes. Pucks don't have holes. They must be thinking of ringette."
   (b) It cuts down travel time for the Ottawa lobbyists using the free tickets they get for pressuring the NHL into awarding a Canadian franchise.
   (c) If Hamilton got an NHL franchise, Toronto would want one.

Dear Diana: Send Money

The Province, December 5, 1991

MR. PAUL ANKA,
c/o Ottawa Senators Hockey Club,
Ottawa, Ont.

Dear Paul,

Sorry to hear about your accidental purchase of part of the Ottawa Senators NHL franchise. At least, I'm assuming it was accidental, since no one in his right mind would do it on purpose.

Truly, it is a marriage made in heaven, the kind that's been known to launch dynasties: You have money, they need money. Who could ask for anything more?

> You're so rich and we're so broke,
> Oh, Paul Anka, what a joke.
> We don't care just what they say,
> Long as you can pay and pay . . .

I gather this is the honeymoon phase, when you and your new partners get all cutesy-poo and blushy at the mention of each other's names, just thinking of the wonderful life ahead with all the really neat people who run the NHL. They'll all love you, too (You really *do* have a lot of money, don't you?), more than you'll love them once you understand the way things work when it comes to welcoming new teams to the lodge.

> And they call it puppy training,
> Except the owners pee on you . . .

Mind you, things will get better once they actually have your money. (You're sure, now? You *can* cover the US$22.5 million due in June, just like your partner, Bruce Firestone said? Or, at least, I assume that's what he meant from that quote in the paper that now the Senators can stop worrying about that money due in June.) Before you know it you'll be involved in the expansion draft where your new NHL partners sell you some of their very own players to get you started.

> Put your hand on my shoulder,
> I can't stand up unaided,
> It's been years since I've skated,
> Hold me, tell me where I sign . . .

The important thing at that point is not to panic. Out-of-shape Senators have always been big in Ottawa, although you may have trouble actually getting them out to games. Then again, in the tradition of Senators through the years they won't get much accomplished when they do show up, so it all kind of evens out.

True, there will always be unforeseen operating expenses (Have they mentioned that you don't have a rink? Or a place to build one?), like jars for the false teeth, individual prune juice glasses and a pros-tate-removal clause in the team medical plan, but think what you'll save doing the anthem yourself and maybe writing a team fight song:

> We've got the fight!
> We've got the fizz!
> Let's go, Senators!
> Zzzzzzzzzz . . . .

Okay, so it will take time to build a winner. What's 30 or 40 years when you're having fun? Just think what it could do for your creative juices, trying to write hit songs fast enough to break even.

And if you don't, if you lose your shirt, well, you've already sort of written a great exit . . .

> And now, the end is near,
> I've got this team, no hope of winning.
> My friends, I'll make it clear:
> They're fat and slow, they're double-chinning.
> The league, it drained my poke,
> I got sucked in, yes, in a square way.
> And now, I sit stone broke,
> I did it their way . . .

Forever House
The Province, February 4, 1993

> *Calgary traded right wing C.J. Young to Boston for left wing Brent Ashton.*
> —Transactions, *The Province*, February 2

SUSAN ASHTON CALLS IT HER FOREVER HOUSE. It sits empty in Saskatoon, waiting for the summers when hockey's over and the family can come home for a few months before the phone rings again and they move heaven knows where.

"We bought it, but we don't rent it out," she says. "It's just there. We open the door, and we're home. And one day when this is over we're going to move in and stay forever."

"This" is the life of a hockey gypsy, where time is measured in packing cases and team jerseys and you're almost afraid to make friends because you know that goodbye comes too soon after hello.

"This is not real life," Susan Ashton says without a trace of self-pity and with a barely detectable hint of regret. "It's like you're waiting for your life to start."

She is on the phone from Boston, where Taylor (four) and Carter (two) and a 125-pound German shepherd named Fletcher make background sounds as she packs for the umpteenth time, heading this time for the Forever House, which will be close enough to Calgary for visits back and forth.

Her husband has just been traded to his ninth National Hockey League club, Boston to Calgary. For Susan Ashton, who remembers the jumps less in terms of cities than moving companies, it is a point of pride that, though he'd begun this season with the Providence farm club, the Bruins weren't trying to get rid of him; the Flames came looking.

But then, it's always been that way. For 14 seasons, from Vancouver to Colorado to New Jersey to Minnesota to Quebec to Detroit to Winnipeg to Boston and now to Calgary, Brent Ashton has epitomized that bedrock of the working class, the skilled journeyman.

Want a winger who'll skate all night, kill penalties, work the power play, check relentlessly, do his share of the rough work and end every game with his uniform soaked in honest sweat? Phone whoever's got Brent Ashton.

Need a guy who can fly in today, play tonight, get along in whatever dressing room he happens to be in, fights for his worth but never whines or goes public, and just might be that extra part you need for the stretch? Where's Brent Ashton these days?

He has the skills that make him handy enough to be valuable, but not too valuable to lose. So the phone rings, the GM gives him the word, and Susan Ashton looks around Whatever House in Wherever City, and calls another van line.

"The kids are still too young to realize," she says. "The dog knows every time. He sees a duffel bag or a packing case, he sits by the door and doesn't move. Me—I've done it so often the moving companies don't tell me how it works, I tell them."

Moves are measured by the places she's unpacked. New Jersey was easy because the whole team was moving from Colorado. Minnesota was six weeks in a hotel and two houses in 18 months. Quebec was moving 11 days before Christmas, farther east than she'd ever been, more snow than she'd ever seen.

In Detroit, they bought a house. Seventeen months later they were in Winnipeg. "You believe them the first time they say you're not going to be traded," she says. "After that, you just wait."

There have been good times. Susan Ashton has learned that every city is beautiful in its way if you take the time to look and savour new experience. "Here in Boston we rented Wade Boggs' condo," she says. "I'm looking out the window right now and can see the beach where we can walk in the winter."

Wednesday she talked to Brent, who'd played his first game as a Flame the previous night. "He said he got to play a lot and was aggressive," she says, the pride coming through. "It looks like it's going to work out pretty well."

She said goodbye and thanks. There were suitcases to fill, and Forever House was waiting around one more twist in the road.

Calamari To Go
Calgary Sun, May 12, 1996

TRUE LOVE, STANLEY CUP STYLE:

In Detroit, a Red Wings' fan prepares for the trip to the Joe to see his team dump all over those Blues guys from St. Louis who had the gall to turn this thing into a series and cost him all kinds of extra ticket bucks.

He stands in front of the mirror, sucking in his gut like Lee Marvin did dressing for the showdown in *Cat Ballou*.

He pulls on his Red Wings' jersey, the one with Stevie Y's name and number on the back.

He paints his face Red Wings' red and pulls on his Red Wings' cap.

He goes to the bathroom. Got to keep the old bladder empty. Leaves more room for the beer.

Then he runs a check list:

Gretzky Sucks sign. Check.

Go Wings Go towel. Check.

Keenan Sucks sign. Check.

White towel. Check.

Hull Sucks sign. Check.

Dead octopus . . .

"Honee! Where'd you put the octopus?"

"They didn't have any."

"They what??? Game Seven, and they're out of octopus? What kinda wimp supermarket you dealin' with?"

"Well, actually, they did have some, but they jacked the price, so I settled for squid."

"Squid! You want me to go to Game Seven with my buddies, and when the Wings score they're all throwin' octopus and I'm throwin' *squid*? What kinda hockey fan you think I am? They'll laugh me out of the Joe!"

"Uh, maybe they won't notice. See, I saw how squishy and drippy and oozy the damn thing was, and I thought 'What the hell, there's got to be a drier squid than this.'"

"And . . . ?"

"And I talked to the butcher, and he said no, there wasn't, and please apologize to you for him, but the rest of the idiots got there first. So . . ."

"Wait a minute! You said you got me a squid!"

"Well, sort of. See, I went over to the specialty counter and they had a sale, so I bought you a whole *bunch* of squid. Here!"

"What's this?"

"It's a bag of calamari."

"Calamari? I send you out for octopus and you come back with deep-fried squid?"

"But honey, they've got holes in the middle! Think of them as squid donuts. They're aerodynamic. You can spin 'em like Frisbees. You'll get lots better distance than your buddies. You might hit the referee right in the head and do some real damage!"

"There is that," he concedes.

"Sure! And what you don't throw, you can eat. Let's see those low-lifes try *that* with their stupid octopus."

"I love you," he says, throwing his arms around her.

"Careful," she says. "You'll squash your ammunition."

She stands in the doorway, waving goodbye and wondering where and when the man she loved became a fruitcake. Then she shrugs. After all, it could be worse.

Her sister is married to one just like him, and they live in Florida. It must be tough finding deep-fried rats.

Winning One for The Lord
The Province, February 6, 1992

> *Pastor calls school's "Sparky the Devil" cartoon mascot "a subtle erosion" of children's defences and wants the school board to cast him out.*
> —*The Province*, February 5, 1992

HALLELUJAH, BROTHER, I have seen the *light!*

It came upon me as a message clearly visible in the peanut butter spread over my morning toast: NHL NAMES ARE TOOLS OF THE DEVIL!

That was it. Nothing more. But any fool can see what it meant.

I have been Called. I must devote my life to changing the name and logo of every team in the National Hockey League, lest this subtle erosion of children's defences continues.

For too long I have watched as teams performed live and on TV before the impressionable eyes and ears of our young people under names like Redskins. And I have done *nothing!* But no more! *No more!* Help me, brethren! Help me strike down the devils in New Jersey and their more subtle but no less insidious fellow twisters and warpers of young minds. Look at these names, I pray you, and tell me why they should not be smitten as David smote Goliath:

New York RANGERS: Named after a masked man who took the law into his own hands, subjugated an Indian and forced him to do all the difficult tasks like going into town and getting beaten up, and was so stupid that when he found a silver mine he used the silver to make bullets.

Montreal CANADIENS: Loaded with players from other countries in an obvious plot to convert children to Separatism.

Edmonton OILERS: With each victory they plant the seed that the people of OPEC are really nice guys.

Winnipeg JETS: Jet plane emissions pollute the environment.

Calgary FLAMES: Flames mean fire. Fire means matches. Matches mean smoking. Smoking means cancer and flipping butts out of cars on vacations and setting fire to Bambi.

Los Angeles KINGS: Foster belief that Americans need a monarchy. Didn't they fight to get *out* of one?

Hartford WHALERS: Whalers kill whales. (See: Aquarium.)

San José SHARKS: Sharks kill people. (I know: People kill whales. But that's different.)

St. Louis BLUES, Detroit RED WINGS, Chicago BLACKHAWKS: Clear cases of colour bias and, in the latter two instances, possible denigration of Indians and/or Indian tribes.

New York ISLANDERS: How long will we allow these people to keep rubbing Indian noses in how they got skunked on sale of Manhattan island?

Philadelphia FLYERS: (See: Winnipeg JETS.)

Washington CAPITALS: Elitist, clearly discriminatory to the cities, towns and villages that aren't the capital of anything but make America great.

Boston BRUINS, Pittsburgh PENGUINS: Demeaning to animals.

Buffalo SABRES: Nickname is okay, but Buffalo has to go. Not the name, the city.

Quebec NORDIQUES: Discriminates against Anglophiles, who don't know what the hell it means but suspect it's code for "Give us everything!"

Minnesota NORTH STARS: So what have they got against eastern, western or southern stars? Obvious subliminal message promoting mass emigration to Canada.

Toronto MAPLE LEAFS: Gives maple syrup a bad name. Children refuse to eat nutritional pancakes and waffles.

Vancouver CANUCKS: False advertising. Team loaded with players from other lands. (But hey—two more Russians and we can win our national game.)

You see? You see the evil that lives among us? And it could be even worse! Tomorrow I'm going to put both peanut butter *and* jam on my toast. Heaven only knows what I'll be afraid of by noon.

Hockey Night in Toronto
Calgary Sun, February 18, 1997

To: ALL STAFF
From: Head Office, Hockey Night in Canada
CC: CBC
Re: Foster Hewitt dead rumours.

It has come to our attention that a radical group of western viewers, upset with our mandate to follow our beloved Toronto Maple Leafs on their inexorable drive to the Stanley Cup, are spreading a scurrilous rumour that Foster Hewitt is dead.

Further, these nagging nabobs of negativism, in league with the national media, are producing on a daily basis standings showing the Leafs in last place in their division, an inept band of underachievers with no chance of reaching the Cup final without buying tickets, and charging that we at HNIC are living in the past.

Their stated objective: To force HNIC to telecast Saturday night games *that do not involve the Leafs.*

Instead, they would have us foist upon this nation games in which participating Canadian teams are actually battling for playoff position, including those based in cities west of the Great Lakes.

Allow me to respond.

1. Foster Hewitt is not dead.

Although we do not attend games personally, we know that he is still in the gondola providing those thousands of children sprawled on the floor in prairie farmhouses with his matchless descriptions of Teeder and Turk and the Big M and awarding the third star to Dave Keon, who always plays a good game. If he wasn't, Harold Ballard or King Clancy would have called to tell us.

2. The Leafs are definite contenders for the Stanley Cup.

Anyone with any understanding of mathematics realizes this. With six teams in the NHL and four of them advancing to the playoffs all we (excuse me, they) have to do is finish ahead of two clubs, which should be even easier with the rumoured injuries to Jean Béliveau and Bobby Hull.

3. Proposed telecasts of games involving NHL teams west of the Great Lakes.

There are no NHL teams west of the Great Lakes—or anything else, for that matter.

Every schoolchild realizes that anyone crossing the Saskatchewan–Alberta border falls off the edge of the earth into a flaming pit, to be devoured by dragons. This is all anyone in the east knows about the west, or cares to.

Westerners, on the other hand, hunger for any crumb of information regarding life in Toronto in general and the Leafs in particular. Here at HNIC that is our mandate, and we are committed to its relentless pursuit.

4. Lost touch with the NHL?

Deep in the Molstar bunker in Toronto, crack teams of trained senior citizens who can recite the rosters of every Leaf team from Conn Smythe to Punch Imlach are crouched over their crystal sets on 24-hour alert for reported sightings of non-Toronto Canadian NHL franchises—all part of HNIC's commitment to remaining on the cutting edge of hockey coverage.

Further to this commitment to stay abreast of the hockey scene, we plan to launch a series of HNIC profiles of up-and-coming players who might some day be Leafs. Segment One: a 14-year-old in Brantford named Wayne Gretzky.

The Curse of the Muldoon
Calgary Sun, January 22, 2001

IT'S A WEEK NOW since Jim Coleman's heart gave out and left the world a lesser place. But he would come back and smack us if we were still mourning.

"I lived 89 years," he'd snort, "and considering the way I treated my body for the first half of them I was damned lucky to make 60."

So, because I was in Mexico when it happened and missed the funeral and the retelling of all the old Coleman tales, let me say goodbye to my friend with a happy story.

On a winter's day in 1994, we were lunching in the Vancouver *Province* cafeteria, where Coleman daily attracted pressmen, circulation types, ad salesmen and reporters smart enough to see it as a chance to go to school. I was loftily explaining how I'd straightened out a bunch of radio guys about the Curse of Muldoon, put upon the Chicago Blackhawks by their first coach, Pete Muldoon, when he was fired in mid-season. The Hawks, he said, would never win the Stanley Cup.

Coleman snorted.

"Had nothing to do with the Stanley Cup," he said. "It was about first place. Maj. Frederic McLaughlin, the first Chicago GM, fired Muldoon in the middle of the 1926–27 season.

"Muldoon got so mad he leaned across the desk and told McLaughlin 'I put the Curse of the Muldoon upon you! This team will never finish in first place as long as you're alive!'

"And they never did," he added.

"How do you know so much about it?" I asked.

"Because there never was a Curse of the Muldoon," Coleman said comfortably. "It's all b.s. I know, because I made it up."

It seems that during his stint as Saturday columnist with the *Globe and Mail*, Coleman was expounding to assistant sports editor Ralph Adams his theory that sports fans were so gullible they'd swallow anything.

"I'll prove it," he said. "I'll write something for tomorrow that is absolute b.s., and I guarantee that people will take it seriously."

And he sat down at his battered old typewriter (to his dying day, Coleman would have nothing to do with computers and wrote his columns on a portable typewriter almost as old as he) and dreamed up The Curse of the Muldoon.

"Not The Curse of Muldoon," he admonished. "The Curse of *the* Muldoon." Coleman was old school. Even his b.s. had to be accurate.

And the people did buy it, and kept buying it no matter how often he explained that it had been a huge joke.

The Curse took on a life of its own. Years later, around Stanley Cup time, Chicago writers would phone him for details. Each time, he told them it was fiction. It was like trying to put out a brush fire with spit.

The story changed with age. Sometimes it was the Hawks, sometimes the Rangers. But the Curse of the Muldoon was a fact. Everybody knew that. It was a piece of NHL history.

Finally, the NHL stepped in. On Page 173 of its 75th anniversary commemorative book, it reports "Muldoon, in fact, said no such thing. The 'Curse' was invented by a sports writer in 1941."

"That's b.s., too," Coleman scoffed. "I invented it 12 years later than that."

Ah, the indignity of it: To be the author of one of the great hockey hoaxes of all time, and not get the credit.

Coleman had a theory about that.

"Muldoon," he said darkly. "It's got to be Muldoon."

Goodbye, 99
Calgary Sun, April 19, 1999

NEW YORK—HE WALKED TO THE RINK this one last time with his dad, the way it was on so many nights and days and early mornings when the air snapped with cold and he and his world were young.

Wayne and Walter Gretzky, strolling from the posh Plaza Hotel to the storied pleasure palace of Madison Square Garden, not saying much, mostly thinking.

In the three years he'd been a New York Ranger, No. 99 had always taken the long way around to the dressing room, up the ramp and past the Rangers' bench, because that way he didn't have to pass the visitor's room and meet some of the players he'd be facing in a matter of hours.

But this time he led his dad through the regular door and walked around the building, looking at the walls and the pictures and up at the ceiling as though storing everything in the memory banks and not wanting to miss a thing.

It was starting to sink in: After today, it really would be all over. Everything he did from then until the final horn, the final wave goodbye, would be for the last time.

He would make the final pass, take the final shot, maybe, if the break came, score the final goal, skate his final thank-you circle with the spotlight showcasing him and the crowd roaring its love.

And then hockey would be over.

Later, he would tell the assembled media that "this is not a passing on, this is a moving on." And he'd be right, and they would come to see it. But this was late morning of the final game of his career, and he wanted his dad there with him, the way he had been since he laced up those first skates and sent a four-year-old wobbling onto the Nith River for his first stumbly strides to immortality.

He didn't know then that in ceremonies before the game, Walter Gretzky would skip introductions of the rest of the family, and reappear as the passenger in a new Mercedes-Benz, a gift from the Rangers' organization.

He'd have laughed at the thought, as the walked from the hotel. One of them would say "Not like the Blue Goose, eh?" And somewhere in there, Walter would look at him and say for the 1,000th time over the past 32 years:

"Long way from the river, Wayne. A long, long way . . ."

He thinks he said it first that night on Nelson Skalbania's plane, when Nelson dictated the terms of a professional contract for a skinny 17-year-old who wrote it out himself on a piece of school foolscap because Wally was shaking too much to hold the pencil.

One plane flight, one decision, and his son's salary had jumped from $22 per game in junior "A" to a guaranteed $820,000 over the next four years. "Long way from the river," he said, looking out the window of the private jet. And, under his breath: "I sure hope we're doing the right thing . . ."

And look at that car!

Never mind that Gretzky has now won 19 cars of various models in his 20 years in the NHL, or that the last one came only weeks ago when he was named MVP in the NHL all-star game. In Walter Gretzky's world—"A blue-collar guy who never made more than $35,000 a year but put it all into his family," Wayne told reporters—you weren't given cars. You saved, and you bought, and you ran them until they dropped.

Like the Blue Goose.

It was old and battered and the odometer had long since given up the ghost and settled on maximum, but it carried the Gretzky kids and as many members of their minor hockey teams as could be crammed in to tournaments all over Ontario.

Wally drove, always. Late at night they'd be heading home to Brantford through the snow, and Brent would lean over the seat and comb Wally's hair to help him stay awake.

One day he came home from work and there was a new car in the driveway wearing the Goose's plates.

"Phyllis!" he screamed as he barged into the living room. "Where's the Goose?"

"I got tired of telling you to sell it," she said, "so I sold it for scrap. The new car is from Wayne."

"Coulda got another 100 thousand miles out of her," Wally muttered.

But now here he was, getting out of a Mercedes at centre ice at Madison Square Garden. And the little White Tornado was a 38-year-old playing his last game.

Wally's eyes stung a little as he climbed to his seat and watched his son get one last assist, miss by inches a pass that might have given him a breakaway for the winner in the third, and wave a long and emotional goodbye to the Garden crowd.

He's back coaching, is Walter Gretzky. Not at 42 Varadi Ave., though. The backyard rink he built every winter is a swimming pool now, a gift from Wayne and Janet the week 99 was traded from the Oilers to the Kings.

Little guys, like Wayne used to be. He is not too sure about the younger generation, these kids who call him "Wally" instead of "Coach," or "Mr. Gretzky," but they love the game, and that's all that matters.

On Saturday, I asked him how many NHL games he'd be watching now that his eldest son had said goodbye.

He gave it some thought.

"Y'know, not many, I guess," he concluded. "It wouldn't be the same . . ."

History Lessons

"Those who cannot remember the past are condemned to repeat it."

—George Santayana

WITH THE 2010 WINTER OLYMPICS BEHIND US, pushing aside the nagging thoughts that we may never know how much they cost, and that the final payment on the 1976 Olympics in Montreal was made in April, 2009 (the Games, remember, that Montreal mayor Jean Drapeau assured us "could no more lose money than a man could have a baby"), let us borrow the Wayback Machine used so effectively by Mr. Peabody and Sherman on the Rocky and Bullwinkle Show in the '60s and travel back through time to view a few pivotal points in the histories of the games we play or pay to watch others play for us.

Don't be afraid. There'll be no exams, written or oral, or detentions for skipping a section. You might even learn something . . .

Let's Hear It for Theodosius
Calgary Sun, February 5, 1998

VANCOUVER—IN THE YEAR 393 A.D., the Greek emperor Theodosius abolished the Olympic Games because they had grown too ornate and besides, some of the athletes were being paid off and using drugs.

Sixteen centuries later, millionaire professional hockey players are Olympians, and the big worry is a cold tablet called Sudafed. The more things differ, the more they remain the same.

Thus, as the world's athletes prepare to gather in the spirit of friendly competition and potential endorsements and the white-coated lab techs huddle in the testing tent, let us pause and compare the old Grecian Olympiad with the current Games. But first, let us sing the unofficial anthem of the modern Olympiad:

> Tinkle, tinkle, little star,
> Please be sure to hit the jar.
> And if your sample be not pure,
> We'll have your gonads, that's for sure.

In fact, punishment might be a good place to start.

False starts (modern): False starters in track events given one more chance.

False starts (Grecian): False-starter horsewhipped on the spot, then allowed to continue if he could.

Clothing (modern): Nike, Puma, Adidas, etc.

Clothing (Grecian): Nothing. Starkers. Buck-naked. Nude. Mind you, there were no Winter Olympics, which was probably a good thing, since naked lugers and cold metal sleds would make for painful dismounts.

Cheating (modern): Athlete sent home in disgrace to seek lawyers, do talk shows and whine that he or she was framed.

Cheating (Grecian): Athlete forced to pay for construction of statue to Zeus, set up at Olympia as permanent warning to potential cheaters. Record for Most Statues, One Athlete (6) held by Kallipos of Athens, who bribed his opponents in the pentathlon.

Sponsorships (modern): Government, equipment and clothing manufactures, corporate support.

Sponsorship (Grecian): Athletes supposedly competed as individuals, but some city-states even bought athletes hoping to benefit from their skills. In the fifth century BC one Astylos of Croton, a double winner from the south of Italy, changed his national allegiance to Syracuse (in Sicily) between Olympiads because he got a better deal.

Rewards (modern): Corporate sponsorships, professional contracts, ticker-tape parades.

Rewards (Grecian): Home states provided cash, estates, theatre tickets and extravagant homecoming processions.

Endorsements (modern): Clothing, banks, hair spray, shampoo, equipment.

Endorsements (Grecian): Limited commercial opportunities due to lack of radio and TV. Athlete pushing products ("Flavius Spears—the Winning Edge!" "Caesar's Sandals—Where the Arch meets the Apia") would have to stand in the market square and shout.

Trophies (modern): Gold, silver and bronze medals.

Trophies (Grecian): Wreaths made from home-grown veggies—olive at Olympia, laurel at Delphi, fresh parsley (and later pine) at Corinth and dried parsley at Nemea. (Scholars remain hopeful that some archaeological dig will unearth a wax tablet containing first scribe-jock Olympic quotes: "That's right, Octavius, I'm going for the parsley.")

Politics (modern): Rumours out of Washington suggest president Clinton has more or less agreed not to bomb Iraq during Olympics.

Politics (Grecian): When his own country was banned from the Games, a Spartan named Lichas entered his horse in the chariot race claiming to be a Theban. He won the race but was caught and horse-whipped. In retaliation, the Spartans invaded Olympia.

Spartans, it seems, had no sense of priorities.

Big Noise in the Valley
The Province, December 18, 1981

> *Larry Holmes and Gerry Cooney to earn $10 million*
> *each for heavyweight title fight. Sugar Ray Leonard*
> *and Thomas Hearns guaranteed minimum $12*
> *million each for middleweight title bout.*
> —*The Province*, December 17

THE SCRIBES GATHERED WITH THE DAWN in the tent in the Valley of Elah. For it was here, on the site of the original battle, that promoter Don King would announce details for the greatest rematch in history, the Return of the Bible Belters—David vs. Goliath.

Because of what he termed "the enormous religious significance of a fight fans have been awaiting for centuries," King had decided to stage the actual negotiations before the world press. You could sense that time had not cooled the animosity.

David: "Still got your coat of mail, eh, Fatso. Better pull it up over your forehead or you'll go down in one like last time."

Goliath: "Sheep lover!"

King: "Gentlemen! Gentlemen! Let us get down to the issues. First and foremost, the purse split."

David: "I don't lift a sling for less than $20,000,000. I'm the champion. Give him $10,000,000 tops. And I get the closed circuit and all ancillary rights including the T-shirts."

Goliath: "No way, Shorty. You get lucky in one fight, and . . ."

David: "One fight! One fight! That's all I ever hear. Before I decked you last time the beef was that I had *no* fights. Even Saul was buggin' me about it. Ask the lion I smote when he stole one of my lambs. *POW!* Right in the mouth! And when the bear got into it I whupped him, too. What about them?"

Goliath: "Big deal. The WBA didn't recognize the lion and you hit the bear when he was hibernating. I asked your whole damn Israeli *army* to come out and fight. *You* only came out 'cause you lost the draw . . ."

King: "Uh, I think we can leave that for the moment, gentlemen. Let us move along to the actual site for the fight."

Goliath: "Right here in the valley, same as last time. I'll whip him on his own turf. I'll fight him right now for *nuthin'!* I'm the *baddest!* I'm . . ."

David: "You're the *dumbest!* Look at this place. Mountain on one side, mountain on the other side, lousy sight lines. This is AD, man! The 20th century! You think people will pay half a grand to stand on a hill for a fight? No slot machines, no johns . . . ? Nah! It's got to be Caesars. That gives us all the comforts plus maximum advertising potential in the major market areas. You wanna fight in front of two camels and an ox, that's your business. Me, I'm goin' for the shekels."

King: "I've been handed a question by the scribes. Goliath, what weight do you plan to come in at?"

Goliath: "I never worry about my weight. Long as I got my six cubits and a span, I . . ."

David: "Sure—and your 5,000-shekel coat and your greaves of brass around your legs, and your spear with the shaft like a weaver's beam—you look like a scrap-iron drive, and me with nothing but a robe and a jockstrap. Whyncha come out and fight like a man?"

Goliath: "People who throw stones shouldn't knock brass housing, creep. You got in one lucky shot last time and even then I had to be out of shape. I didn't sweat a drop during the whole fight. I think it was my pituitary medicine. All that trying to put on an extra cubit in a hurry left my forehead weak. But this time I'm ready. Say goodbye to your sheep, baby. It's *over!*"

King: "Goliath, the scribes note that in the first fight David took your own sword and cut off your head. How do you respond to doctors who say if you fight again you're risking permanent damage?"

Goliath: "Listen, for ten million dollars they can cut off whatever they want and I'll come back, fight, and do the anthem as a soprano."

King: "And for you, David—is there any truth to published reports that God will be in your corner?"

David: "We're workin' on that. We figure He'll be worth four points in the Nielsens. Last time we fought for nothing. This time we're gonna do it right."

Genesis
The Province, November 14, 1985

1. IN THE BEGINNING, there were Teams.

2. And Teams begat Cheerleaders.

3. And General Managers said, "Let them be built, that our male customers would salivate and dream great dreams and pay money to come back and watch them inhale and exhale every playing day."

4. And they were built.

5. And it was good.

6. And the Marketing Men said, "Lo, for the fans who are not of the

male persuasion and dream not dreams of Cheerleaders builteth fore and aft, let there be Cheerleaders of the male persuasion.

7. "And let them dress in cloaks of many colours, or torn jeans and numbered sweaters; and let them waddle like ducks or cluck like chickens; or beat upon a drum and make a great noise, so that the multitudes will know when to create bedlam and confound our enemies."

8. And the Earth was struck by a plague of ducks, chickens, lumberjacks, gophers, dogs, bears, armadillos and humans whose elevators reacheth not the top floor.

9. And they clothed themselves in strange raiments, and waddled like ducks, and clucked like chickens, and smote upon their drums to confound the enemy.

10. And it was God-awful.

11. And the Leaders were a Chicken who was funny, and a Schoolteacher named Krazy George, who was not.

12. And the Chicken and the Schoolteacher begat Ralph the Dog, who begat Gainer the Gopher, who begat the Ipsco Goose, who begat Jerome, the Gnome Who Lives Under the Dome.

13. And from their figurative loins sprang a host of humans who made waves and funny sounds and clothed themselves in gorilla suits and did other things that caused attendants from nearby Hospitals to yearn for their butterfly nets.

14. And the People, being foolish, forsook the ways of spontaneity and cheered only on cue.

15. And the Lord looked down and said, "Enough is enough. Let the Angel who created this abomination come down with the shorts."

16. And it was so.

17. And Krazy George awoke from his bed five days before the Big Game and learned that he was out of work.

18. And he was sore anguished, and just plain sore.

19. And Krazy said unto the Lions, "Why hast thou forsaken me? Have I not served thee well for a decade? What is this contract I see before me? Wilst not thou honour it?"

20. And the Lions said unto Krazy, "There is no more bread to cast upon your waters. Our Angel has tapped out. Thou art history, babe."

21. And Krazy rent his garment, and was sore afraid.

22. And a Radio Station, seeking to ride upon the fame of the Cheerleader, offered to pay his salary to cheer at the Big Game. But the Lions said, "Nay! We will play the game without thee."

23. And it was good.

24. In fact, it was great.

Holding A Kicker
Calgary Sun, June 7, 1998

SO HERE WAS EDWARD III, staring down from the palace window onto the fields where his troops were supposed to be practising their archery.

It was 1337, he had the big war coming with France, and if his troops couldn't shoot the thing could drag on for 100 years. But were they practising?

Hell, no. They were playing football.

What was it about this damned game? A dozen years earlier, Eddie II had decreed imprisonment for anyone playing it. Yet here were his own troops, kicking away.

So Eddie III drafted a law of his own.

"It is forbidden, on pain of imprisonment, to indulge in football, stone-throwing, catapulting wood and iron objects and all such frivolous games without gain."

It didn't work for Eddie III any more than it had worked for Eddie II. Nor would it work later work for Richard II or the Henrys IV, V and VIII, who all made similar laws, or for James I, who ruled in the Scottish parliament of 1424 "That na man play at the Fute-ball."

If there was something to be kicked, men were going to kick it and others were going to gather to watch and sometimes to riot.

As the greatest kickers of 32 nations gather in France and billions around the planet make camp in front of television screens to put their hearts and wallets on the line; as French shopkeepers put the valuables and breakables on the back shelf and tavern owners haul in the money with fingers crossed, it is a thing to remember:

The World Cup, the most-watched event in television history, is merely an extension of a sport spawned on the far edge of history, all its variations based on a single, basic rule: If it moves, kick it; if it doesn't move, kick it until it does.

There are pictures from 17th-century China showing men trying to kick a ball through two bamboo posts in a game called tsu-chu. Military manuals from the Han Dynasty list the game as part of the physical education program.

A thousand years earlier, Berbers in north Africa played a game called koura, apparently part of a fertility rite to encourage crop growth. ("Aw, c'mon, honey. I'm goin' on a road game. And it's for the crops!")

Balls have been found in the tombs of Egyptian pharaohs, the walls covered with game drawings. The ancient Greeks played something called episkyros.

Name a country, and it had a game in which object A was kicked to or through target B. And if you didn't have a ball—or even if you did—use a human skull.

Roman legionnaires are said to have used the skulls of conquered foes. In 11th-century England, at Kingston-on-Thames, residents celebrated a victory over Danish marauders by decapitating the Viking captain and starting a pick-up game with his head. Mayan legends tell of games played between cities, with the losing captain getting to be the next game ball.

Over the centuries, rules evolved. The mob-football street game, little more than an excuse for violence, moved into the parks and left the mobs in the streets. The simple booting of a ball became an art form, and the game grabbed the heart and squeezed.

It's a simple game, really. A ball you can see, two big nets—what's not to understand?

But there is a magic to it.

Wizards named Matthews and Pelé and Maradona and so many more have cast their spells and moved on, leaving the field to the new young sorcerers like Ronaldo, who can drift through defenders like mist across the moors.

And somewhere, on a playground with a $100 Umbro or on a packed dirt street with a ball made of rags, the new wizards are dreaming potions of their own. The names change. The world game goes on.

The Cup of Life
Calgary Sun, May 17, 1998

THIS IS A TALE OF TWO TROPHIES, a war, two kidnappings, a shoe box, a burial, a blast furnace, and a dog named Pickles.

Pickles didn't know he—or possibly she—would become a part of sporting history. Then again, had the Germans bothered to look in the shoe box under the bed, Pickles would have been just another pooch in search of a bone and we'd have no story at all. Except for the second kidnapping, when the victim was thrown into a furnace.

And soccer's World Cup '98, starting next month in Paris, just wouldn't be the same without the Legend of Pickles.

The tale that wagged this particular dog actually begins in 1928, when FIFA, the governing body of world soccer, grew weary of losing arguments with the International Olympic Committee on the question of amateurism—essentially keeping many of the greatest players out of the Games—and decided to hold an "international championship" of its own, starting in 1930.

Well, you can't have a championship without a trophy. With an eye to cultural and artistic merit and a trophy that would essentially tell the IOC to look in a mirror and multiply, FIFA commissioned the French sculptor Abel Lafleur.

Lafleur's creation: a gold-plated sterling silver statuette of the goddess of Victory, holding aloft an eight-sided chalice, set on a four-sided blue base of semi-precious stone, a gold plate on each side on which to etch the names of the winners to be declared every four years.

There were three names on it when world war came to Europe for the second time.

It was precious, it was valuable, and it was in Italy. So were the German occupying forces. Desperate to keep it from falling into enemy hands, FIFA vice-president Dr. Ottorino Barassi cast around his home for a safe hiding place. Finally he stuffed it in a shoe box and shoved the shoe box under his bed. It stayed there until June of 1945.

As it turned out, the good doctor should have left it there.

In 1966, now known as the Jules Rimet trophy, it disappeared while on a tour promoting that year's acrimonious World Cup competition between Germany and England. ("Should Germany defeat us at our national game," wrote a British journalist, "let us ever remember that we twice beat them at theirs.")

Enter Pickles.

Scratching around in a field, the wonder dog unearthed the trophy at the base of a tree, apparently buried by the thieves until they could retrieve it once the heat wore off. The trophy was saved—but only for 23 years.

In 1983, in Rio de Janeiro, it was stolen again. With Pickles long since gone to a just reward, police were left to handle the case on their own. They were not equal to the task. Neither kidnappers nor trophy were ever found, although word did leak out of the underworld that it had been melted down for the gold and silver.

The Brazilians, particularly upset since their third cup victory had just earned them the right to keep the trophy forever, ordered a replacement. It is called the FIFA World Cup Trophy, and it is what all the fuss will be about in Paris.

It's valuable enough in its own right, this statue of two athletes reaching out to embrace a world globe: 36 cm high, 4,970 grams of solid 18-karat gold on a malachite base with room for championship names stretching through 2038.

But it is not its value that has triggered barroom brawls, stadium riots and more than one suicide. It is the undeniable fact that the country that gets to wave it aloft is, for four years at least, the land of the greatest team in the greatest and most popular game in the world.

Bigger than the Stanley Cup. Bigger that the Super Bowl. Bigger than the World Series. For, after all, they are merely about games. In countries where generations of barefoot children have sewn rags into a ball and dreamed of kicking it to glory, the World Cup is about life.

When in Doubt, Punt

AS A SELF-CONFESSED CANADIAN FOOTBALL LEAGUE ADDICT I took a lot of flak from fans of other sports whining that I wrote too many football columns. Guilty as charged, but what the hell. Canadian football is the only game left that is ours and ours alone.

Hockey, you say? Fugeddaboutit. Yes, it holds unchallenged sway in our hearts, but the National Hockey League is so well stocked with players from other countries that even in the Pavel Bure days the Vancouver Canucks went something like "Two more Russians and we can win the Stanley Cup."

Curling? The 2009 women's world championship was won by a rink from China, the 2010 women's Olympic gold by Sweden. Lacrosse, supposedly Canada's other national sport by Parliamentary decree? There's now a flourishing professional box lacrosse league—in the US.

But Canadian football is unique in rules and field size, a virtual Mom and Pop corner store compared to the National Football League colossus—but it is much the better of the two games. And wouldn't I love to see Peyton Manning or some other hotshot quarterback try to get a play off in the CFL's 20 seconds instead of the NFL's 40.

No less a CFL star than Doug Flutie (and, incidentally, one of the finest ambassadors the league has ever had) once called the Grey Cup "Canada's Super Bowl." But the first Grey Cup game was played in 1909, the first Super Bowl in 1961, which means that the Super Bowl is actually America's Grey Cup. And the game from which US college football and the NFL evolved was actually brought south from Montreal by a team from McGill University for a two-game series against Harvard, where the game was a kind of cross between rugby and soccer. They played one game under each set of rules, and the Harvards liked the Canadian game so much they adopted it. Soon it spread throughout the Ivy League schools, then gradually across the US. It is no real stretch to say Canada gave the Americans two of their major sports: basketball, invented by Canadian James Naismith, and football, borrowed from McGill.

I never put down the NFL. There's no need. Any fan who watches both games would have to agree that the NFL has many, many more of the greatest players—and that we have the better game. And some of the stories you wouldn't believe . . .

500 Air Miles from Home
The Vancouver Sun, March 30, 1978

> *MONTREAL—Police say three-month investigation turns up no proof of plot to weaken key Edmonton Eskimo players with sex the night before 1977 Grey Cup game.*
>
> —News item

THE NEXT SOUND YOU HEAR will be the voices of 32 Eskimos trying to convince wives and girlfriends that they are not and have never been key players.

"Key player? Me? Hell, honey, I barely got out of training camp. I was a *rookie*. Rookies don't get to no parties, 'cept the rookie show, and even then all they let you do is drink and throw up. Aw, c'mon, honey! Open the door . . ."

Fortunately, winter is all but over in Edmonton. Had the Montreal story broken in February instead of yesterday, coach Hugh Campbell would have spent all summer chipping his starters out of the ice that had formed around them and their living-room chesterfields. As it is, the 1977 Eskimos—however innocent—will be subjected to a lot of winks and elbows in the ribs in the coming months. Nothing in sport titillates the imagination more than a suggestion that a man's playbook may be X-rated.

The story itself has just enough innuendo to conjure up scenes of lechery and debauchery, with booze flowing like water and hard-eyed girls plying football players with invitations to study their statistics.

Police in Montreal say their street contacts claim a group of girls had banded together on Grey Cup Eve to make sure the Eskimos left their game in the bedroom. Recalling that the score *had* been 41–6 for Montreal Alouettes, and that the Eskimos did play like 32 guys who'd spent the night in a steam bath, they launched a three-month investigation that ended yesterday with assurances to CFL commissioner Jake Gaudaur that "nothing criminal had occurred."

In theory, that ends it. But of course it won't.

Disgruntled westerners who mortgaged the farm to bet on Alberta Crude will always wonder whether the dice were loaded, not to mention the players. They'll start asking questions—preceding them with "Of course, I don't believe it, but just suppose . . ."

There will be no shortage of questions.

Was it a plot by the bookies? Were the girls mob-hired or merely dedicated Alouette fans ready to give their all for the team, luring the innocent Eskimos with promises of a bicultural relationship that would melt the ice off their moustaches?

The suggestion is not without historical precedent—as commissioner Gaudaur is well aware. Legend has it that, in his days as general manager of the Hamilton Tiger-Cats, his team had a big game coming up in one of the other eastern cities against a club possessing an exceptional quarterback. And that several days before said game, a Hamilton miss with a leaning toward football players decided the team needed a little help.

She boarded a train, the story goes, rode to the rival city, struck up an acquaintance with the quarterback, stayed with him for several days, then sent Gaudaur a wire that said, approximately:

HAVE TAKEN CARE OF QB. REST UP TO YOU!

The Eskimos' problem is twofold. No one is ever totally cleared of such a story, no matter how clean a bill of health the police and league officials issue. Besides, in matters pertaining to the pursuit and conquest of broad and/or booze the football player is the victim of his own image. Football players and girls *always* chase each other. Joe Namath said so.

Was it not Jim Young who said in his autobiography, *Dirty 30*, that the unwritten rule of all professional football teams is "Five hundred air miles from home, everybody's single"? It's not true, of course. Some of them aren't married in the first place. But the image is there, fleshed out yearly by curfew-breaking training camp escapades dutifully reported by the ever-vigilant media, who happen to be in the same hotel checking on the supply of Gideon Bibles.

I myself recall the memorable day a veteran player announced his retirement and, as a farewell gesture, listed on the dressing-room blackboard the names and numbers of girls he knew in every league city. The players, who'd seen the girls he dated, rose as one man, and rubbed them out.

Not that it's all the players' fault. Some of those girls just won't quit. They buy club press guides, which list the hotels of visiting teams, and lurk in the lobby ready to pounce. There was a girl in Winnipeg once they called the Avon Lady because she knocked on every player's door and offered samples. Then she . . . oh, never mind.

The point is, the poor Eskimos of '77 are left with Hobson's Choice. Do they plead innocent and blow the image just to keep peace in the family? Or do they snigger suggestively and blow their home life just to keep the respect of other teams in the league?

Will it be the ladies, or the Tiger-Cats?

If only the game had been closer. But 41–6 . . . hell, they'd have been better off with a shutout. That way they could look their sweeties straight in the eye and swear they'd never scored at all.

Draft Dodger
The Province, June 14, 1981

ONCE UPON A TIME there was a little boy who wanted to be a shoemaker.

All his life, while the other kids were out playing games or stealing hubcaps, he'd be at his little toy workbench making little toy shoes. Eventually, people were offering him scholarships to make shoes for them.

All the big schools—Vanderboot, Oxford, Arkanshoe, Mississlipper, LSshoe—had scouts on his doorstep promising him groupies, under-the-table leather and peach cobbler. But he was a California boy. For him there could be only one school: ShoeCLA.

Because he was on scholarship his course load wasn't heavy (Lacing 10, Leatherpunch 91) and the coach didn't seem to care whether or not he attended classes. "Just keep those cordovans coming, kid," he said. "You're our ticket to No. 1 in the polls—*Gentleman's Quarterly*, *Cobbler's All-America*, you're gonna make us the Really Big Shoe."

But college was not without pitfalls. He fell in with the wrong crowd at first. For a while it seemed that if the dean didn't get him the Dubbin would. But he persevered, because he had a dream: He was going to turn pro! He'd already picked the spot for his shop, close enough to Beverly Hills to lure the high-class trade but not too far from the haunts of the leather-and-spike-heel set.

He graduated *summa cum toecap*. He'd given it his awl and now it was going to pay off. He was packing his apron and last when the word came.

"Congratulations, kid," his coach said. "You've been drafted by the Boston Bootblacks."

"Uh, gee, that's nice, coach," he said. "But I don't want to work in Boston. I've got this shop picked out right here in LA. All my plans are made. The Bootblacks will have to get someone else. A lot of good shoemakers have graduated this year. They'll have . . ."

"They'll have *you*, kid," the coach interrupted. "All the shoe factories are in on the draft. They take turns picking and they've agreed that no one tries to hire the other guys' pick. Cuts down overhead and makes it a hell of a lot easier to keep good help."

"But . . . but . . . I don't know anyone in Boston! Nobody asked me if I wanted to go there or work there or even visit there. I've *seen* Boston! Who wants to go through life making sensible shoes? I want to be on the coast where I grew up. I want to benefit mankind. I could be the guy who makes the big breakthrough: the beach thong that doesn't split the skin between your toes. I'm not *meant* for spit-and-polish! I won't go!"

"Oh, you'll go, kid," the coach replied. "You'll make shoes for the Bootblacks or you'll make shoes for no one. Because the National Footwear League won't let you work for any of its other teams. It's Boston or nothing and you might as well get used to it."

"But that's restraint of trade! That's slavery! That takes away a man's freedom of choice! There's got to be a way around it!"

"Well, you could jump to the Canadian League, if you wanna spend your career making second-rate mukluks. Up there you're on the negotiation list of the Hamilton Highbuttons."

He signed with the Bootblacks. At least there he could make shoes. Hamilton meant a career in workboots. And after all, it was a two-year contract. He'd do his time, then move to California. He could do two years standing on his head.

Two years later he tried to move to the LA Lacers. They wanted him. They'd pay him far more than he was getting in Boston. But they couldn't take him.

"Compensation," they said. "If we take you we'd have to give up our entire pump line to the Bootblacks."

"You mean," the kid said, "that I can never work where I want to work—that my career is always going to be in someone else's hands? That's ridiculous!"

"Sure it is, kid," they agreed. "But that's shoe biz!"

Please Pray Quietly
The Province, September 10, 1981

> *But thou, when thou prayest, enter into thy closet, and when thou hast shut thy door, pray to thy Father which is in secret; and thy Father which seeth in secret shall reward thee openly.*
> —Matthew 6:6

It's time to get God out of football games.

Not that He won't be there anyway. It's His world, His universe, His cosmos, and we learn from childhood that He is everywhere. But I wish football players would stop talking about Him as though He's stickum on the hands or the extra deep back on second and long. It's, well . . . *arrogant*.

Case in point: Brian Kelly, wide receiver, Edmonton Eskimos. Monday in Hamilton he made a marvellous, one-handed catch for a touchdown. "Congratulations on that great catch, Brian," said the TV man on the sidelines.

"Well, thank you," said Brian Kelly. "I guess the Lord had a hand in there, too."

Now, I am not a particularly religious man. I profess no special understanding of His eternal plan. But I doubt it includes much about a professional football player running a down-and-in.

I also question both the logic and sincerity of a boxer who spends 15 rounds obliterating another man's face, then falls on his knees to announce that "God was in my corner." What happens when two good men of equal religious fervour and depth of belief fight one another? Is it a draw? Does God take sides? Or does He look down and say:

"I've given you the skills. I've put the desire in your hearts and the strength in your bodies. Go to it. Now, if you'll excuse me, I've got a universe to run . . ."?

The Jocks for God groups are sweeping through the ranks of professional sport. Fellowship of Christian Athletes, Athletes in Action . . . whatever the name, the game's the same: Play your sport, do your thing, then tell everyone you couldn't have done it without the Lord.

Well, of course not.

The Lord put us here, set up the rules, laid out the Commandments. It's like saying "If it wasn't for the air, I couldn't breathe." There's no need; it's self-evident.

Individually, Jocks for God tend to be good, bad or indifferent in about the same proportion as newspapermen, milkmen, insurance salesmen or plumbers. Collectively, I don't trust them—maybe because I've been unlucky.

Most of the ones I've met fall into two categories: ex-drinkers, chasers, carousers and curfew-breakers who now run around polishing their halos; or guys who were jerks, got the halo, and feel that the fact that they've got it entitles them to go right on being jerks. It's like an insurance policy, a Pearly Gate pass.

"I try to live a good life inside," a guy told me once. Inside he was Oral Roberts. Outside he was Harold Robbins. Just following him, you'd get old.

Certainly there are athletes in AIA and other groups whose sincerity you cannot doubt. But of the Christian athletes I've come to respect, most didn't go around preaching about it. They just lived it.

It's almost become a game in itself. Athlete makes big play, athlete comes to sidelines, athlete gets in front of camera, athlete says

God was there with him. It's become an annoyance, an interruption, another commercial. Head for the fridge, boys, here comes the God bit.

In the end they defeat their own purpose.

In 1975, Long Beach State had a running back named Herb Lusk. Whenever he scored a touchdown he'd fall on his knees in the end zone and pray. "I just love to get into that end zone so I can thank the Lord," he said.

A year earlier, the BC Lions had a running back named Johnny Musso. He'd come out of Alabama and Bear Bryant said he was the greatest football player he'd ever coached. Now he was packing to go try it with the Chicago Bears, and the things he packed most carefully were the Bibles belonging to him and his wife.

Johnny knew about the end zone. He'd knock you flat to get into it. But that was for touchdowns and talk and games and TV. The Bibles were for living. He never forgot the difference.

Back To You, Al
The Province, August 18, 1982

> *Saskatchewan Roughriders seek ban on sideline player*
> *interviews because they interfere with the game.*
> —News item

THERE ARE SEVERAL TYPES of TV sideline interviews, each packing the intellectual wallop of a conversation with your pet rock.

1. I Couldn'ta Dun It Without My Bible.

"Joe-Bob, a great catch out there for that all-important first down in the opening seconds."

"Thank you, Al. I guess the Good Lord had his hand in there, too. I know I couldn't have made that catch without Him and I just give thanks that He was there when I needed Him."

"A great pick play, too. by your teammate, Fred Fleet-foot, to get you open. Of course, we all know (ha ha) that pick plays are illegal, but I guess you'll take it, eh?"

"Well, Al, if the pick was there I guess it was because the Lord wanted it to be. He runs our plays and sets our picks and I certainly thank Him for it."

"Thanks, Joe-Bob. Great play. Up to you, Frank."

2. Inside Football, or, Wha'd He Say, Frank? Wha'd He Say?

"I have Joe-Bob Lobotomy here with me, Frank and Dale. Joe-Bob, that certainly was one super-great catch. How did you get so wide-open so fast?"

"Well, Al, they were showing zone and we came out in ace, so we overplayed left and fluctuated our freeb while the two back hit the four hole to draw the linebacker in and enable us to overblast with our end and cheat with our Y. Now, had we not read zone we have an option to go against a man defence which is the same except that the guards stay in and sock and the tackle traps and I run a post curl to hit the seam. We just executed real good and fortunately they fell for it."

"Thank you for sharing that with us, Joe-Bob. Good luck the rest of the game."

"Thanks, Al."

3. Hello, Central? Give Me Everybody.

"Frank and Dale, I've got the man of the hour here at the bench. Joe-Bob, I guess you feel pretty good about making that catch when you were wide open like that."

"Sure do, Al. I couldn't have done it without my quarterback, my teammates, my coaches and all the people who've had faith in my abilities through the years. I'd specially like to say hello to my mother down in Bug Tussle. Kentucky—Hi, Mom!—and my married sister in Arkansas, and my dog, Fang—Y'all stop bitin' the baby, y'hear?—and my high school coach and most of all to my girl, Belinda—It ain't true, honey, I never even left the ho-tel."

"Thanks, Joe-Bob. Super play!"

4. Where Is Marcus Welby When You Really Need Him?

"Frank and Dale, I'm here at the Argonaut bench with Joe-Bob Lobotomy, who has just been helped off the field and now has a huge icepack on his right knee. Joe-Bob, I see your leg below the knee is at a 45-degree angle. What seems to be the problem?"

"Well, Al, my cleats kinda locked in the turf, y'know, and when I turned just as I got hit I, uh, heard something pop, y'know? The trainer says it's probably, like, a torn cartilage or ligament, y'know, if I haven't like busted the kneecap."

"Tough break, Joe-Bob. Any chance you'll be seeing action later in the game?"

"Gosh, I sure hope so, Al. Y'know, I had the hip pointer and then the pulled quad and I was just, y'know, gettin' to where I thought I could, y'know, go full out."

"Best of luck the rest of the way, Joe-Bob."

"Thanks, Al."

5. You Can't Fool a Four-Year College Man.

"Joe-Bob, your team has gotten off to sort of a bad start here, falling behind 42–0 in the first quarter. What sort of adjustments do you have to make?"

"Well, Al, we had a few bad breaks, what with the four fumbles and the five interceptions, but we're a good team with a lot of heart. We just have to get out there and kinda suck it up and play with intensity, cut down our mental errors and put some points on the board."

"That's it from down here, Frank."

God willing.

Ms. QB Knows Her Rights
The Province, April 18, 1985

ALL HER LIFE she'd dreamed of playing quarterback for the BC Lions. What could be so tough? She could yell "Hut one! Hut two!" as well as any guy. What else was there?

On the morning of April 16, she read the words that would change her life:

> 15. (1) Every individual is equal before and under the law and has the right to the equal protection and equal benefit of the law without discrimination.

And, buried in the big story about something called the Charter of Rights and Freedoms:

Discrimination based on race, national or ethnic origin, colour, religion, sex, age or mental or physical disability will be outlawed . . .

She thought it over carefully, chose her lawyer, and demanded an appointment with Lions' coach Don Matthews. When he refused, the lawyer read him the Charter clause covering the rights of women to equal employment opportunities.

She got the appointment.

She announced that she wished to try out for quarterback. When Matthews said "But you're a girl!" she called him a sexist pig, turned to the lawyer and said "Shut down this pop stand."

She got her tryout.

She couldn't see over the tackling dummies, let alone a defensive lineman. She threw a football as though she was shot-putting a bean-bag. Sometimes she threw it up to three or four feet. When they threw it back she caught it with her head. When Matthews laughed, she threatened him with a charge of mental cruelty and sexual harassment on the job site.

She got a contract for training camp.

On opening day in Kelowna her time for the 40 was an hour and 10 minutes including coffee break. When Matthews questioned her speed she pointed out that she'd broken a nail after five yards and the Charter clearly stated that there shall be no job discrimination based on physical disability, and if he expected a poor girl to be seen in public with a jagged edge on a fingernail and the polish chipped to boot, well . . .

He listed her time as 4.4.

The day of the first exhibition game against the Winnipeg Blue Bombers she noticed she was listed eighth on the depth chart at quarterback and demanded to know why she wasn't starting. When Matthews pointed out that Roy Dewalt and Tim Cowan were returning veterans and the other five were graduates of top-rated college teams she sniffed enough to get the mascara running, conferred with her lawyer on the sidelines, and returned to Matthews.

"Coach," she said sweetly, "I can't help but notice that Mr. Dewalt and Mr. Cowan and all those other young men are Americans. I am a Canadian citizen. In giving them preferential treatment you are clearly violating both the spirit and the letter of the Charter in that this is a Canadian league and I am a Canadian and therefore I should be given first opportunity at any jobs available. Now, you are perfectly free to take this matter before the courts, but you know how they're backed up and I assume you want to start tonight's game before Christmas. Therefore, on the advice of my solicitor, I suggest . . ."

She was moved to No. 1 on the depth chart and named the starting quarterback.

When they handed out the game uniforms she refused to put on shoulder pads because they made her head look small, rejected her jersey because orange wasn't her colour, and asked for something chic and summery. When Matthews threatened to bench her she reminded him that job discrimination based on clothing or hairstyle was clearly another violation of her human rights.

She was given a charge card for a local high-fashion boutique and started the game in a yellow pant suit, the Lion logo on the side of her helmet replaced by a mug shot of Cyndi Lauper. And her number read "Like, One."

On the Lions' first play from scrimmage she tapped centre Al Wilson on the shoulder, demanding that he hand her the ball like a gentleman because no lady ever reached between a man's legs on the first date. Wilson picked up the ball, turned, and handed it to her. Linebacker Ty Jones charged through the hole, tackled her and threw her to the turf. She awoke in a chic body cast.

"Baseball . . ." she whispered to the battery of lawyers, civil rights and women's action group reps leaning over her bed. "I've always wanted to pitch for the Blue Jays . . ."

Two were trampled in the rush to the phones. She lay back on the pillow, a faint smile touching her lips. Baseball would be fun. Oh, she hated spitting and cussing and chewing tobacco, but she'd soon make them stop doing that. After all, she knew her rights.

First and Life for The Flea
The Province, August 4, 1988

TERRY EVANSHEN PUNCHED HIS WIFE last week. She was so happy, she cried. He wasn't supposed to be able to punch her, or hold her, or maybe even speak to her. In the minds of a lot of people, he was supposed to be dead.

One month ago tonight the paramedics hauled what was left of Terry Evanshen out of the wreckage of his car, did the best they could while rushing him to the intensive care unit, and began thinking of him in the past tense.

He was in a coma. He had eight broken ribs, collapsed lungs, a spleen damaged beyond saving, a broken ankle and a right arm that had to be opened end-to-end because it had blown up like a balloon. Those were the injuries they knew about. The brain was jungle country, with unknown tigers crouched and waiting in the darkness. The only thing anyone knew for sure was that if he hadn't been an athlete he'd be dead.

Some day, Lorraine Evanshen will give her husband all the gruesome details of the accident his mind has blocked out, the July 4 nightmare outside Oshawa, Ontario, when a man drove his truck through a red light and smashed Evanshen's car on the driver's side.

But not now. Not when he is standing up in front of the TV set, dropping into a boxer's crouch and tossing mock jabs at any shoulder within range. Not when the doctors say he's got 65 percent of his mental faculties back, with a good chance of regaining most of the rest. Not when they say that far down the road after restructuring and therapy the right arm could be almost good as new, that the vision in one eye is normal and that some of the blurring in the other could recede.

Now is for letting go, ever so slightly, of that breath she's been holding for a month. Now is for daring to allow the luxury of real hope. "That old bugger of mine," she says fondly. "I always said he had nine lives, and I guess he's used up half of them on this one."

There is a quaver in her voice, a threadbare sound that tells of the daily 14-hour stretches at the hospital, so many of them beside a loved one in a coma from which he might never recover. But mostly there is amazement mixed with joy.

"He wants to jog," she says. "He's using those grips to exercise his hands. He wants to be out and doing things. We're not kidding ourselves. We know there's a long way to go, and no guarantees. But he's up, and he's *talking*."

For those who knew Evanshen in his 14 years in the Canadian Football League, that's the most encouraging sign of all. He always was a yapper, a needler, a flea of a flanker who'd never use one word when 30 would do. Tongue-tied, he'd never have played. "He's talking a mile a minute," Lorraine says. "Not all of it makes sense. There are periods where he'll just—go away—in mid-sentence. And he'll need speech therapy. But it's coming back. It's coming back!"

She can only shake her head at the response to word of her husband's injury. Prime Minister Brian Mulroney called. So did Harold Ballard. Bernie Faloney, who played his last season in Montreal, dropped in to talk to him. Bernie recalled a play they used to run, and gave the signals. "Sure," Terry said, "but how about this one?"—and made the calls for another route.

Wires and letters arrived by the hundreds, mostly from BC and Calgary, but some from all over Canada and one from Australia. "Tell them thank you for me," she says. "They'll never know how much it meant."

The miracle comeback is a daily, ongoing battle. And every day there are little signs of progress.

The other day, Lorraine Evanshen took her husband to the washroom.

"They need a urine sample, honey," she said.

He thought it over for a minute.

"The people around here are crazy," he complained. "There's nothing wrong with my urine. It's my goddamn head!"

Hang in there, you guys. Both of you.

Quintuple Threat Man
The Province, January 21, 1990

As A 1983 BC LION, Sammy Greene was a quintuple threat—kick returner, pass receiver, boozer, pill-popper and cocaine snorter. "If it would make me feel good, I'd try it," he says.

Feeding his abuses cost him about $2,000 a week—probably a lot more than the other users on that 1983 team that went to the Grey Cup game without him. "Yeah, I wouldn't say I was the only one," he admits. "We kept it in the closet pretty good. I'd do something [get drugs] for them; they'd get something for me. We were a close-knit family."

He is speaking quietly. We are, after all, in church . . .

"Sammy Greene's turned preacher," the caller said. "He was at the Lux Theatre over on East Hastings, on the stage with the microphone talking to the street people. They say he's found God."

Sammy Greene? The BC Lions' Sammy, who tried out with about 14 teams in three leagues and was chopped by all of them? Sammy Greene, who tore up the CFL for 14 games in 1983, then got cut, and Don Matthews would never say why? Sammy Greene, who tried a comeback in 1988 and was doing pretty well at training camp until he told coach Larry Donovan that he couldn't play with Matt Dunigan?

You're kidding.

"Another one," I thought. "Another jock in big trouble who probably found God 20 seconds after the cops found him. A scam. It's got to be a scam . . ."

"I have trouble watching football games on TV," Sammy Greene says. "It hurts too much. I look at Merv [Fernandez] playing for the Raiders, and I know he wasn't that much better than I was. Ronnie Lott ['49ers safety], he'll be in the Super Bowl. I played against him in college. And I know I could have been there, and I threw it away."

The face above the shirt and tie with the blue blazer looks less lived in than abandoned. In 48 hours he'd be hitting the streets of Skid Road again—talking to the hookers, the homeless, the winos, the drug pushers with whom he used to deal. After that, he'd be on the stage at the neighbourhood Salvation Army branch, trying to pass along the message he says has worked for him.

But now, sitting on one of the fold-away metal chairs that stretch row upon row at the Vancouver Christian Centre that has become a home and refuge, Sammy Greene is laying out the other story, the one about the football career he couldn't handle.

"The day coach Matthews cut me, I'd come to practice under the influence. I said I didn't see why I should have to go play the next game in Regina when we already had a playoff spot clinched. Heck, all I wanted to do was get back to my room and finish what I had. We argued, and I said some rude things, and he cut me."

Matthews took a lot of flak for refusing to say why. "He was protecting me," Sammy says. "The coaches always protected me. I was spending more than I was making, so every time I reached an incentive point in my contract, for passes caught or something, I'd go in and ask for it then. And they'd give it to me. They were protecting me. I just wish that once somebody would have quit protecting me. Because then maybe I'd have gotten some help and . . ."

"Sammy's crazy," one of the '83 Lions told me back then. "You know, one time he left his helmet in front of his locker and somebody peed in it. He put it on, got all that stuff all over him and yelled. But then he just went on out to practice."

"Every team I went to it was the same," says Sammy Greene. "Every team! I'd start off good, but I'd always feel like there was something missing. And I'd go to the booze and drugs trying to find it, and my confidence would go, and I'd be gone."

But no one ever blew the whistle. Not on him, not on the team-mates he says were using the same stuff, although perhaps to a lesser degree. Even in college, they were "helping" him. Because Sammy Greene could play football, and if you could perform between the white lines on the field, the white lines you were snorting didn't matter.

As a high school hotshot in Santa Barbara, he went on a recruiting visit to the University of Nevada, Las Vegas, in 1978, and came home with five bottles of Jack Daniels. When the college coach questioned him, he said they were for his mother. "Okay," said the coach, and he got his scholarship.

Stardom in college was a two-edged sword, because now it wasn't just booze, it was drugs. "People gave me things," he says. "Money, everything. And my dosage increased with my popularity."

The Miami Dolphins drafted him third in 1981. ("There I was," he says, "a guy with a cocaine habit, in the drug capital of the world.") He played the pre-season, then bounced from team to team, league to league. In Regina, on one of his last kicks at the cat, he met a girl named Carol who became his wife, hung in there through the troubles and a move to Vancouver, and eventually led him to the church.

"If you ever play again," she said, "it's going to take an act of God."

By this time he was trying to quit, and even telling himself he was making progress. He'd go to prisons to speak out on the dangers of substance abuse. On the way home in the car, he'd have a drink.

Crunch time came at the church.

"At first I sat in the very back row," he says. "Then, gradually, I started moving up. And then I back-slid."

That was when Pastor Henry Hinn took him aside.

"You need a change of environment," he said, and hauled him off to Florida for a church convention. There he heard Jimmy Swaggert, Oral Roberts and other evangelists, and came home determined to carry the word to Skid Road. "That *is* Hell down there," he says. "I know it. I've been there."

Sammy Greene removes the TV mike from his lapel. "Thank you," he says, and shakes hands. His life, he says, is just beginning. In two weeks, he'll be 30 years old.

Victor Had A Little Lamb . . .
The Province, June 16, 1991

KELOWNA—Out on the lush green turf of the Apple Bowl the would-be BC Lions cavort in the morning sunshine, perhaps relishing their final day of freedom before the veterans arrive to teach them the facts of pro football life.

On the sidelines, Vic Spencer is talking not of Lions but of lambs—one particular lamb, in fact—the one that became the Lions' first-ever mascot of their first-ever training camp right here, 27 years ago.

Mr. Spencer is an authority on the subject. If he hadn't had the DeSoto and hadn't been there to help sweet talk the little girl into giving up her lamb . . .

But I digress.

Suffice it to say that Vic Spencer was a Lions' director before there were any Lions, back in the early 1950s when those s.o.b.'s from Winnipeg and Regina kept shooting down a Vancouver entry in the Canadian Football League, first because they didn't want to travel this far and later out of fear that with a stadium the size of Empire the new team could generate enough money to buy the best players and (sob) win the Grey Cup every year.

But they got their franchise, and now here sat Spencer and a few of the other directors at that first training camp in 1954, eagerly awaiting the team's first intra-squad game the following day. It can safely be assumed that the odd glass was lifted in anticipation of the big event.

Somewhere in the course of the afternoon they had a great idea: What the team really needed was a mascot for the first intra-squad game. Lions being hard to come by on such short notice, they opted for a lamb.

"Well, we piled in my DeSoto and headed out into the country," Spencer recalls, "and eventually we came to this farmhouse where a little girl had a pet lamb, so young that they were nursing it with a bottle."

The little girl would not sell her lamb. After much negotiation, she did agree to rent it for the weekend, as long as they agreed to take the bottle, feed it regularly, and take really good care of her pet.

"Absolutely," they said. Then they drove back to the city and had it dyed orange and black.

"Vegetable dye," Spencer says virtuously. "Didn't hurt the lamb a bit and it made a lot better mascot wearing the team colours."

Now there was a problem. The game wasn't until the next afternoon. Where was the lamb going to spend the night?

"By this time she looked thirsty," Spencer says. "But that's all right, because so were we. So we took her back to the hotel with us and sneaked her into the bar while we talked it over."

They got a break. The bartender had his back turned, bending over digging out some ice. Spencer sat down on one stool and parked the lamb on the next one, front hooves on the bar.

"Scotch for me," he said, "and a double mint sauce for my friend!"

Strangely enough, they were asked to leave.

They retired to their rooms to mount the search for a proper place for the lamb to spend the night. Their choice was perfect: the hotel manager's bathroom.

"It got kind of messy, her doing what lambs will do," Spencer concedes. "But she stayed in there quiet as a lamb, you might say, and the next day we trotted her out for the game. She was a big hit, and we took her back to the little girl good as new once the coloured hair grew out."

We stood for a few minutes more watching the rookies—the talented, the tryers, the dreamers, the ones who'll make the first cuts and the ones who'll pack their hopes in athletic bags and look for another team or another line of work the way Lions' rookies have done now for better than a quarter-century.

"Vic," I asked, "why do you suppose they threw you out of that cocktail lounge?"

He gave it some thought.

"I guess," he concluded, "they only served lamb in the dining room."

Bum Steer in Mississippi
The Province, September 16, 1992

FOOL THAT I AM, I thought the high-school football coach who bit the head off a toad had achieved the ultimate in inspirational speeches.

It happened in Texas a few years ago. Come to think of it, maybe it was a newt. Whatever it was, it wandered across the practice field while he was whipping his boys into a frenzy over what they were gonna do to those pissants in the Big Game come Friday night, and he just flat grabbed that sucker and chomped.

There was considerable fuss.

They might still be talking about it down there if it wasn't for another high-school coach whose team was about to play a team called the Eagles. He painted a chicken in the school colours, threw it out onto the field and screamed at his players to "Stomp that eagle!"

A surprising number of people took offence, which makes me wonder how Jackie Sherrill is going to fare at Mississippi State now that he's castrated the bull.

Well, what else was he supposed to do? The damned thing was too big to bite its head off. It might not have liked being painted Texas burnt orange and white, and probably wouldn't have stood for a stomping.

Besides, those are high-school stunts. This is university. You've got to think grown up and big. So, when Jackie Sherrill was psyching up his Bulldogs in the days before the big game against Texas Longhorns and they admitted they didn't even know what a steer *was*—well, hell, he had to do *something*.

So, he had a calf castrated by its owner on the practice field. Presto: instant steer.

Now that a complaint has been filed with the state Animal Rescue League, and the associate dean of MSU's school of veterinary medicine has deemed the event "out of place" on the practice field, Sherrill has felt moved to justify his actions.

"One, it's educational," he said. "That's probably the biggest reason. And motivation."

Asked how he thought viewing a castration would motivate his players to go out and beat Texas, he replied: "That's everybody's different perception."

Yes, indeed.

"Uh, coach? I been studyin' the Texas game films and I notice the QB tends to stand a little bit spready-legged. If we were to get in there quick-like and combine this castration thing with the chomp that high-school coach put on the toad, we could maybe get him out of his offence real fast."

"Hot damn, Billy-Bob, you're right. Hit 'em low, hit 'em fast, and chomp, that's the stuff! It's like that Churchill guy said: 'Give us the tools, and we'll finish the job.'"

Sherrill stands by his motivational techniques. "They were going to perform the castration anyway," he says. "We didn't do anything inhumane to an animal . . . I don't think the calf was embarrassed by anyone watching him."

Besides, didn't his Bulldogs beat those Longhorns 28–10? Just goes to show you: There ain't nuthin' beats a college education.

Joshua
The Province, November 1, 1993

HIS NAME IS JOSHUA, and he is three.

On nights when his daddy works at home instead of out of town, Joshua gets to go to the office with him. He sits and watches him work, and when the job is done he takes his hand and walks with him to the place where he gets out of his work clothes.

Joshua sits there quietly next to his daddy, wondering, maybe, why it's taking him so long. If *he* took that long to dress in the morning, Mom would tell him to get a move on. But people keep stopping him to poke the microphone-things and the camera-things at him and ask him the same questions, over and over again.

Through all the questions and the noise and the people swarming around, Joshua says not a word. It's late, and he's tired, and he's waiting for his daddy to finish so they can go get Mom and go home.

His name is Joshua, and he is three. He doesn't know about roll-outs and slants and fly patterns and blocking assignments and the mental "Thousand-one, thousand-two, thousand . . ." that is all the time his daddy has before he hits the artificial turf really hard and his ribs hurt or his shoulder pops and he hears the ugly sound of 35,000 wolves in full cry.

All he knows is that this is where Daddy works, and Daddy is the greatest football player in the world . . .

Danny Barrett brings his son, Joshua, to every home game the BC Lions play. He calls him "my perspective." When things have just gone badly, as they have so often lately, he can look down at the small figure next to him and feel his universe jolt back into orbit. When Joshua smiles, the microphones and the cameras and the notepads disappear and he is not Danny Barrett, quarterback, any more. He is Daddy, and life is good.

A curious and terrible thing has happened to Danny Barrett this season, an incomprehensible, festering something that burst and spewed its poison in a 54–14 loss to the Edmonton Eskimos. The customers weren't just booing him any more. They were waiting for him to fail.

He expected the boos. He's a quarterback. Booing is part of the package. As Doug Flutie's replacement he's been two incompletions away from booing every home game he's played. But that was just frustration. This is something else.

The good games, the record-setting 601 passing yards against the Argonauts, the comeback in Ottawa—all old news, tossed aside and forgotten during a half-season in which he has struggled along with the rest of a team turned old and tired. They want Danny McManus as their starting quarterback. Danny Barrett they just want gone.

He has never mentioned it. Not once. No one has to tell him he's going through a bad patch, or that as the quarterback he is the focal point win or lose, or that he's getting the big bucks to win. He has never questioned the customers' right to boo.

But there is something different about this. The booing that rolled down on him Friday as he trotted off the field at half time had an ugliness to it that took it beyond football into a personal attack.

Maybe it would be best if the Lions didn't win this bush-league squabble over who gets the semi-final at home. If there's a way out of this, maybe the path starts in Edmonton. On the road, the blessed road, the boos are for somebody else . . .

His name is Joshua, and he is three. If he were six or seven he would know about the boos and the losses and endure the jeers and insults at school, and feel the sting of tears. But he is three. And his daddy is the greatest football player in the world.

Danny Ray
Calgary Sun, October 3, 1996

MY FRIEND DANNY RAY KEPLEY went into Canadian football's Hall of Fame this week, still without confessing whether or not he really bit off that guy's ear.

The affair of the missing lobe came in the oft-troubled retirement years, after the medical problems and before the broadcasting career, when he went through the not-uncommon trauma of life after jock-dom. He hit the trauma with the same force he'd hit everything else, and one of the pieces that allegedly came off during a misunderstanding in a bar was a chunk of his opponent's ear.

"Well, maybe a little bit of the tip," he conceded one night after a broadcast. "And it might have been an accident."

Today's Danny Ray is one of those Dorian Gray types who looks younger now than he did in his decade as middle linebacker for the Edmonton Eskimos. You hardly notice the hearing aids, made necessary by a stubborn refusal to go to hospital when an infection was still treatable. Single guys want to troll him through the singles bars in hope of catching the ones he throws back. He has built a solid career as CBC colour commentator, and when he pulls on the blazer he looks like one of those people in the TV commercials who just sold you a house, or maybe a bridge.

But the Danny Ray I remember best is the other one, best personified during a play in 1982, when he played the entire season with a torn left shoulder. If he hit a man straight on, he was fine. If he had to arm-tackle him, the shoulder would pop out and the arm hang there like a spaghetti strand until he popped it back in.

He'd just made a tackle in front of the Edmonton bench. Coach Hugh Campbell, who knew about the shoulder, saw him trying to pop it back and tried to grab him to bring him off.

Danny Ray stepped over the sidelines and glared at him.

"What the hell do you WANT?" he screamed.

Campbell looked at him. "You're okay," he said finally. "Get back in there."

Campbell understood two things: that Kepley wouldn't play if he thought he was hurting the team; and that his career was based on the theory that pain is a matter of mind over matter—if you don't mind the pain, it doesn't matter.

You can get arguments about the greatest linebacker ever to play in the CFL. Given the new pass-happy offence, the wide open spaces of the Canadian game, more telecasts, better isolated cameras and a proliferation of quick, mid-sized players deemed too small to play in the NFL, there is no shortage of current candidates.

But those who've watched the game for a long time narrow the choice to two: Wayne "Thumper" Harris, eight-time all-Canadian and a western all-star in every one of the 11 seasons he played (1961–72) for the Calgary Stampeders, or Danny Ray Kepley. The argument inevitably ends with the assertion that, even today, there isn't a coach in the league who wouldn't kill to have the loser.

Harris was quietly deadly. Legend insists that his pre-game ritual included emptying tins of tape rolls and using the tape to attach the tins to his arms. Kepley was louder, on and off the field. The Eskimos were family, and he considered it his role to bring recalcitrant family members into line.

At one training camp some 20 years ago he decided a rookie wasn't doing his part in holding the tackling dummies, volunteering his body for skeleton drills, and basically running his butt off. So one night he went to the rookie's dormitory room and knocked on the door.

Actually, it was 3 a.m. and he didn't knock on the door, he kicked it in.

Before the rookie could get off the bed, Kepley had flipped on the light, grabbed a water glass, smashed it on the edge of the dresser, straddled the kid's chest, pulled his head back by the hair and begun gently stroking the jagged glass across his exposed throat.

There was no danger. It caused just enough of a scratch to get enough blood on Kepley's fingers to show the kid. He then explained that, as a veteran, he didn't appreciate the rookie's deportment on the practice field, and suggested that it had best change the next day.

The kid never did make the team. But boy, did he work at it.

There are all kinds of stories like that. The danger in telling too many of them is that they might obscure the fact that Danny Ray was one of the greatest players, never mind the position, ever to grace Canadian football.

But let me tell you one more.

We were working on a book, sitting in my living room on opposite sides of a coffee table, the tape recorder between us, discussing the jocks-for-God movement. My head was down as I made backup notes.

"It's okay," I conceded, "but sometimes I think athletes find God right after the cops find them."

I heard a shuffling noise. Danny Ray had come off the couch into what looked like a three-point stance. There was a snarl on his lips. He looked ready to come over the coffee table.

I remembered the rookie and the broken water glass.

"But maybe not," I concluded weakly.

"Damn straight," said Danny Ray Kepley. In life, as in football, the man competes.

Position Filled
Calgary Sun, November 23, 1996

HAMILTON—IT'S A TRICKY WORD, "GREATEST", and naturally it was being thrown around with abandon here last night as Doug Flutie, the tiny perfect quarterback, graciously accepted his fourth outstanding player award in five years.

Nothing wrong with that, as long as you broaden the definition with "greatest modern-day", "greatest of the '90s" or even "greatest thing to happen to Canadian football since they heated the press box in Saskatchewan." In BC, in Calgary and now in Toronto, Flutie has been little short of marvellous. Had he not missed seven games last season he'd probably be riding a five-year run.

But in the days preceding this latest foregone-conclusion coronation—and even during the season—commentators have been suggesting that when it comes to the Canadian Football League, Flutie should now be considered "the greatest player of all time."

Sorry. That position has already been filled.

It belongs to a drawling, jug-eared, hunch-shouldered, semi-bow-legged assassin named Jack Dickerson Parker, and until someone else comes along who plays four positions well enough to be an all-star at any of them and kicks field goals on the side there is no earthly reason why he should not continue to fill it.

It's not Flutie's fault. As a quarterback he's done everything anyone could humanly ask.

But he has yet to play both offence and defence. He hasn't won three Grey Cups (although No. 2 could come Sunday), or made eight straight all-star teams, let alone made them at various times as quarterback, running back and defensive back, or become one hell of a receiver when pressed into service, or produced perhaps the all-time finest one-line defence of the British people: "Any country that invented Beefeater cain't be all bad."

He hasn't led his team to three straight Grey Cups, as Parker led the Edmonton Eskimos in 1954–55–56 over luckless Montreal.

In the first, Parker played offensive and defensive halfback, and scooped up a late fumble by Montreal's Chuck Hunsinger to cart it 84 yards into the end zone in the game that first truly burned the national final into the national psyche. When Bernie Faloney left after the one season, Parker slid over to quarterback—or running back, when coach Frank "Pop" Ivy felt moved by whim or circumstance to insert Canadian Don Getty at QB and let Parker wreak his particular brand of havoc elsewhere.

There used to be arguments over what was Parker's best position on offence—quarterback or halfback. The New York Giants, who had the Mississippi State phenom locked away until the Eskimo brass dumped $10,000 on his hotel-room bed ("I swear I 'bout fainted"), had him pencilled in as a receiver.

CFL coaches, however, had no doubts. They wanted to see him anywhere but quarterback because at quarterback he handled the ball on every play. Nobody ever ad-libbed better than Parker, although Flutie could give him a run.

Like Flutie, Parker had other attributes. He didn't play guitar, but giving him a deck of cards was like handing Capone an extra gun. His brother, Fred, wasn't an athlete like Darren Flutie, but he was competitive. Parker still has a hairline scar from the night a football argument ended with Fred firing a bullet pass with the telephone.

Different times, of course, and a different game. Greatness is produced by being the best of your era, its rules and its circumstance. Comparisons are for bull sessions and Grey Cup Week, when the memories flow like fine old wine and the old stories are buffed to a new lustre with the retelling.

Normally, you would not read them here. But in these wobbly, uncertain times for Canadian football, when even a game like this one with its Fluties, its Plesses and its Pinballs cannot totally erase the worry of tomorrow, there is comfort in recalling that we did, indeed, have a wondrous yesterday.

You Gotta Have Heart
The Province, July 31, 1992

SONNY HOMER IS MILDLY CLAUSTROPHOBIC, throws up on airplanes, played 10 years of pro football with one kidney and has a heart that now contains eight bypasses and one metal valve. If he were a used car, he'd be sitting in a scrap heap somewhere compressed into a foot-square metal block.

Instead, he is recuperating at home from the last operation three weeks ago—the one that put the five bypasses in to go with the three he had in 1973—taking blood-thinners, and debating the relative merits of a pig valve vs. the metal one that went in with the latest five detours.

"Metal is more trouble because it causes stuff that means you have to take the thinners," he says. "But the pig valve lasts only five years and the metal is lifetime.

"However the hell long that is . . ."

Lawrence "Sonny" Homer is 55 years old, a BC Lions' receiver from 1958 through 1968, a Vancouver kid who ran so fast he seemed to float over the grass without disturbing a blade. He might have been even faster if he hadn't had to lug that extra pad around, the one that covered the only kidney he had left.

He had the surgery after his rookie year. He'd been squeezed between a tackle and a running back in his senior year at Grays Harbor junior college and emerged with one kidney squished to the thickness of a 50-cent piece. The doctors removed it and said he was nuts to play pro ball. Get hit just the right way at just the wrong time, they said, and you could run out of kidneys. "Right," he said, and played 10 more years.

The playing was the easy part. Getting there was something else.

Sonny hated to fly. His stomach hated it even more. These days he'd be selling monogrammed NIKE barf bags. Those days, he just threw up.

The claustrophobia became public knowledge on a road trip to Winnipeg, where he was trapped between floors in a stalled elevator loaded with Lions' linemen. Sonny began to freak. Fortunately, his buddy Jerry Bradley was on the floor above to talk him through it.

Bradley leaned into the shaft.

"Homer!" he called. "You're gonna DIE, Homer! You're gonna be trapped down there until you run out of air!"

"You sonofabitch," Homer screamed. "I get outa here, I'll show you who's gonna die!"

It took about 30 minutes. Bradley maintaining a running commentary on Homer's life expectancy. When power was restored, Homer burst out in pursuit of Bradley, who says to this day he only did it to take Sonny's mind off his problems.

But then, as now, Sonny never much stopped to realize he *had* any problems. He just played—and smoked, maybe a pack a day. The first bypass operation didn't convince him to quit, but five more bypasses have now done what three could not. He's been a non-smoker for three entire weeks. Eight hours on an operating table ("It was scheduled for five and a half, but they hit scar tissue") does tend to get your attention and shuffle your priorities. He dreams of cigarettes now, but dreams contain no nicotine, and he has other things to keep him busy.

The first is a projected walk around the block, and two blocks the week after that, and so on. "Don't worry about it," he says. "I wouldn't have much resale value on the car lot, but the motor's still running."

And hey—if he needs encouragement, he can always call Jerry Bradley.

Rider Pride
Calgary Sun, November 16, 1995

THE CYNICS INSIST that the Grey Cup game should never have been awarded to Regina, where the snow blows and the winds howl and the chill factor can freeze the balls off a Christmas tree. The cynics have never heard the voice of Taylor Field.

It's not an easy thing to do, listening to a building. You have to cock your ear for the creaks and the groans of shifting timbers or settling concrete, and open your mind to the voices of players and coaches who've come and gone. Do that, and the walls will tell you stories . . .

There was the afternoon in 1970 when the snow was blowing and the wind was doing its worst, so malevolently cross-field that Calgary's Larry Robinson, lined up for a last-second field goal with his team trailing 14–12 in the deciding game of the western final, actually had to kick the ball *away* from the goalposts.

Robinson kicked, and the crowd went dead silent—so silent that one man's voice echoed across the park: Roger Kramer, the huge Stampeder offensive tackle, shaking his fist and screaming into the wind: *"Bend, you sonofabitch! Bend!"*

The ball listened, bent left, and dropped through the uprights for a 15–14 win. The Riders had gone 14–2, Ron Lancaster would win the Schenley as the league's outstanding player—but the Stamps were going to the Grey Cup.

The crowd went home stunned. But they would be back. In Saskatchewan—not just Regina, but all of Saskatchewan—they always come back. In Saskatchewan you are not merely for the team, you are *of* the team. Sandy Archer, the Riders' trainer from 1951 through 1980, remembers one game against Hamilton when the rain came down so hard that all the towels were soaked and there was no way of keeping the kicker's shoe dry. A fan noticed the problem, came out of the stands, peeled off his angora sweater, and wrapped it around the kicking shoe. "The guy kicks the field goal," Archer says, "and we win 5–3."

Archer's first year was also the rookie season for a quarterback named Glenn Dobbs, lured out of a two-year retirement as an answer to the hated Indian Jack Jacobs in Winnipeg. He'd been a college All-American at Tulsa, an all-pro with the Los Angeles Dons in the old All-American Conference. The man was a *star*. "I went to my first practice," he recalled years later, "and they handed me a bucket of paint and a brush. The Riders' job that day was to paint the Taylor Field fence."

He stayed two years and loved it as the city loved him. Saskatchewan issued vanity licence-plate holders labelling the province as "Dobberville." The battles with Jacobs were classics. Taylor Field had itself another legend.

Not that there was ever a shortage. This was a team that had its offices and dressing room at the city race track, dressed there and bussed to the stadium on game days, and had to beware of oncoming horses as they crossed the track to practice in the infield. For years the only heat in the dressing room was provided by a pot-bellied stove. But even then there was tradition: A support beam in the middle of the room was festooned with the name tapes ripped from the helmets of players cut or released over the seasons. Sometimes they'd add the name of a hotshot rookie, just to watch him turn green.

Once, when trainer Dale Laird had a heated argument with coach John Payne over dressing-room territory, Laird hid the footballs for an afternoon game, which didn't start until they found replacements. Laird was also a key figure in the development of a country-western record: Tim Roth on guitar and vocals, Nolan Bailey on drum, and gigantic Clyde Brock singing and pounding a wrench on a steel pipe. The title was to be the combined weight of the three players, but Laird's dog wandered into the cover picture, so they added his weight and called it *800 Pounds of West Country Rock*.

More than anything, the Riders are a team that makes do, a team that became the green-and-white in 1948 because a team director found two sets of nylon jerseys in a surplus store in Chicago and couldn't resist the bargain; a team that exchanged tickets for wheat in a year when times were tough in Saskatchewan; a team that survived for years on the funds from civic dinners, in a province where employers used to give their help one day off if they bought a season ticket.

In those years, Taylor Field has grown from an 8,000 capacity to the 55,000-plus for the Grey Cup game, thanks to those cold metal scaffolding temporary seats. Last October 14 they did a dry run with the new seats—and drew 55,438. Somebody figured that on that day, not counting Regina and Saskatoon, Taylor Field was the largest community in Saskatchewan.

The cynics have it backwards. Saskatchewan isn't lucky it has the Grey Cup game. Canadian football is lucky it has Saskatchewan.

Language Barrier

Calgary Sun, July 11, 1996

IT IS NO SECRET that in the minds of many professional athletes the word "Mother" ends with a hyphen.

No, wait: not ends, exactly. The hyphen is more of a bridge to another word, the combination then taking on a meaning that has no connection whatever with mom, affection, Chevrolet or apple pie.

While students of the language remain uncertain of the hybrid word's origin, historians have traced it back as far as 1873 to the southwest corner of Arizona, where a US cavalry private, assured by his sergeant that there were no Indians for miles around, stepped outside the fort, where arrows made him an instant pincushion.

Falling back inside, he glared at the sergeant.

"You muh . . . !" he groaned. "You muh . . . !"

And thus did the city of Yuma get its name.

All of which is a roundabout way of noting that mother has fallen into disrepute yet again. This time, the blame falls on the Canadian Football League.

A bunch of nervous Nellies upset at some aspects of the league's Radically Canadian ad campaign—to wit, the T-shirt bearing the message Our Balls Are Bigger—are approaching cardiac arrest over phase two, a shirt informing the world that CFL players are Tough Mothers.

"First balls, now mothers," they bleat. "Where will it end? Stamp out these smutty T-shirts before our young women reject motherhood and our young men go blind!"

Psssst! Folks! Yeah, you there, with the blue noses. Got a bulletin for you:

The kids know about the hyphen. They don't care!

What they see is a cool new line of sports gear with a slogan across the front that might shock a parent or two—which, of course, is another neat reason to be wearing one.

What the parents should be seeing, particularly those who've followed the CFL's historically stumbling course through the marketplace, is a campaign that's catchy and innovative and has every chance of giving the league a shot at a new fan base it ultimately must tap if it is to survive.

This is the league whose idea of marketing in the past has been to get a connection with a greengrocer and bill meaningless pre-season exhibition games as a fight for the coveted Salad Bowl.

This is the league so weighed down by an inferiority complex by that bigger league and lesser game to the south that its theme song should be "I Surrender, Dear."

This is the league we've pleaded with for 30 years to stop apologizing for the differences in our game and start boasting about them, to quit genuflecting in front of the Super Bowl and start reminding people that the Grey Cup was a football tradition for better than half a century before the NFL's big-deal trophy was a gleam in Pete Rozelle's eye.

And now, finally, it's come out swinging instead of begging for crumbs, going for a chunk of the clothing and paraphernalia market that has been worth billions to the NBA, the NFL and even the NHL—quality stuff, as good as any out there—and people are *bitching?*

Tacky? Of course it's tacky.

Off-colour? Not unless the dye runs. And it won't.

Look around. Check out the messages on T-shirts these days. Double-entendre is not a football formation, it's a fact of life.

Some of it goes too far. But I would rather see a kid in a shirt that said CFL Players Are Tough Mothers than in some I've seen that said Kill Whitey, or Screw the World or (Bleep) the Olympics.

What we have here is a nifty campaign that is having an impact. People are talking about it, and thus about Canadian football—the league, not the collapse. When was the last time that happened?

Those who fear that their children's moral fibre will melt at the first touch of a new CFL T-shirt, golf shirt, sweatshirt or cap have the answer in their wallets. The merchandise—more's the pity— is available only by credit-card mail order through toll-free numbers. You don't want it in the house, don't let your kid have your card.

But think about it first.

What's the greater worry: that your kid wears slightly risqué gear that brags about a Canadian game and Canadian sports heroes; or that he grows up worshipping at the shrine of American jock millionaires and believing that when it comes to sports, Canadian is an eight-letter word for bush?

The Late Starter
Calgary Sun, July 26, 2001

THE WIRE STORY said the Winnipeg Blue Bombers had released Garry Sawatzky (6'3", 300 lb., Stonewall Collegiate), which pretty much writes *finis* to a tale that surely is the stuff of movies.

You see, there is a Stonewall Collegiate, but Garry Sawatzky never attended. His life school was Stony Mountain Penitentiary, where he was doing life for second-degree manslaughter when he decided he'd like to try pro football.

There was no logic to it. He was 27 and hadn't played since high school. There was no way of knowing when or if he'd get out. Life 10, they call it: life in prison and the chance of parole after 10 years hanging out there like candy you can't quite reach.

But he'd lived in the weight room for three years, building a physique and a reputation. "In prison, lifting defines who you are," he told me six years ago, "but it doesn't matter a damn if you can't fight."

Few people believed he'd ever get the chance. Too old, too green, too much baggage. What were the odds on a team taking a chance on a guy doing time for a bikers-vs.-townies brawl in which a 19-year-old boy died from a flailing knife as Sawatzky went down under a pile of adversaries?

Sawatzky knew all about odds.

Figure the odds on his girl, Colleen, marrying him in prison and hanging in through nine years. Or on staying sane in conditions so vile he once plucked threads from his prison overalls, trying to make a noose. "I wanted to catch a rat," he said, "to prove they were there."

It's an oft-told story now. Six years ago he didn't want to tell it at all. But he did, and never once did he say he didn't deserve anything that happened.

"I'm not a victim," he said right off. "That's crap. I was a kid who grew up angry. My parents split, my dad and I had it out physically. I was 17 when I finally won one, and that's when I left home."

He got his football shot because a guy who used to play for the Bombers visited the prison, saw the physique, and passed the word. His evaluation was held on a day-pass. A year later, in 1994, he was at the BC Lions' training camp, the next year on the roster and in the press book, the rookie from Stonewall Collegiate because a PR man thought Canadian Penal System wasn't cool.

He was big and green, but Canadian. He parlayed that into five years' worth of pro as an offensive lineman, never a star, seldom a first-stringer, but handy enough to keep. Had he not been injured in training camp, he might have made it six.

Sometimes, playing might-have-been, you could wonder what sort of career Garry Sawatzky might have had. There could have been college, and with four years of collegiate ball to rub the moss from the antlers, at least a CFL shot when he was 22 instead of a decade later. A quick Canadian kid who weighed 300-plus? Who wouldn't have taken a look?

But in prison, might-have-beens and might-be's are among the first things to die. "He never let me dream," Colleen Sawatzky said of those prison days. "I'd talk about the future and he'd get upset. Dreaming was a luxury we couldn't afford."

There was talk about a movie once. It never happened, which is probably just as well.

Movies feed on heroes and happy endings. They'd have had him scooping up a fumble and scoring the winning touchdown in the Big Game. Prison would have been a Club Med with bars, full of loveable characters who'd all been framed or misunderstood. *The Longest Yard II.*

The thing of it is, there was a happy ending.

No big money, no fame, no glory. Just a second chance and five years of making it work. Not a big finish. A real one.

"You Wanna Write About *What*???"

GIVE OR TAKE PARROTS, macaws and a parakeet named Petey I knew once who could recite his name and address until the city changed the name of his street, very few birds or animals can talk. They may discuss things among themselves, but as far as English goes they're pretty much tongue-tied—except for rats, of course, and rats who talk are soon fitted with tiny cement shoes and sent skin-diving.

One fateful day it occurred to me that there were a lot of birds and animals involved in sports. Dozens of teams were named after them, billions of dollars were bet on them. They probably had *lots* to say. So I started giving them a voice.

Same with kids, who have a society of their own in which Big People are not allowed unless they know the password or secret grip, which they never do. Them I *could* speak for. Hell, I used to be one. I could remember the way it was, playing games and trading stuff. Why not play those memories against the world of kids as it is today?

So, there I was, venturing into major market sports column writing armed with notebook, pencil, a better-than-average comic book collection, childhood memories and a certainty that there was room on the sports pages for talking birds and animals and the wisdom of small children.

It didn't happen overnight, but with minor early success and managing editors who shook their heads but never stopped me, I slowly worked make-believe into the mix . . .

Revenge of the Devil
The Province, April 19, 1988

I'VE ALWAYS BELIEVED that when it came time to design the thoroughbred race horse, God took the day off and gave the job to the Devil.

He probably said something like "Look, I know I've banished you to the depths of Hell and all that, but no hard feelings, right? So on your way down, how about stopping in on Earth and doing one last Good Thing? Who knows, (well, I do, naturally, but who *else*?) come Judgment Day it might do you some good. At worst, it shouldn't hurt."

"What in Hell have I got to lose?" the Devil snarled. "Whadya want?"

And the Lord sayeth unto the Devil, "Build a creature designed to race around in circles so that Man may have sport to behold at the day's end to his tilling of the fields, and perhaps even place a friendly wager on the outcome."

"You got it," the Devil promised. And, for perhaps the first and certainly the last time in history, he kept his word. He did, indeed, design a creature that would race around in circles for the sport of Man. But he was, after all, the Devil. So, he built in a few flaws.

First, he took this barrel-sized body and rested it on four legs so slender and delicate they could have done ads for pantyhose. Briefly, he considered adding training wheels, then shrugged it off as too Christian.

He added flowing mane and tail accessories, all part of the package price. Then he built a gorgeous, big-eyed head with generous lips and sexy whicker—and placed in it a brain so tiny that small men had to climb aboard during races to show the silly thing which way to go. And even as the earth opened to swallow him forever he added the final touch: feet so devilishly fashioned that men had to pound nails into them to keep their shoes on.

The Lord put in the heart and the courage and the spirit, the Devil having none in stock. You can get arguments over which side brought in the tote board and the bookie, or, worst of all, implanted in the mind of man that watching the creatures race in circles didn't matter as much as having the money down on the right one.

Maybe it was the Devil, planting the seed of temptation. Maybe it was the Lord, testing his flock as to righteousness and handicapping skills. It matters not.

From that moment, the creature called Horse had no say in its destiny. It was there to run for money, eat oats, provide fertilizer and keep its trap shut.

It was proven again on the weekend when the jockeys at Ex. Park refused to ride because they considered the track conditions poor enough to be dangerous. Six races were called off on Friday, along with all of Saturday's card. Reporters, some of whom were counting on the weekend to get even, rushed around taking statements from all concerned.

The jockeys were quoted. So were the trainers and the track operators. We heard nothing from the horses. They probably weren't even asked.

The trainers don't have to tramp around in the mud ruining two pair of brand new shoes. If they choose, they can watch from the clubhouse and get plastered while they're doing it. The jockeys get muddy and wet—but at least they're dressed for it. And when they don't feel like riding, they stage a walkout.

The horse has to go out there stark naked except for a bitty little blanket, a saddle and a sweaty jockey who keeps saying things like "Whoa" and "Atta boy," and is heavily into whips and leather. Everybody talks about cushy stalls and stud fees and candlelight and whinny, but nobody ever mentions *that*.

Just once—maybe this time when the jockeys are ready to go back— I'd like to see the horses go on strike. It would be worth it, if only to see, in this sport of kings, how many would pay to watch the jockeys race.

Things Go Better With . . .
The Province, February 16, 1989

THE HEADLINE IN THE AFTERNOON PAPER was a shocker: Trainers face hearing into coke use by horses.

Well, I guess so! Since the "c" in coke isn't capitalized and hasn't got that teensy little TM near the bottom, we can safely assume we're not talking soft drinks here. We're talking cocaine, which is a horse of a different colour.

And if it's true that several California horses have flunked urine tests and stand charged with running on cocaine booster shots, questions arise that must be dealt with immediately.

How do they pick up the razor blade with their hoofs?

Snorting would be no problem—not with nostrils that size—but how do they roll up the dollar bill to form the tube?

And the urine tests. You ever take a close look at a horse in action? What did they use for sample bottles—wine barrels?

The story says the samples were frozen. Was that done while they were in the horse—in which case I suppose the sample could be squeezed out like a popsicle—or later, which would allow the horse to claim they got them mixed up and that wasn't his at all, it was that cheap little claimer's two stalls down?

More importantly, what made them do it? They had everything: fame, fortune, posh stalls, the best of hay and grain, grooms and trainers to wait on them hand and hoof. And, at the end of the rainbow, retirement at age three or four to a lifetime of the choicest fillies being led to the finest studs like an endless parade of Playboy bunnies to a four-legged Hugh Hoofner.

What drove them to dance with the White Lady? Boredom, perhaps. Or, the old story, the drive to compete. The neigh-sayers deny the stuff has ever touched their muzzles, but get them under oath before the California Horse Racing Board and it'll be the same tired excuse:

"Some of them eastern horses use the stuff alla time, so any western horse that wants to do better than show money has gotta use it or scratch.

"Me? Nossir, never touch it myself, but I know horses that do. It's the pressure. You either use it or finish up the track with nuthin' left but a moth-eaten blanket and a milk route. All that trainin', you think they wanna wind up carryin' some fat New York cop through Central Park, chasin' muggers with knives?

"So maybe they take a chance, y'know? Grab a garden hose and switch urine with some wimp track pony or somethin'. I mean, what are the odds? Everybody knows all those stories about side effects are garbage . . . what's that?

"Well, yeah, those are Teflon implants in my nostrils. Sinus condition, judge. I usta sniff somethin' terrible. Why am I shakin'? Well, I gotta see a groom about a curry job, and I'm late, so if you don't mind could I leave like, right away?

"My oath, judge, I never used the stuff. Not knowingly, anyway. The white stuff those other studs say they saw around my nostrils? My trainer did that, judge. Told me it was face powder, make me look good in the winner's circle. Me, I'm as pure as the driven snow . . ."

Donald, Where's Your Trousers?

The Province, December 17, 1992

PERSONALLY, I'M *GLAD* that the NHL has gone Mickey Mouse and let in The Mighty Ducks of Anaheim. Maybe now we'll get some answers to the questions that really matter, like how come Donald Duck doesn't wear pants?

Everybody from the late Walt Disney himself to current Disney boss Michael Eisner has dodged that one.

Here's this duck with no visible means of support, living with and apparently raising three little boy ducks named Hughie, Louie and Dewey who are supposed to be his nephews (although we've never been offered one shred of proof) *and all four of them are wandering around without pants.*

In fact, if memory serves, when Donald's girlfriend, Daisy, drops in she doesn't wear pants, either. And in the last few years there's been a little girl duck named Webbigail wearing nothing below her waist but shoes.

So where are the social workers when you really need them? Why hasn't someone noticed that the kids are hardly ever in school? Where does Donald get the money to feed them? Aside from a Navy hitch and some factory work during the war, what's he ever done? Is he exploiting the kids? Is it blackmail? Has he got pictures of Uncle Scrooge McDuck (the world's richest duck) getting it on with a teenage mallard?

Are the NHL governors really sure they want to climb into bed with people who condone behaviour like that? Or are they tolerating Donald in the hope of getting next to Scrooge and his money bin in much the same manner they have tapped into Bruce McNall?

There's something else the governors should be asking, a question that has plagued mankind almost from the day Mickey first appeared in *Mickey Mouse Magazine* in 1935:

If Mickey is a mouse and Donald is a duck and Pluto is a dog—what is a Goofy?

Pluto barks and chases cars. Goofy talks and drives cars. He looks like a dog—beagle-ish kind of face, big black nose, long floppy ears—but he walks upright. (Okay, he wears pants. A good thing, too, because he spends all his time on his hind legs. It's either pants or a trench coat.) He has a home. He goes skiing and sky-diving. What kind of an animal is he?

You know what we're talking here, don't you?

Steroids.

If this is a dog, he's on something. The folks at Disney have built themselves a better dog. Not a smarter dog, but bigger and a shade more dexterous with his front paws. And you know what that could mean.

Think about it. Here we have a big, ungainly, tangle-footed creature who falls down a lot but keeps getting up and in his very ineptitude comes off both lovable and marketable. Is that or is it not the perfect player for a team destined to lose game after game?

Maybe, all these years, the Disney people haven't been building a movie and entertainment empire after all. Maybe it's been a cover-up. Maybe what they've really been building toward all along is an all-Goofy NHL franchise.

Is it coincidence that in several Disney cartoons Goofy has been seen ice-skating? Not very well, but on an expansion franchise who'd notice?

Lovable dogs, half-naked ducks, and Mickey Mouse at the ticket window. Look around the NHL and tell me it wouldn't work.

Overs Here, Overs There
The Province, September 21, 1994

> *Australian cricket officials plan to experiment with revolutionary new rules that could transform the limited-overs game. Under the new format, limited-overs will be split into four innings instead of two.*
>
> —News item

"GUESS WHAT?" I shouted across the newsroom. "Australian officials are going to experiment with revolutionary new rules that could transform cricket!"

"Cricket? Didn't she used to be on *77 Sunset Strip* with that Kookie Byrnes. She must be—what, about 112? Kind of old and breakable for experimenting."

"What are they going to do, put in a rule that says the game has to end in the same decade it starts?"

Clearly, they didn't understand the magnitude of the moment.

"It's the limited-overs," I explained. "They're splitting them into four innings instead of two."

"Well, you know what Yogi said: 'It ain't overs till it's overs.'"

Frankly, I do not understand their indifference. How can any sporting heart not beat faster upon reading the details of the proposed revolution in a game so historic that one of its most hallowed competitions is for an urn full of ashes, reportedly those of early spectators who withered away waiting for the first match to finish.

Just listen to the proposed changes and tell me this will not raise the adrenalin to the pulse-pounding levels of a Stanley Cup final or a heavyweight title fight:

"In a 50-overs match under the experimental rules, the team batting first will face half its allotted overs before effectively being forced to declare. The opposition will then take its turn at bat for 25 overs before both sides bat again for the remainder of their allotted overs . . ."

Got that?

The move to loosen up the game has come, explains Australian Cricket Board chairman Alan Crompton, because "there's a suggestion that some matches lose their interest early in the piece, particularly if the team batting first are about 70 for six after 25 overs."

I couldn't have put it better myself.

Oh, we could argue about the precise point where the matches lose their interest. Mr. Crompton opts for the point where the team batting first are 70 for six after 25 overs. My own interest wanes when the team batting first actually shows up. But then, as Mr. Gershwin put it so well, "You say toMAHto, I say toMAYto." In cricket, as in any sport, the dozing-off point is in the eyelids of the beholder.

My own exposure to the game has been limited by a frightening experience in the early '80s.

I was sitting in a bar in Australia waiting for Rick Hansen to get his wheelchair fixed for the next 70 miles of the Man in Motion tour when the bartender turned on the telly.

"Cricket," he explained. "Give it a go. Good way to get your feet wet. It's one of the short matches."

"How long?" I asked.

"One day," he replied.

Suddenly, I felt dizzy. A game that took a whole day to play? That could be slower than baseball.

"You *like* this stuff?" I asked.

"Not really," he said. "But I sell a hell of a lot of beer."

Let The Games Begin
The Province, April 5, 1995

> *Ballroom dancing and surfing granted provisional recognition as Olympic Games events.*
> —News item, *The Province*

"GOOD AFTERNOON, LADIES AND GENTLEMEN. This emergency meeting of the Canadian Olympic Association to discuss the critical ballroom-dancing issue will now come to order.

"As you know, both ballroom dancing and surfing have been given provisional status in the Olympic Games, meaning that it is only a matter of time before they become medal events. Upon hearing the news, as is our policy, your executive immediately called for White Paper, Green Paper and Blue Paper investigations and a series of progress meetings on the Riviera and the Costa del Sol. The Chair will now hear the report by the ballroom-dance committee."

"Thank you, Mr. Chairman. Your committee has toured the dance centres of the world in an attempt to rate possible competing countries. We even took wives and/or girlfriends along in order to properly assess dance-floor facilities and compare them with our own. You'll find our expenses under Appendix A.

"Our findings are as follows:

"Spain is going to kick our butts in the tango. If Cuba is allowed to compete, we can pretty much write off the samba. The lambada is a possibility because it died off so quickly most countries don't even know it exists. The downside is that it's so steamy there'd be no TV and at the end of the event the couples would have to be hosed down and separated."

"Are you suggesting that we do not bother flooring a team in the dance events?"

"On the contrary, Mr. Chairman. It would be unfair to deprive some of our members of the right to those expenses-paid trips in supervisory positions."

"Not to mention the competitors themselves."

"Yeah, right. Them, too. No, sir, the trick is not to skip the competition, but to limit ourselves to events where we feel we have the best medal opportunities. For example, the Viennese waltz competition. Austria has a lock on the gold, but given that the people of this country have been waltzed around the block by assorted governments for the past 30 years, the committee feels we should be able to come up with a Canadian couple or two who've come to enjoy it. Silver would be iffy, but bronze is a definite possibility. And a bronze to go with our gold . . ."

"Excuse me? What gold?"

"The gold medal we win in the one dance that Canadians do better than anyone in the world. In fact, we may be the only people in the world who do it at all."

"You mean . . . ?"

"That's right: the bird dance. The bird dance is our ticket to Olympic gold."

"Explain."

"Mr. Chairman, how many times have you gone to hockey games or watched them on TV and heard that stupid song with the buck-buck-buck-buck at the end of it, and watched people stand up and flap their arms like chickens to keep time? In Edmonton, it's practically the Oilers' national anthem.

"You give me a few hundred thousand dollars and some airline passes and I'll form a committee that will scour the Coliseum for the best bird-dancers in Edmonton. We'll take them to Hawaii for extensive conditioning in the sand and surf—which I myself will supervise on a daily basis—and by the time the Olympiad of the Year 2000 is upon us we will be ready to bird-dance our way to glory!

"I've taken the liberty of moving ahead with this project, Mr. Chairman. Our bird-dance coach will be that fine Canadian and mascot extraordinaire, Ted Giannoulas of Windsor, Ontario, also known as The Chicken. Our medical support team is in training even as we speak, memorizing the official statement in the event of any sort of inadvertent stimulant usage: 'I didn't know those Odour-Eaters were loaded. She should have read the label.' In short, Canada stands ready to dance!"

"Uh, thank you. But don't you think your preparations are, well, bizarre?"

"Mr. Chairman, they've made ballroom dancing an Olympic event. Don't talk to me about bizarre."

Daddy's Boy

Calgary Sun, May 1, 1996

IT'S MAY, that wonderful time of year when college freshmen, sophomore and junior basketball stars must decide whether to stay in school or skip their remaining collegiate years and take the NBA money right now.

It is also the time of year when educators—many of whom have spent the year fighting to maintain the athletic eligibility of gargantuans who believe staying above C level means keeping your head above water—suddenly feel the PR department knives poking into their spines and trumpet to these young men the virtues of staying in school as poverty-stricken Oral Communication, Kitchen Management and Psychology of Square-Dancing majors.

"Get your degree," they plead, "and some day, should you come upon a square-dancing bus boy longing to communicate, when he says 'Alaman left to your corners, y'all,' you'll be able to answer right back: 'Dosie-doh, bro!' With an education, you can make a difference!"

It is a stand supported and appreciated by coaches who were fortunate enough to have out-bribed other coaches to get these phenoms into their program and who can see a shot at the Final Four flying out the window if they leave.

"You've been like a son to me, Alonzo, and . . ."

"Al-FRAY-doh, coach. Mah name's Al-FRAY-Doh, with a r-a-y in the middle and one of them aitches on the end."

"Whatever. The important thing is, you stay around one more year and you'll go even higher in the draft. Go now, and long-term you lose BIG money! Think of your future, son! More important, think of MINE!"

So far, 10 collegiate stars and one kid fresh out of high school have resisted the temptations of more years avoiding the study hall and declared themselves eligible for the NBA's June draft. The high-schooler, one Kobe Bryant, has seen Kevin Garnett make the leap and believes he can, too. The scouts say he's wrong, that he needs collegiate competition, so he's probably making a mistake.

But the rest of them?

If I had a son who'd completed one, two or three years of college and stuffed enough leather balloons through fishnets to attract the attention of NBA scouts, I would sit him down and give him one of those pieces of survival lore that have been passed from father to son since cavemen first began exchanging pretty pebbles for pieces of T-Rex meat.

"Son, this is your father speaking, so listen carefully: TAKE THE MONEY!

"I know you're really enjoying that sociology course, Baywatch: Cultural Landmark or Skinflick?, and I'm not saying that Gym Decoration won't be of great value down the road. And there's no denying you owe Embraceable U a debt of gratitude for getting those nerds to take your other exams so you could concentrate on your jump shot. In fact, you'd make your mother and me really proud if you went back to college in the off-season and took some courses in a foreign language like, say, English.

"But the NBA will pay you *now*. How much is it going to pay you in a year if you blow a knee playing in college for nothing?"

And if he agreed, with tears in my eyes I would reach up, pat him on the head and say, "There's a good boy. Now you go right down to that agent, sign that letter saying you're turning pro, and stay there until draft day.

"And on the way home, stop in and buy your old dad a Mercedes."

Hello, Dolly
Calgary Sun, March 10, 1997

ONE OF THE SIDE EFFECTS of the birth of Dolly the Duplicate Ewe is that sports fans the world over are dreaming of all-Jordan, all-Gretzky, all-Maradona, all-Griffey Jr. teams laying waste to sets of athletes unfortunate enough to have been conceived in passion rather than in a petri dish.

Even allowing for the obvious flaw (cloned M.J.s would grow and develop at the same rate as the original, and what franchise, let alone coach, can afford to wait 20 years?) they are missing the point: If cloning athletes ever becomes possible, the people doing the cloning *will become more important than the athletes themselves.* Figure it out— who would you rather have, one Gretzky or the guy who can build you as many as you like, Gretzky willing? No, the key figures in sport's Brave New World will be the scientists, not the athletes.

Some of us have seen it coming.

In 1992 two Alberta university professors, Ed Krakiwsky and Gordon Rostoker, told the Canadian Space Agency meeting in Edmonton that Canada's brightest young scientists should be drafted and paid like NHL stars. They were a decade late. In 1982, I myself devised a marketing plan for the Faculty of Science at Simon Fraser University, whose funding slash was taking a back seat to the save-the-football-team campaign.

Hold an academic pep rally, I said. Cheerleaders, marching bands, the whole thing—and tailor the cheers to fit the need:

> Look up-court and whadya see?
> The boys from Biochemistry!
> They've cloned a guy who's 9 foot 3
> And now he's jumping centre.
>
> They've made a tackle five feet wide,
> Designed for speed and action.
> Except, they put the feet inside,
> And he can't get no traction.
>
> They'll cure that cancer, wait and see,
> It's there on their agenda.
> Right now it's no priority,
> They're building a tight enda.

I was ahead of my time. But Dolly has changed everything. Maybe it is time scientists were paid jock money, despite the inevitable salary disputes.

Who should get more—a scrub nurse who wins the Golden Rubber

Glove Award for keeping the operating theatre germ-free for an entire season, or the superstar surgeon who goes one-for-four on tummy tucks?

How would you judge the relative worth of the scientist who perfects the gene-splicing technique that crosses Lee Iacocca with Julio Gallo to produce a car salesman who'll never sell you a lemon; and the developer of the spray for telephone mouthpieces that burns out the tongue of any caller who begins with the words "Is this James. E. Taylor? And how are you today? That's great! James, I'm calling on behalf of the Association for . . ."

There is, however, the problem of acceptance by the general public of intellectual superstars who haven't broken a sweat since the day they found out they had tenure.

I would suggest a program in which they learn to do the things that set athletes apart in public perception. They could start by learning to pout and spit.

Not in the Cards
Calgary Sun, May 25, 2001

> *Tiger Woods signs five-year autographed photo and trading card deal with Upper Deck for reported $4 million a year and percentage of sales.*
> —News item

My first memory of sports trading cards involved bubble gum that defied chewing, let alone blowing. It was prissy pink and tasted like sweat socks dipped in cotton candy. You could pave roads with it. Add rivets, you could build fighter planes.

In our town we'd buy it, tear off the wrapping, and either throw the gum away or masticate it just long enough to make it worthwhile sticking it in Bobby-Joe Woodman's hair.

We had a name for kids who actually chewed the stuff. We called them "Stupid."

The rest of us, looking cool in out-at-the-knee blue jeans and runners with the peeling rubber edges and the grommet holes in the canvas sides, knew it was never about the gum. What counted was the cards.

Truth be told, we didn't know all that much about the athletes on the front, or care about the stats on the back. We wanted the cards because guys with the biggest collections ruled recess.

That 15-minute break was the greatest learning experience in elementary school. Trading cards taught us avarice, lust for power, leverage, blackmail and the art of grinding an opponent into the dirt once you had him down. Business school should be so informative.

We would have laughed at suggestions the day would come when trading cards would be a zillion-dollar business with three-dimensional cards and million-dollar fees for the guys in the pictures, or that there'd be a 100-card set of doggie trading cards from the Iditarod dogsled race.

Believe that, and you'd believe that some day athletes would be charging for their autographs.

As for encasing cards in plastic or putting the most valuable ones in bank vaults, how dumb was that? Everybody knew that your best cards were pasted in a lined notebook, your traders went into your pocket, and the lousy ones were pinned to your bike spokes so you could make a lot of noise and annoy the big people.

In our town, annoying the big people was almost as important as finding a hot horse on a cold winter day so you'd have a hockey puck.

If there'd been elephants on the prairies instead of horses, our national game might be soccer.

Today, anyone over 30 can tell you woeful tales of the card collection they used to have, and how if mother hadn't thrown it away they'd be sitting in the Bahamas clipping coupons. In these stories, every collection had Bobby Orr's rookie card, or a vintage Mickey Mantle. Memories, like rookie cards, grow greater with the years.

In our town, we never thought of the cards as commodities to be stored away between cardboard sheets lest, God forbid, a corner should be turned or torn. They were just things to have, like yo-yos or a big brother whose skates you might one day own.

But even back then, recess economics would have told us that the Tiger Woods autographed stuff would have no long-term value. Not when there'll be millions of it out there.

Down the road, the most valuable trading card of them all might be the signed Wayne Gretzky Indianapolis Racers rookie card. That's because he signed only one, and kept it.

One Tiger Woods card would be beyond price. A million Tiger Woods cards are spoke ammo for your kids to annoy the big people who bought them, years ago. Poetic justice.

Corn on the Cobb

Calgary Sun, May 31, 2001

HONEY, CHECK THE AIR FARE to Cooperstown. Ty Cobb's dentures are going into baseball's Hall of Fame.

Not as an honoured member. That would be silly. As a display, a curiosity, something thousands of dads can show their baseball-minded sons as they tour the Hall this summer.

"Look, son. See those ugly, old-fashioned dentures? Yessir, the great Ty Cobb used to chomp on those as he glared out at the pitcher or took his lead off first and measured the second-baseman or shortstop for spiking.

"Sometimes at the plate he'd turn his head and spit tobacco juice through them. Can't you just see him, son? Bat cocked, snoose juice dribbling down his chin . . ."

"Dad! You're makin' my hot dog taste funny."

Granted, it would have been so much better if the dentures could have been inducted to the Hall with the rest of him in 1936, but he was alive at the time and probably using them. At best, we'd have caught no more than a titillating flash of incisor.

Now, The Georgia Peach being long-since one with the worms, fans everywhere can trek to Cooperstown to view the dentures at their leisure, circling the exhibit to peer from all angles at every stain and filling, their minds wandering back to the game's golden age, when these same dentures were in semi-permanent residence in a Hall of Famer's mouth.

Great moments, well worth the wait.

Thus, a debt of thanks is owed to one Karen Shemonsky of Clarks Summit, Pa., who wandered into a baseball memorabilia sale in 1999, saw Cobb's dentures, and just knew she had to have them. And, $7,475 US later, she did.

It is fair to say her purchase triggered much speculation at the time.

What does someone do with used dentures? Even if she wanted to go to the ball park to munch a weenie or whistle "Take Me Out to the Ball Game" through a Hall-of-Famer's teeth during the seventh-inning stretch, the odds were against a decent fit.

If she wasn't going to wear them herself, what was left? Passing them around at a party in search of the Prince Charming who'd find them a perfect fit? Touring Little League diamonds to point to the old-fashioned fillings and warn of the dangers of not flossing en route to the majors?

But, no. She just wanted them, she said. Besides, it certainly one-upped her sister, who wastes her money on cruises. You can't put a price on that.

Now, she is realizing her other dream: to see Ty Cobb's dentures in the Hall of Fame. "It's such a thrill!" she burbled, which may offer a clue as to how swinging things get in Clarks Summit, Pa.

For five months they'll be on display for the world. Then she gets them back to fondle and perhaps to celebrate their homecoming by changing the water in their glass. Kodak moments, all.

There is, of course, the chilling possibility that Ms. Shemonsky has been had—that Cobb left his dentures in the locker room and therefore they cannot be credited with even one major league appearance.

But let's not be picky. Instead, let us leave Ms. Shemonsky to her moment and her dreams—a far prettier mental picture than one of a toothless Cobb, at bat in Heaven or Hell, glaring at the umpire and gumming:

"You caw that a stwike? It was miw ouside!"

The Old Name Game
Calgary Sun, June 16, 2001

WHEN IT COMES TO NAMING NEW STADIUMS ("Stadia! Stadia!" my old Latin teacher used to scream) I modestly admit to being years ahead of my time.

Nor is the talent restricted to the naming of sporting facilities.

Long ago when twin elephants were born during our visit to Thailand, I told my elephant jockey that they should name both of them Gerald in honour of the great jazz vocalist, Elephants Gerald. "Get off my elephant," he said.

In 1980, when BC was trying to decide what sort of stadium to construct, I campaigned for an all-wooden dome on the grounds that they could get all sorts of sponsorship bucks by naming it Lumberland.

They opted for an air-support dome.

Undaunted, I entered the name-the-stadium fray with a suggestion that they cover the dome with huge Styrofoam anchovies and olives and call it Pizza Hut.

There was heavy competition, and considerable lobbying for the guy who noted the steel cables criss-crossing the vast expanse of roof and suggested they call it Marshmallow in Bondage.

But it seemed like a lock: a stadium roof as the world's biggest billboard—a giant pizza beacon for tourists flying in from all over the world.

Pizzerias would be falling over each other, waving six-figure cheques for the naming rights. Godfather's would put contracts out on the other bidders. It couldn't miss!

They called it BC Place.

These people who once held a contest to name the new hockey arena, then called it Pacific Coliseum ("Coliseum after those Roman places, and Pacific 'cause, like, that's where we are"), were now applying the same irrefutable logic in naming Canada's first domed stadium ("See, it's a Place to watch football, and it's in BC, so . . .").

Meanwhile, much scorn was heaped upon my innocent bod. Name a stadium after a company? Boy, how dumb are you?

Well, ha ha on all of them. The 28-year-old Providence, R.I., Civic Centre has just been renamed the Dunkin' Donuts Centre.

The deal is for 10 years for $4.25 million plus a $400,000 share of revenues from the sale of the aforementioned donuts and an agreement, valued at $4 million, that the DD people will promote at least two events in the arena each year. For DD, a slam dunk.

And, in case you'd like a little ketchup with that, the H.J. Heinz Co. has just signed for $57 million (presumably $1 million for each of its 57 Varieties) over the next 20 years for the right to call Pittsburgh's new 65,000-seat stadium Heinz Field.

They are merely the latest to jump on the bandwagon I tried to get rolling some 25 years ago.

At last count there were nine North American sports facilities named after airlines, three after Pepsi. Dot-com companies have stamped their corporate initials on dozens more.

Some sports fans hate the trend, flatly refusing to utter the sponsor's name. (To the chagrin of the General Motors people, Vancouver fans call G.M. Place "The Garage.")

But as the beloved, hoary sports shrines of old are torn down and replaced with faceless, interchangeable, cookie-cutter models of glass and steel, more and more companies are shelling out millions for the privilege of having them named after the products they're flogging.

It doesn't always work. A lot of these same companies with their names emblazoned across sporting palaces have balance sheets red enough to set Dracula a-drool.

But at Dunkin' Donuts, they don't care. You can't make donuts without being in the hole.

Way To Go, Winfield!
Calgary Sun, August 5, 2001

DAVE WINFIELD goes into baseball's Hall of Fame today. I just hope the seagull goes, too.

Seagulls don't get much recognition. Red Skelton did a marvellous impersonation of a gull called Heathcliffe, and on a bad day a businessman or two has been known to glare up at one and scream "Go ahead! Everybody else does!" But that was pretty much it.

Until August 4, 1983, when Winfield made one famous by skulling it in Toronto's Exhibition Stadium and rendering it seriously dead.

Winfield was a Yankee at the time, shagging flies in the outfield. He threw a practice ball in the general direction of a seagull standing about 80 yards away.

Unfortunately, he hit it dead on. The bird died, and some yo-yo laid charges.

Winfield said he was only lobbing the ball out there to make the seagull move. The bird-lover apparently believed the action was deliberate.

My own reaction: "Lord, I hope so."

I was kind of hoping the case would go to court and Winfield would confess that, under his breath, he'd muttered:

"This is for the statues! And the bald guys! And my car! See how good it feels when something lands on *your* head, you bleeping feathered flush toilet!"

If he'd missed on the first try, I'd have expected the Jays to do the humane thing, and keep tossing the ball back to him until he got it right.

Instead, the hills were alive with the sound of sanctimonious claptrap:

"Omigoodness! He killed a helpless little bird! Burn in Hell, Winfield! God sees the little sparrow fall, you creep!"

What he should have received was a standing O.

Officials estimated that there were 88,000 mating pairs of seagulls within a mile of the stadium, most of whom hung around until the crowds gathered, then used it for a missile range. Winfield lowered the count by one plus however many more it may have engendered. Good on him.

Not that you could blame the gulls.

In Mother Nature's great plan it obviously stipulates that their mission in life is to eat garbage and dump on anything stationary. Since baseball proceeds at such a glacial pace you often have to line a player up with a stationary object to ascertain whether he's moving, the game and the gulls were a natural fit.

Two nights earlier, one had spent an entire game in centre field, presumably falling asleep about the third inning. Trying to roust Winfield's victim to do its excreting elsewhere seemed a logical decision.

But, no.

He was charged, taken to a police station and made to hang around for three hours while the paperwork was done, in which he swore to come back to Canada on a specified date to face charges under the Criminal Code of "causing unnecessary suffering to an animal."

Later, the charges were dropped. Cooler heads had decided that the issue was less whether God saw the little sparrow fall than whether He saw what the little seagull drops.

A good thing, too. With seagull homicide on his resumé, Winfield might never have been signed by the Jays, and thus wouldn't have been around to hit that 11th-inning, two-run double to win Game 6 of the '92 World Series.

It seems only reasonable, then, that the seagull be inducted today along with Winfield, and have its own little bronzed seagull bust.

They could even put a ladder next to it so thousands of Hall of Fame visitors could climb up, lean over, and . . . oh, never mind.

You Gotta Have the Contacts
Calgary Sun, October 18, 2001

WHAT SAYS "I LOVE YOU" best of all?

Roses? A sweet card? A charge card? Cash? They're all good. But if you're a National Football League fan and you want to send that special message to that special someone, nothing says it better than contact lenses.

Not ordinary lenses. That would be dumb.

If you're a hard-core NFL fan, the kind who thinks that on the seventh day the Good Lord put his feet up on a cloud to watch the Angels kick Devils' butt, the last thing you want to give the girl you expect to share your life and bed and keep the beer cold is something that will help her see you as you really are.

But imagine the look of pure joy that will come over her face when she opens that little velvet box and sees a set of NFL Crazy Lenses with the name and logo of your favourite NFL team imprinted in a circle around the edges.

"Oh, you shouldn't have!" she'll coo, pawing through the box in search of a second set, or possibly a ring.

"You're worth it, darling," you'll say suavely. "Every time I look into your eyes and see that Buffalo logo, I'll remember that wonderful Sunday afternoon when we sat here in the snow and saw Doug Flutie beat the Redskins.

"Honey . . . ? Where you goin'? When you come back, bring me a beer and a hot dog?"

Don't worry. She'll just be overcome.

Once you explain that the lenses aren't prescription, have nothing to do with improving your vision, they're tinted in your team's colours, you got them for only $120 to $150 US and you've got a set, too, so you can attend all the games together, she'll melt in your arms.

You don't think so? You don't believe there are enough fans out there who'll shell out that kind of money for two pieces of clear plastic with a team logo that they're expected to stick in their eyes?

Keep in mind, we are talking here about a league where fans routinely wear pig snouts and dog masks, paint their faces in team colours, shake their fists while yelling "Woof! Woof!" and sometimes strip to the waist in blizzards and line up to misspell the team name across a series of pot bellies.

Clearly, the NFL knows its market.

So it's made a deal with CooperVision, which will begin shipping the Crazy Lenses this week—selling them as accessories, not as lenses—to fans who want to show their team loyalty and somehow find spilling beer and belching doesn't get it done.

For now, supplies are limited to a few teams. But by next season every team logo will be available to jam into a devoted fan's eyes. Before long, fans who don't have them—the old guard, with their snowballs and klaxon horns and hard hats that shoot flame from the top—will be so sick with envy they'll be skulking across the border to watch the CFL.

For a fan wanting to put a move on his intended, or even his second-stringer, the advantages are obvious. In fact, they've got a couple of things going for them.

First of all, it puts you on the cutting edge.

That guy Steve, who held up a "Marry Me Wilma!" sign and waved it at the camera? Wilma would need her head read.

But contact lenses? Perfect.

They're cheaper than team jerseys. If you give her a set, she's not likely to find herself sitting next to another girl who's also wearing them. If you're caught putting the leer on the babe in the next seat, you can always say you were checking her lenses to make sure she wasn't actually a Cowboys' fan.

But the best part, the sheer genius of these accessories whose time has come, is that they're good whether your team is hot or cold.

If it's winning, you're showing team colours. And if it's lousy—hey, they're contact lenses. Every morning, before you put them in, you can spit on them.

If the Shoes Fit . . .
Calgary Sun, October 25, 2000

THE TALK WAS OF SPORTS SHOES—runners, we used to call them back in the days before cool became a mantra and the swoosh inherited the earth.

We'd been wandering the sporting goods stores, staring open-mouthed at the price tags that could have made my father's mortgage payments, tacked to shoes so colourful Joseph would have killed to have a pair to go with the coat.

"Remember the North Stars?" someone asked.

At least, he thought they were North Stars. They might have been early Converse or, given the perpetual state of the family economy, generics from the Eaton's catalogue. Who knew, or cared?

Buying them was simple. Your parents took you to the store, picked the most inexpensive pair available, and told you to wear them until the sole fell off or your toes pushed through the front, whichever came first.

There was no colour selection problem. They came in black with a white rubber strip around the bottom.

They were canvas because it lasted forever and had one hole with a metal grommet around it on each side on the theory that if some air got in there your feet wouldn't smell like you'd used dead rats for insoles.

If someone suggested the day would come when you had to—absolutely *had* to—buy a different kind of shoe for every sport or be some sort of social misfit, we'd have knuckled his head or locked him in the outhouse.

Cross-trainers? ALL our runners were cross-trainers. They had to be. They were the only shoes we had. We lived in them.

They were our baseball shoes, football shoes, soccer boots, hiking shoes, gym shoes, every-day-but-Sunday shoes. They waded creeks, tromped mud puddles, shinnied up trees, and ran miles down back alleys and dusty dirt roads.

Not that it was all play.

Getting your first pair meant you had to learn to tie double bows—big ones, because laces cost money and the first ones were always twice as long as they had to be to allow for breakage. You could practise weird knots on your sister's.

They also taught you cool scientific things like the friction effect of rubber on hardwood floors. When the soles reached a certain smoothness they could make a floor squeak like chalk on a blackboard. The black streaks made the big people angry, another plus.

The older they were the more comfortable they got. It made getting a new pair a mixed blessing.

Sure, the treads were better on the new ones, but there was a certain status—cool, we'd have called it had we known the word—to having the rubber strip flap when you walked because it had ripped at the front and was working its way down the side.

The other thing about new ones: Nobody stole them, or grabbed them, or beat you up or killed you if you wouldn't let go.

Our runners were not signs of where we stood in the street culture. How could they be? They all looked the same. Throw them into a pile in gym class and you might wind up wearing a left from one pair, a right from another, and neither of them yours. If they fit, who cared?

Nobody endorsed our runners. We would have—a nickel might well have been involved—but nobody asked us. Besides, who cared what it said on the side? Simpler times, of course. No organized leagues, no sculpted fields. Just a bunch of kids on a vacant lot with jackets for bases. If you were lucky, yours was first base. Nobody slides into first.

They were runners, not shoes. And we never had to worry about being like Mike.

Lie Detector
Calgary Sun, November 30, 2000

Mr. Martin Hudson,
Sports Editor,
The *Calgary Sun*

Marty: I need $80. A guy named Amir Lieberman has invented a pocket-sized portable lie detector.

This is true. If you don't believe me, buy one yourself and use it on me. Besides, it says so right here in the morning paper, and we all know newspapers never lie.

It's called the Handy Truster Emotion Reader, it can be plugged into telephones or just held under the guy's nose like a tape recorder, and the manufacturer says it can spot eight lies in 10 tries.

The way it works is this. When people lie, the blood flow to their vocal cords is restricted by stress, which causes faltering changes in the voice at such a low frequency we can't hear them, so your basic lie-in-his-teeth ratfink gets away with it.

But not with the Handy Truster Emotion Reader, boy. Not only does it pick up the falter, Amir claimed in a press conference in London, it can tell if the stress is caused by lying, excitement, exaggeration or emotional conflict.

You stick it in front of a guy you think might be lying and as he's talking you look at the little screen, which has an apple icon on it. If there's doubt that he's telling the truth, a bite is taken from the apple to a maximum eight bites, Dodging a question produces a half-eaten apple, and a flat-out lie flashes a gnawed apple core.

So I was thinking: Wouldn't it be handy to have a Handy Truster Emotion Reader at sports press conferences?

Wouldn't it be great to be able to rely on Actual Scientific Evidence that someone is lying to us? Isn't it time we stepped into the new millennium and scrapped the current system where we assume he's lying because his lips are moving?

Think of the age-old questions that could be answered—and all for $80 (batteries not included):

Do coaches really believe that when the going gets tough, the tough get going, or that it ain't the size of the dog in the fight, it's the size of the fight in the dog?

How great would it be, when a coach says he went to the opera and it ain't over till the fat lady sings, to be able to jump up and scream: "Apple core! Apple core! You've never even BEEN to the opera!"

Wouldn't you like to have a Handy Truster Emotion Reader handy when professional sports teams announce their losses for the season to justify ticket price increases? Or when a team owner swears he has no intention of moving his franchise?

How about when a boxer, having just beaten an opponent senseless, thanks his Maker and says he owes it all to Him? Or when Gary

Bettman says the pro hockey talent pool is deep enough to stock 30 franchises and the game has never been in better shape?

How many bites would come out of the apple, do you suppose, when athletes who blow the pee-pee test swear they thought they were taking a flu shot? Or when some 19-year-old holdout who barely finished high school, majored in gum and thinks principle is the guy who expelled him says it's not about the money.

Eighty bucks, Marty! I blew more than that on Grey Cup taxi fares to hear BC Lions insist they always knew they were a great team and there was never any dissension. Core, hell. Halfway through sentence one, Handy would have been spitting apple seeds.

So kindly send me the $80, post haste. Also round-trip ticket to London, where they're being sold. Business class is fine.

—JT

PS: The Handy Truster monitored the US presidential debate and indicated that Bush told 57 lies and Gore 23. So we'll have to remember it registers on the low side. Or maybe it ran out of apples.

Okay, Sometimes I Got Mad

THERE WAS A TIME in the newspaper business when the column reaction mail took three or four days to arrive and there wasn't that much of it because outrage seldom lasted long enough to sit down with pen and paper, find a stamp and then a mailbox. E-mail changed all that, for which I am eternally grateful.

On days when the idea tank hit empty, rescue was often a computer click away. Hate mail was the best, once you got past the misspellings by people who clearly thought grammar was grampa's wife. And there was a bonus: A column answering the letter would trigger a letter in response, which provided yet another column.

To a guy writing five columns, fifteen radio shows and five TV editorials a week, as I did for three years, the hate-mailers were as vital as the fifteen-cup coffee maker. (In our house we had a rule: The coffee maker was constantly to be in one of three states—full, perking, or broken, in which case the trip to replace it was mandatory within the hour.)

I treasured the mail no matter how it arrived, particularly the letters from English teachers saying they were using the columns to encourage their classes to use the language as it was intended. That was almost as big a thrill as the day I learned that the Hotel Georgia was hanging my columns on the wall over the urinals so men could read as they peed, and occasionally get pissed off. But a few years into the column biz, there was what you might call a humour backlash: If I wrote two serious columns in a row, people wrote in demanding that I knock off the deep stuff and get back to making them laugh.

Well, that wouldn't work. Yes, I wrote a lot of sports humour—some it a dismal failure—but that was just the way the column evolved. I never, ever, woke up and asked myself "What will I be funny about today?" If something struck me as funny, I went for it. Same thing with the snarly stuff. Writing diatribes, no matter how serious the topic, is a bit like getting a mule's attention with a two-by-four. Pretty soon, he's ignoring you.

The trick was to strike a balance, to have people picking up the column never knowing what to expect. On the heaven-sent days, I could mix the two and harpoon with laughter. Nothing stings like ridicule.

But in the ongoing process of learning what made a successful column work, I made a discovery: If I stuck mainly to humour, when something upset me and I reared back and cut loose with the fastball, the reaction was that much more vociferous . . .

The Good Old Days
Calgary Sun, December 17, 1998

REMEMBER WHEN GAY MEANT HAPPY?

Remember when colour meant flair or style?

Remember when black was the colour of my true love's hair?

Remember when you could write "canny Scot" without someone threatening to hit you with a civil suit or a bagpipe?

Remember when sports pages were full of sports?

Remember when months would go by without some pug-ugly jock beating on his wife or girlfriend?

Remember when muscles came out of the weight room and not out of a pill bottle or a needle?

Remember the NHL when everyone who was in it had the talent to be there?

Remember when you could refer to a loan shark as a Shylock and people knew you were referring to a character in *Merchant of Venice* and not slagging a race?

Remember when games belonged to the athletes and kids' sport belonged to the kids?

Remember when suits were clothing, and not a bunch of glad-handing, dead-eyed sharpies pouring millions on athletes who think fiscal responsibility means showing up on time at the gym?

Remember when fans mattered?

Remember when the headline "IOC URGES HONESTY" would have been funny?

Remember when professional athletes were both professional and athletic and weren't insulted if their contract offer didn't match the gross national product of North America?

Remember when Mark Tewksbury was an athlete, performed as an athlete, marketed himself as an athlete, and lacked the arrogance to think that anyone would give a damn whether his sexual preferences leaned toward women, men or sheep?

Excuse me. It's been a long week.

Mark Tewksbury "came out" this week. He came out on television, in newspapers, on stage and in a media press conference.

He's gay. Hooray. Next.

Brian Orser didn't come out. He was ratted out by a former partner in a palimony suit. It was sad on two counts: He'd always figured, correctly, that it was no one's business but his, and the grubbiness of the suit would mean another hell week for young male figure skaters who would hear the old homophobic taunts all over again.

Mark Tewksbury wasn't outed. He stepped out of the closet with teeth agleam into a self-created spotlight to confirm an open secret as though the world was dying to know.

When Ellen did the same thing, it boosted her sagging TV ratings for a week or so. Then the show died, not because she was gay, but because it hadn't been funny for a couple of years and no amount of nudge-nudge-wink-wink single-entendre was going to save it. And she still looked lousy in a tie.

If Tewksbury had made the announcement from the top step of the medal podium at the '92 Olympics in Barcelona, if he'd waved his 100-metre backstroke medal in the air and shouted "This one is for the gay community of which I am a proud member!" it would have made waves big enough to empty the pool.

In those days, coming out was rare, the world less accustomed or inured to it. Today the world in the main has come to the conclusion that it doesn't matter and that the whole thing is growing a tad tiresome.

What was it Dorothy Parker said: "If all the girls at the senior prom were laid end-to-end, I wouldn't be a bit surprised."

There are gay athletes and ex-athletes. Always have been, always will be. Come out or stay in, it's their choice, and an agonizing one.

But outing, like sex, is a participant sport. Save us, please, from those arrogant enough to think we care.

Selective Grieving
Calgary Sun, November 2, 1999

> *Robert Fraley*
> *Van Ardan*
> *Michael Kreig*
> *Stephanie Bellegarrigue*
> *Bruce Borland*

RECOGNIZE THE NAMES?
Probably not. It took a long internet search to find them. Mostly they were buried, afterthoughts in the other, bigger story.

Five relative unknowns who died with Payne Stewart last week when his Lear jet drifted aimlessly through the skies with no one at the controls, then crashed into that South Dakota field.

Five ordinary people with hopes and dreams and aspirations and friends who will mourn their passing. Five ordinary people who did not wear designer plus-fours or hit a golf ball the way Payne Stewart could, or come remotely close to his celebrity.

There was no bagpiper for them, marching into the mist playing "Going Home." No black arm bands, no celebrity eulogists. If there were television cameras or media people with tape recorders and cameras present when their friends and loved ones said their goodbyes, it didn't make any network television I saw.

They died as people die in plane and automobile and motorcycle accidents; as soldiers and civilians and children are dying every day in wars they don't understand, some on foreign soil in countries they'd never heard of until the day they were ordered to go.

Payne Stewart's death was tragic and wasteful, but no more so than theirs.

Payne Stewart won the US Open. Bruce Borland was a 40-year-old golf course designer who cancelled his commercial flight ticket so he could ride with Stewart and discuss one he wanted to build in Dallas.

Payne Stewart had found a new peace in recent years that allowed him to put his game and his life into perspective. Stephanie Bellegarrigue, commercial pilot with 1,700 hours of daylight flying logged, had her life ahead of her. Stephanie Bellegarrigue, dead at 27.

Payne Stewart was famous, a man of charm and style with flaws and faults and foibles, just like the rest of us, and just like Robert Fraley and Van Ardan, the sports agents who died with him.

Five ordinary people and one celebrity. All dead in the same accident for the same reason, whatever it proves to be. But one is worth a week of mourning and sorrow by media people who mostly didn't know him but follow professional instincts that tell them the people want every detail and stop-action shots of every trickling celebrity tear.

It is, I suppose, the last price tag of fame for the departed, the last chance for the people who come to view celebrities as family to peer into the fishbowl at a life they'll never know or ever really understand. And so the focus narrows.

When Lennie Bias, the kid tabbed as the next great Boston Celtic, died of a crack overdose, Jesse Jackson flew in to do the eulogy. I was in Miami, sitting next to a city cop, watching it on television.

"You know how many kids die of crack overdoses in Miami every year?" the cop asked. "You know who comes to their funerals? Nobody."

When Philadelphia goalie Pelle Lindburgh, intoxicated far beyond acceptable limits, died in a two-car crash at the wheel of a sports car he couldn't control, there was the same preoccupation with an athlete's life cut short. A week later it took half a day to track down the hospital where the victims in the other car had been taken, to learn that they had survived and eventually would be fine.

Lindburgh was a celebrity. They were just the people in the other car, as Robert Fraley, Van Ardan, Michael Kreig, Stephanie Bellegarrigue and Bruce Borland, except to the ones who knew and loved and lost them, have been reduced to the five other people in Payne Stewart's plane.

It is not callous disregard. It's just the way we are. A defence mechanism, perhaps, against contemplation of the inevitable day our own turn comes.

Stay as Small as You Are
The Vancouver Sun, October 28, 1978

THEY'RE SHAKING THEIR HEADS in Strasbourg over the sins of Nadia Comaneci.

The cute little kid from Romania who captivated the world with her elfin charm and her string of perfect scores in the 1976 Olympic Games in Montreal isn't leading the world gymnastics championships, and people are wondering why.

The kid has no class. Do you know what she's had the gall to do since 1976? She's *grown up.*

She's absolutely refused to remain 14 years old as she was in 1976. She has (Omigod!) developed a figure! She has slipped away on dates! With a rock singer! The ungrateful little wretch.

Judy Garland didn't grow up. Mind you, she was 17 when she played a 14-year-old kid in *The Wizard of Oz* in 1939, but she looked like a kid and stayed a kid years after she was dead. We can still see her every year on TV—cute little Dorothy, looking for Kansas, cute little Toto barking behind her.

Shirley Temple is nine years old. Ask anybody.

So what's gotten into Nadia, anyway? She isn't posting perfect scores in Strasbourg. Elena Mukhina of the Soviet Union, the European champion, is ahead of her in individual points after the team championships.

What's going on here? The next thing we know, Karen Kelsall is going to be 16, Elfi Schlegel will be running around demanding to be 15. Whoever heard of a 15-year-old elf?

Where will the adults be if the crop of cute little kid gymnasts dies out? One bad season and we could be left with a bunch of amateur athletes who think they're people, with normal drives for normal lives.

Remember Nadia in '76? So tiny and doll-like and mechanically efficient?

You couldn't design a better gymnast. She was tiny, compact, aerodynamically sound. Months after the Olympics there was even a suggestion in a medical journal that she'd been given some form of medication to inhibit the growth of the long bones in her body to keep her tiny and perfect as long as possible.

Her coach said he found her in a kindergarten and began working with her way back then. And just before the Games, which television has made part show biz, there was a major mechanical breakthrough.

They taught her how to smile.

She'd come rocketing off the beam or bars to a perfect landing, throw her arms to the heavens and flash this precise, machine-tooled, perfect little smile at the judges. It was important. Without it a 10 might be a 9.9. Teeth: the final frontier. She was Nadia. The Little Swallow. The Romanian Barbie (Pat. pend.).

Had she been American, Christmas 1976 would have brought a flood of Nadia lunch kits, Nadia clothes and track suits, Nadia dolls ("Push Nadia's navel! Watch her do the uneven parallel bars routine! See the 10s flash on the little Nadia scoreboard! Bars and scoreboard sold separately, batteries not included.")

But she was a star! How come she couldn't be satisfied with that?

We prefer our sporting idols in one of two models: forever young, in which case they have an obligation to remain that way as though dipped in amber at birth, or old yet ageless, as in Gordie Howe or Muhammad Ali. Howe can't play hockey the way he did years ago. Matched against the films of the young Cassius Clay or even the Muhammad Ali of the three Joe Frazier fights, the Ali who cast aside an inept Leon Spinks is a hollow mockery. But we identify with them, credit them with skills long since departed. Because if they stay young, then so do we.

And if the Nadias of the world are growing older . . .

Olga Korbut was Nadia once. She wowed the world in Munich in 1972 as Nadia did in Montreal four years later. She toured the US and made it a personal triumph. On one day at Disneyland she was bigger than Mickey Mouse. She was pert and pretty and superbly talented—more animated, perhaps, more bubbly and outgoing, but an instant child star nonetheless. Until she committed the ultimate indiscretion. She grew up.

Olga was in Montreal, too—a tired, wan 21. She was virtually ignored, shoved into the shadows while the lights played on her successor. She had aged. How dare she do that to us?

And now Nadia is going the same way.

Commentators have referred to her as "older, heavier." The tone was faintly accusing. The wire service flashed a picture of the new Nadia working on the balance beam. By any definition it was a leg shot of someone who was total girl. Guys in the office looked and letched.

Then the story came in about the dates with the rock singer. It was a shocker. The guy's 20, for Pete's sake! What's a 14-year-old girl doing, hanging around with a 20-year-old guy?

She was a star and she's throwing it all away. She's growing up and acting like a normal 16-year-old. The kid's got a lot of nerve.

Weep for Peter Schnugg

The Province, January 27, 1980

> *"We are being sacrificed because we are front page news. The whole world is watching, and you know this is a political year."*
> —Peter S. Schnugg, San Francisco water polo player

IN THE HILLS OF AFGHANISTAN, where the rebels reload guns so old they may explode in their faces and aim them at Soviet armour, they're probably thinking a lot about Peter S. Schnugg and his chances of winning an Olympic water polo medal. In the cities, where knots of Afghans watch as Soviet tanks roll through their streets, there will be but one topic of conversation today:

"Psst! Peter Schnugg might not get to play water polo in Moscow! Pass it on!"

"Nine years he's been playing, and now the president's telling him to clear the pool. No free trip to Moscow to play games!"

And the shock waves will roll down the streets in the wake of the tanks, jarring people's minds away from the minor irritation that they are no longer free . . .

It's not difficult to be cynical about the Olympic Games boycott. The very design of the threat lends itself to cynicism.

In the United States, President Carter gives the Soviets until February 20 to pull troops out of Afghanistan or face an American boycott of the Summer Olympics. He does not mention the Winter Olympics, which open in Lake Placid eight days before his deadline and will be attended by Soviet athletes. Translation: "We'll screw up your Olympics by not attending, but there's no sense screwing up ours by making you stay home."

In Canada, Prime Minister Joe Clark plays follow-the-leader: If Soviet troops aren't out of Afghanistan by February 20, Canadians won't go to Moscow, either. Originally he said he favoured moving the Games, but not a boycott. Then Pierre Elliott Trudeau announced that he didn't want any part of a boycott. Now Clark does. And the deadline is set two days after a federal election that could make it meaningless if Mr. Trudeau means what he says.

So I can forgive the Peter S. Schnuggs of the world their cynicism. But I cannot forgive their tunnel-visioned fatheadedness.

It will hurt to give up a target that's been shining out there in front of them for years, the chance to represent their country against the best in the world. But there are different ways to represent your country. The hill rebels are representing theirs. When the game is over there'll be no shaking hands and swapping sweat suits. For many, their badge will be an unmarked grave.

Peter S. Schnugg is not being asked to pack a rifle and go to a foreign country and die, as were the best and the fittest of generations past. At worst he is being told he'll have to play his water polo in a different pool. How tough is that, really?

There are world championships now in virtually every Olympic event. They draw the same group of athletes. The Olympics are one major step on the tour. How big a sacrifice is it, really, for an athlete to stand up and say:

"I do not compete in countries whose leaders send troops and tanks through the streets of free people. I live in a free country. I will not compete in a country that denies others that freedom."

Somehow, that sounds better than "To hell with somebody else's freedom. To hell with tanks over the border. Clear the pool. It's time for the water polo finals."

Because that is the issue. Sport is not above politics. Sooner or later the people in it have to drop their discus or their track shoes and say, as Sebastian Coe said the other day, "An athlete cannot stick his head in the sand. This is a decision I'll have to make as a human being."

Certainly the issue is political. Certainly it is easy to say that if this wasn't an election year and if the country being invaded wasn't cheek-by-jowl with the country that produces a large part of the world's oil, perhaps President Carter wouldn't have been so quick to jump, or Joe Clark so anxious to follow. But does that make it any easier for the Afghans?

The posturing of the International, US and Canadian Olympic Committees is ludicrous. They are penny-ante players in a game turned table stakes. Let the world turn into a radioactive slag heap and once the air cleared you'd find two guys in blazers organizing the Geiger Counter Games.

The IOC says the Games "can't" be postponed. The USOC says it doesn't know whether it will go along with the boycott or not. The COA says it will think about it. The president and the prime minister admit they cannot flat-out order the Olympians into line. And Peter S. Schnugg says he wants to play water polo, and that the whole world is watching to see whether he can.

The athletes are upset and understandably so. But there is something they should consider: There will be no lifting of passports, no troops stopping them as they board the plane. The country might withdraw its financial support, but in the end the individual athlete will be free to go to Moscow if he or she chooses.

It is called freedom of choice. Nobody asked the Afghans if they wanted the tanks.

The Baby-Killers
The Province, March 3, 1985

I'VE DISCOVERED A WONDERFUL PLACE to watch whales. It's called the ocean. Maybe you've noticed it on your way to the aquarium. Big, roomy place. Old, sure, but the plumbing works and you don't have to scrub, drain or refill it. And as far as I know there hasn't been a single instance of a whale getting a bruise on its brain by bashing its head into the wall.

The whales seem to like it, too, probably because they were born in it. You know how it is when you grow up in a neighbourhood.

Funny thing about whales. They never run away from home. Oh, they wander around checking all the rooms and poking in the corners. But, barring the occasional crazy or careless type who gets washed up on the shore and can't get back, you don't hear much about the kids running away from home to have a look at the big city.

There are no street whales hanging around the corners offering to do it for a fin. Whales don't knife each other to raise money to suck strange chemicals up their blow holes.

But little whales do disappear. One day they're there, the next day they're not. The People get them. They throw nets around them and haul them off and stick them in jails called pools so more People can come and stare at them and make them parade themselves for pay, jumping in the air to earn the fish they eat while the Person at the wicket takes all the money.

I don't know what the whales call that, but I know the People term for it.

I wonder what the other whales think, back there in the ocean? I wonder if there are any who still remember Sanaq, the year-old baby who was kidnapped near her home of Churchill, Manitoba, in 1976 and carted off to Vancouver to do her tricks for money? I wonder if any of the old beluga group remember her or Kavna, the little boy beluga taken at the same time?

Is there a case file somewhere, listing the unsolved disappearances? I suppose not. Whales would have no way of knowing that five of their number have died here since the Vancouver Aquarium first got involved in kidnapping and confining whales in 1967.

They just disappeared. Swam off one day and were never seen again. And what the heck—they were only whales.

But still I wonder. Do whales cry? Do they mourn for the lost ones? Are their lives ripped apart, as human lives are torn by the disappearance or death of so many kids?

The scientists tell us no. They give the kidnap victims cute names, sometimes chosen in contests by newspapers or radio stations. They put them in tubs and tell us this one is frisky and this one is playful and this one really enjoys jumping up and grabbing that fish.

When one of the whales gets sick and dies, the scientists have all the answers. It was a parasite or a fever or some sort of pneumonia. They lay the whale out as they did Sanaq, and they slice it open and do a post mortem and come up with a good, scientific reason or guess as to cause of death. And then they get themselves another whale.

They have the pat answers, the People do. They have the numbers to show how many People came to see Sanaq and Kavna. They talk of the "impact" the close-up view of a live whale has, and how it's so much better than a picture in a book or on TV.

It's all very glib and professional—and a lot easier than discussing a nine-year-old female kidnapped at one and caged in a tub until she died.

Plain Jane
The Province, January 20, 1994

PRETEND FOR A MOMENT that she wasn't Nancy Kerrigan and she wasn't defending the US figure skating championship. Her name was Jane Plain, and when the guy stepped out of the shadows and slammed her across the knee with the steel bar, she was on her way to her as-sembly-line job at the widget factory.

Would it have made headlines in Detroit, where the parking lot outside Joe Louis Arena has to be floodlit or you might not make it to your car, and if you do get there it might not have wheels? In a major American city where muggings are the *assault du jour,* would it have made the papers at all?

Would the FBI have been involved? Would a federal law-enforce-ment agency with no logical jurisdiction in what was essentially another street crime, have arrived with its computerized photo-enhancement equipment to try and pull the phantom attacker's face from a muzzy amateur camera shot?

Would there have been press conferences in which the head of various law-enforcement agencies pledged that the attacker would be brought to justice. Would the head of Widgets R Us International have said, "Jane Plain was about to try for a position that's now been taken by someone else, but we're going to let her share it."

Would there have been days of time-consuming police work as far away as Portland, Oregon, to try to pull the net on a one-time mugger from Detroit when the victim, shaken and distraught for two or three days, was back to work in less than a week?

No way. Timing, celebrity and the terrifying prospect that there might be a copycat assassin out there emulating the wacko who knifed Monica Seles made the Nancy Kerrigan story a worldwide sensation. It was treated accordingly by a nation that, for all its might, had been unable to protect one of its athletes from an assault right there in the rink on the eve of its most important skating event.

Jane Plain would get a case file number and questioning from an overworked police department that deals with a dozen such muggings every day. Shortly thereafter, her file would work its way from pending to open to dead. Nothing against old Jane, but widget-making is not a medal event.

I will make you a bet about the Nancy Kerrigan story: It will generate a book and at least one prime-time network TV dramatization. If she wins Olympic gold, make that two or three books, two network specials and maybe a movie.

This is not to suggest that the law should have laid back. The cold, mindless brutality of planning and executing an attack of this nature—apparently to push a competitor forward for a better chance at the estimated $5,000,000 or more in endorsements that comes with Olympic gold—is enough to chill the blood.

But it's turned soap opera.

The bodyguard and the estranged husband of the skater who went on to the American title with Ms. Kerrigan sidelined, both charged in the plot? The skater herself going 10 hours with the FBI, then emerging to announce that although she still believes he had nothing to do with the attack, she thinks it's best that she and the former husband—divorced but living together—should part company so she can concentrate on the Olympics?

It took the LA earthquake to shift the Nancy Kerrigan story from the front page. It will return. The supermarket tabs may run it forever. All it lacks is Michael Jackson. For now.

Pared of the glitz and avarice, what happened in Detroit that day was another assault with a club, metal and high-tech retractable, but nonetheless a club. Apparently they have the people who planned it and the man who did it. Book 'em, Dano. We've got to get to the widget factory.

Intelligence Test
The Province, February 16, 1994

REALLY, NOW, ONE MUST OBJECT to the blatantly sexist "Are you a Tonya Person?" quiz run on these pages.

Nancy and Tonya. Tonya and Nancy. Two references to her

"ex-bodyguard" without so much as a mention of Shawn Eckhardt's name. Of estranged husband and freestyle plea-bargaining champion Jeff Gillooly and the alleged hit team of Shane Stant and Derrick Smith, not a single word. On this evidence, figure skating's greatest crime since the men began dressing like begonias was all Bonnie, no Clyde.

Credit where credit is due, I say. Herewith, The Gang That Couldn't Think Straight Intelligence Test:

1. Shawn Eckhardt's method of finding a hit man was to ask people whether they'd be interested in taking the job for X dollars.

2. Once the hitter was found (allegedly the aforementioned Mr. Stant), the conspirators discussed the game plan on the telephone. Apparently fearing that one of them might forget some of the key details ("Like, who's this dame we're supposed to slug again?"), someone taped the call.

3. Eckhardt felt moved to tell someone. Well, wouldn't you? ("Hey, guess what we're gonna do this week? We're gonna smack that Nancy Kerrigan across the knee so she can't skate no more.") The person he chose was a minister.

4. "Let's make it look like a mugging and robbery attempt," someone said. Great idea. So where do they put the smack on Ms. Kerrigan? In the skating rink, as she's coming off the ice. Would she be carrying any money on her? Would she be carrying a purse? So how will it look like a robbery? Oh, yeah . . .

5. Having done the dirty deed, the assailant Gets Rid of the Weapon, a key move in any great crime. He gets rid of it in the dumpster behind the rink. ("They'll never think of looking for it there!") Strangely enough, the police find it. There are fingerprints. ("Hey, you bring the gloves?" "*Me* bring the gloves? I thought *you* were bringin' 'em!")

6. "Imagine that! A mugging—and in Detroit," cry the local police. "Who'd ever have believed it? This looks like a job for the FBI!"

Shortly thereafter, Messrs. Eckhardt, Stant and Smith are in custody.

7. Too young to remember Jimmy Cagney movies ("You ain't gettin' nuttin' outa me, copper!") they take the high road to repentance by saying they're sorry and apparently ratting on Gillooly. (Hey, what are friends for?)

8. All parties, including Ms. Harding, are grilled by police. Gillooly rats on Ms. Harding, claiming she was in on the plan all along and gave final approval. He only ratted on her, he insists, after the police showed him her statement in which she'd ratted on him first. Her disloyalty shakes him. Had they not promised not to rat on each other? Boy, you just can't trust anyone these days.

9. Gillooly, facing seven racketeering charges, plea-bargains his way down to one by providing police with details of the Master Plan and implicating Ms. Harding.

   His contribution to the hearing is one word: "Guilty." Through his lawyer, he also says that Ms. Harding shouldn't be allowed to skate for her country in the Winter Olympics. Those who've been keeping track recall that getting Ms. Harding into the Olympics was the objective of the whole exercise. Of course, that was before they got caught.

10. At last report, all four men were out on bail. Police aren't worried about them trying to run. On their record so far, they'd just get lost.

Brave New World
The Province, April 26, 1994

THE HOTEL WAS BATHED IN SPOTLIGHTS. An army truck with a machine gun mounted on the back circled it 24 hours a day. Inside, the Israeli swim team kidded and kibitzed as kids have done since road trips began. But they never went near the windows. Framed in a window, you could be inviting a bullet.

Belgrade, 1973. The first World Aquatic Games, a gathering of the finest in the spirit of friendly competition. Except that, mere months earlier in Munich, 11 Israelis had died under terrorist bullets at the Olympic Games, and now teenage kids had to be kept under guard just in case the murderers weren't through.

We talked about it, munching our mixed grill and knocking back our plum brandy in the cafe across the street. "War correspondents," we grumbled. "Come here to cover a swim meet and we could wind up dodging bullets." We laughed and agreed that any bullet that found us would have to find its way through a basement window and under a bed.

Because we thought that the horror of Munich was a one-time thing. The precautions were understandable, but something like that would never happen again. How many loonies could be out there?

Twenty years later we have our answer: lots of them. Too many to identify, let alone watch. Terrorist loonies like the ones who killed at Munich. Mind-warped loonies like Günther Parche, who leaned out of the stands and plunged a kitchen knife into Monica Seles at the Hamburg tennis tournament. Looney Tunes loonies like the wing-nuts who whacked Nancy Kerrigan's knee in the slapstick comedy that was Skategate.

We know these people only because they were caught. But who else is out there? Of the thousands upon thousands of cranks who write threats to public figures every year, how do you separate the dreamers from the doers?

The extortionist who threatened to kill Boris Becker, his wife and baby son, his manager and his manager's family probably was a dreamer. He made no specific demands and hasn't been heard from since. But what if he wasn't? What if he's out there, waiting . . . ?

The person or persons who sent the note threatening to kill Steffi Graf at the Hamburg tournament might be pranksters, giggling at the fuss they've caused with words like "This time the slimy Graf will be the target . . . and we are not playing with kitchen knives." An extra 150 guards for the players. Undercover police all over the court. Beefed-up security everywhere. "We did that," they can chortle. "We made them do all those things, and all it cost us was a stamp."

And they can do it again, at any major sports event, anywhere. Because, as much as trained experts in the field can decide that this threat might be serious and this one is some passive sicko's lash back at the world, they have no choice but to treat every one as serious. Because it might be.

It is such a handy weapon. No storage, no upkeep, no ammunition required and, if they're careful, little danger of discovery. They write the note or make the call, and crawl back into the woodwork until they get the urge to do it again. Hey, world, I'm doing this. And you'll never find me!

The nuts behind the letter to Hamburg police warning that Graf will die if she plays may be copycats. Cases like Skategate and the Seles stabbing invariably breed wannabes who take the initial step and tell themselves that they could follow through if they wanted to. But sometimes, one of them will see a nobody like Günther Parche suddenly famous, his picture on TV and magazine covers, and decide that the exposure might be worth the cost. And who better to attack than a famous athlete at a televised event?

For decades, athletes have heard that they don't live in the real world. At these times, in these circumstances, they do now. And it's not a pretty world at all.

Pushing The New PC
Calgary Sun, January 7, 2000

> *Lord Sandwich: "Wilkes, you will die either on the*
> *gallows or of the pox!"*
> *John Wilkes: "That must depend on whether I embrace*
> *Your Lordship's principles or your mistress."*
> —Parliamentary exchange, *circa* 1785

IN SIMPLER TIMES, the answer to an insult was a better one, a poke in the snout or pistols at 20 paces. Today it's "diversity training"—whatever the hell that might be—and a mandatory trip to the local shrink.

In simpler times, PC stood for Progressive Conservative, then for personal computer. Today it stands for Politically Correct, and heaven help you if you're not.

That's what bothers me about Thursday's hand-wringing, omigoodness pronouncements from the people who run pro hockey and baseball: the feeling that they were made not because they needed to be made, but because the people felt that they needed to be seen making them.

John Rocker, the redneck Atlanta relief pitcher, insults New York, homosexuals, AIDS victims, foreigners, a black teammate and the driving habits of Asian women in a *Sports Illustrated* interview.

"Get thee to a psychological evaluation," thunders baseball commissioner Bud Selig.

Vaclav Prospal, the Ottawa Senators' centre, calls Montreal's Patrice Brisebois a "frog," adding a liberal profanity garnish.

"Go to the diversity trainer," says the NHL. "Go directly to the diversity trainer. Do not pass go. Do not collect $200." Whereupon baseball and hockey stand back in all their self-satisfied righteousness. There will be no protest groups to placate, no picket lines to cross. No one can accuse them of insensitivity. They have Done the Right Thing, and they've got the media coverage to prove it.

Question, Mr. Selig, sir:

What happens if the psychologist checking out Rocker comes back and says, "After extensive testing, it is apparent that Mr. Rocker really *does* loathe New Yorkers, homosexuals, AIDS victims, foreigners, blacks and Asian women drivers."?

What do you do then? Ask him if it affects his fastball?

Suspend him, and you'll be up to your ass in lawyers. The best you can do is tell him to keep his prejudices to himself. Unless he has the cranial capacity of a tuberous begonia, he'll already have figured that out.

Question, Mr. Bettman, sir:

You appointed this Zach Minor as league "diversity trainer." You sent him around to all 28 clubs, complete with educational video, to talk to your players about racism and other forms of intolerance.

Commendable—but do you really believe the lesson will sink in faster than it would if the insultee dropped his stick and beat the crap out of the insultor?

If Vaclav Prospal truly dislikes French-Canadians, Russians, Swedes, Finns or those Mickey Mouse gloves on the scoreboard telling people when to clap, do you honestly think you'll change his outlook by making him stay in after class?

Epithets are the second language of sport, and always have been.

Pro football players think "mother" ends in a hyphen. Hockey players curse as well as they spit.

But insults are settled individually as they are hurled. No one yells "Wait till the commissioner hears what you said, man!" or waits for the Language Police to decide whether the words were appropriate to the occasion.

John Rocker needed no hangman. He tied his own noose and kicked over his own chair. Better to let him swing quietly.

Help for the Needy
Calgary Sun, January 19, 2000

DOWN AT THE FOOD BANK, the word will be spreading like wildfire. "PSSST! The feds are gonna help out the Canadian NHL teams!"

In the hospital halls where patients are parked because there's neither money nor room to put them anywhere else, the hands not hooked to the I.V. units will be raised for feeble high-fives.

"Thank God! The Canucks are saved!"

"Yeah. What a shame John didn't live to see it. If they could have scheduled his surgery, he'd be clapping his hands today."

"Poor John. He never actually *saw* them play, of course, except on the television when the other people in the home didn't want to watch *Jeopardy*. But he had his radio, and when Jim Robson said his special hello to shut-ins, well, John said it was like having somebody who cared."

In hundreds of rental units, mothers fighting to stay off welfare will take a break from worrying because the daycare centres are closing for lack of funding and how to juggle the day job and the night job when there's no one to mind the kids, and they will smile and tousle the baby's hair.

"We might have hard times," they'll think. "But at least Mark Messier won't have to move to another city to make his $6 million."

On the Granville Mall, the street kids crouched on the sidewalks muttering "Spare change?" to people who hurry past pretending not to notice, and the hollow-eyed teenager hookers who've wandered in from small-town Somewhere because anything is better than what they had will nod and say "Cool! Somebody's finally helping the kid millionaires."

Oh, yeah. Happy days are here again.

Of course, none of those people are hockey's problem.

Hockey didn't put the hospital system in near-collapse or create the economy that made the Food Banks necessary. Hockey didn't do in the daddies who were injured or died, or urge on the ones who crawled out from under their responsibilities and fled. Hockey didn't tell the kids to leave home, or play pimp to the under-age desperate, or sell the drugs from which society cannot protect them. Hockey is just another business looking for ways to get out from under, a business disguised as a sport that, having peed in its own bathwater, now wants someone else to clean the tub.

Hockey is an American-run conglomerate with six Canadian branches that are failing for a lot of reasons, including a lousy dollar—a conglomerate stupid enough to end a lockout by signing an agreement that gave its employees the key to the cash register without limiting how much they could take, and now wants the country to cover its losses.

Hockey is a business that cries out about the millions in tax dollars it hands the government every year and warns—not threatens, oh my, no—that it will have to leave for friendlier US climes and take those dollars with it if help isn't forthcoming, and soon.

Hockey is a business that has priced itself beyond the reach of the very people who love it and who built it with their support and now whines because so many seats are empty, a business now based on luxury boxes leased by corporations and big shooters who write off the evening's frivolity as business and entertainment expenses while the guy sitting at home looks at his kid and wonders how he can scrape up enough for two in the greens.

Hockey is a business that waves the spectre of failed franchises in Winnipeg and Quebec City where the help wasn't provided, that musters political clout in Ottawa and backs the government into a corner by telling it to put up or watch Senators fly south.

Hockey is a business until it needs money. Then it whimpers that it is a game, a vital thread in the nation's cultural fabric that requires and deserves public support lest it be torn out and the nation come asunder.

Hockey is correct: It is a game, and it can be wonderful and it can unite a nation like nothing short of war. But hockey is not life. Life is in the streets and the homes, the schools and the hospitals. Solve the real problems, Mr. Manley. Then we'll talk.

Paging Mr. Manley
Calgary Sun, January 21, 2000

Mr. John Manley,
Industry Minister,
Ottawa

Sir,
In the last 10 years I have grossly mismanaged my business, overpaid and pampered my employees and shown little but contempt for my customers. Please refund half my tax money or I'm moving to the US.
—Weeping in Winnipeg

Mr. Manley,
I wanna tax break like you just gave those NHL guys. People ain't coming to my donut shop anymore just because the donuts are stale and they cost too much and I don't give a damn what they think.

Is this fair? I'm a Canadian citizen. I deserve to be protected from my own stupidity just like those hockey guys.
—Victim in Vancouver

P.S. Please send my cheque in American funds. I go down there to buy my gasoline and groceries.

Mr. Manley,
Delighted to see you say your duty is to protect jobs endangered by failing companies. I used to work in Eaton's. I'd like a tax return retroactive to the day they were forced to pull the plug when the government didn't step in.

There's a hockey connection. Without the Eaton's catalogue, hundreds of kids who went on to play in the NHL wouldn't have had anything to stuff in their stockings for shin guards and we probably never would have beat those Commies in '72.
—PO-D in Prince George

Mr. Manley,
Never mind all these people bitching about you helping out the poor Inhalers. My family and me, we identify with them, particularly the 27 Dallas Stars who spent $22,000 on dinner the other night in Vancouver, including $648-a-bottle wine.

You have to splurge once in a while, right?

Just the other night the wife and I went out to Joe's Pasta Place, completely ignored the $4.95 meatloaf special we usually split, and ordered two full servings of the rigatoni and meat sauce.

And when I saw the light in my wife's eyes I thought "What the hell!" and ordered a glass of domestic red each from a bottle that came with a cork instead of the screw-on plastic cap.

The bill, including tip, came to $21, which meant I pumped $3.00 into the tax coffers. I await your cheque for $1.50.

—With You in Yorkton

Mr. Manley,

I don't like to threaten, but my in-home envelope stuffing business isn't going too well because of the internet so I need $100 million to sue Bill Gates and AOL-Time Warner for popularizing e-mail.

It being your mandate to save Canadian jobs and all, I see no reason why you shouldn't send the cheque right away before the postal workers go on strike again and I'm really screwed.

If I don't hear from you, my employee and I will both move to the Cayman Islands, and then you'll have to deal with my wife. Trust me, you do not want that. Plus, we won't be sending you any tax dollars, ha-ha.

—Ticked Off in TO

Mr. Manley,

Sorry, I can't send you any income tax payments unless you start taxing welfare cheques.

I'd like to, really I would. But my husband ran away and left me with three kids and I have to stay home with them because the daycare place lost its government grant.

Best of luck with keeping the NHL in Canada. I'm sure they're nice young men. I watch them every Saturday on *Hockey Night in Canada.* I'd watch the other games, too, but I can't afford cable.

—Welfare Mom in Moncton

John,

Well, it worked.

Kindest personal regards.

—Rod in Ottawa

Yes, Yes, Nanette
Calgary Sun, February 11, 2000

ONE DAY, NO ONE IS CERTAIN JUST WHEN, a word disappeared. Dropped out of the sports lexicon, just like that.

No one is quite sure where it went, or how we let it get away. But we did, and now we're paying for it.

The word is "No."

No, as in "No, you can't wear a beard when you box, because the rules say you can't. Now, go away."

No, as in "No, Mama, we're not going to change the rules of judo because you and your little girl say bowing to the mat before a bout violates her freedom of religion."

No, as in "No, we're not going to spend time and taxpayer dollars on court hearings and human rights tribunals every time someone doesn't like the rules and wants us to change them because they want to play by their own."

Poof! Gone. Just like that.

And we'd better find it, fast, or amateur sport in this country is going to die not by the sword but by the niggle.

In Vancouver this week the BC Human Rights Tribunal has been hearing the case—now adjourned to a later date—of one Leilani Akiyama, an eight-time US judo champion from Bellevue, Wash., who was disqualified from the semi-finals of a tournament in Abbotsford, BC, because she would not bow to the mat as called for by judo rules.

Bowing to the mat, she told the tribunal, "is against my religious beliefs."

She did not believe in bowing, she said. It made her feel "silly and uncomfortable."

Leilani Akiyama is 12 years old. The incident took place in 1996, which would make her eight, perhaps just turned nine.

The human rights complaint against Judo BC now being heard was filed by her mother, Mariko Akiyama, on behalf of Leilani and her brother, Jimmy, an elite competitor who is now 15. Certainly no one disputes her right to do so.

But you have to wonder what the case, win or lose, is going to teach her children.

Mrs. Akiyama says that bowing to inanimate objects in judo has similarities to the Shinto religion, which she was raised on in Japan but rejected as an adult.

Judo people scoff at the suggestion. Bowing to the mat as they enter or leave the competition area, they say, like bowing to opponents before a match or practice, is a sign of respect for their sport and their fellow competitors.

For this argument, a Human Rights Tribunal had to be convened. Lawyers had to be hired, briefs prepared. One newspaper calls it "a landmark case."

And Judo BC, no doubt as cash-strapped as any other amateur sports body in this country, has to take the time and the money to defend its right—not to mention its duty—to teach its competitors to play by the rules.

Because one woman sees a bow as a gesture of a religion she no longer espouses, a centuries-old sport has to come to heel and defend its rules and its onus on respect.

In a country where political correctness has so often replaced common sense, Mariko Akiyama could win this battle in which her daughter seems both her weapon and her shield. You have to wonder if Leilani Akiyama—pigtailed, smiling, bright-eyed,12-year-old Leilani Akiyama—truly understands all this. She's a little girl playing a sport in which she excels. Is this whole bowing thing her issue? Does she really want to be the symbol of her mother's discontent? Which would teach her more, a human rights victory that could make her a pariah in her own sport, or an understanding that sport is about rules and discipline and sportsmanship as much as about competition?

A simple "No, this is frivolous, we will not hear it," from the Human Rights Tribunal could have scotched this mess on Day One. But we don't say that anymore. It isn't nice.

How sad.

All for the Love of the Game
Calgary Sun, June 10, 2000

WE WERE IN THE TRAIN STATION in Rome when we saw him, a Brit kid of 19 or 20 huddled dazed and battered on a bench, blood splattered on his England shirt.

Police separating fans by nationality after the England-Germany 1990 World Cup soccer match had accidentally shoved him onto a bus full of the Germany supporters.

They saw the England shirt. They beat him and took his money and passport. Then they threw him off the bus.

Same tournament, a few days earlier. We're in a crowded first-class coach when the door is booted open by a bunch of British fans cursing, waving beer bottles, shouldering their way down the aisle, clearly hoping someone would be silly enough to object.

A Canadian reporter is wearing a German team shirt because it looks good. They see it, and curse her as she sits there. No one objects. No one dares. It's what they want.

"You coming to the Cup in the US in '94," I asked.

"Bleeping-A," he shouted. "Why?"

"Well, just a tip: When you get to Los Angeles make a side trip to a place called Watts. Great fans there. They love to see guys waving flags and singing songs. And if you get to New York, try Harlem. Guarantee you a lot of fun."

"Watts and Harlem," he repeated. "Thanks, mate!"

Then they headed off to trash another coach.

Lord, I hope he remembered. I like to picture him leading his mob into a gang bar, waving flags and singing. And coming out on a gurney with his banner protruding from a fundamental orifice.

It's not just Europe.

In Team Canada's stop in Jamaica during its unsuccessful qualifying bid for the last World Cup, the chief of police issued a front-page plea for fans to leave their guns at home or, if they must bring them, to check them at the wickets as they entered.

The day before the match in El Salvador, Team Canada was promised there'd be no repeat of the riot during the Mexico game two weeks earlier because soldiers in full body armour would surround the pitch, shoulder to shoulder.

"But if you should win," Canadian coach Bob Lenarduzzi was told, "do not go to the dressing room. Stay in the middle of the field, and we will take you out by helicopter."

It all came back this week with word that police in Belgium and the

Netherlands are gearing up for the violence they know will accompany Euro 2000, which opened today.

The cost will be prohibitive, the violence impossible to cap. At some point before or after one of the 31 games, in the crowd outside the stadium or the street riots that follow, it's almost odds-on that someone is going to die.

Soccer will be blamed, this game that for some reason inflames national passions like no other. But it will not be soccer's fault.

Soccer is not the cause, it is the excuse, the alibi that allows thugs and craven cowards to band together, drink themselves into a stupor, mug strangers, destroy bars and set fire to cars, all in the name of supporting their team.

Alone, they'd never dare. But lost among hundreds like them, they can be the big, macho guys they are in their dreams.

We gave the boy in the train station money to get home. He took our addresses, promised to pay it back, and did.

He'd saved his money for the trip to Italy. It had taken quite a while.

"I din't want no trouble," he said softly. "I just wanted to cheer for England."

He waved one last time as he boarded. The bloodstains had dried on his shirt.

Tradition Rightly Screwed
Calgary Sun, May 30, 2001

TAKE YOUR BELT, wrap it around your right leg at the highest pressure point and tie it off so tightly that your blood can barely make it down to your knee. Drink enough coffee to give you the caffeine shakes and send your heart into overdrive.

Now play 18 holes of golf, and tell me you'd trade places with Casey Martin for the right to use a cart.

There's no doubt that the US Supreme Court's 7–2 ruling that Martin has a right to ride a cart between shots on the PGA tour will open a bag full of worms.

Is a bad back a disability? Is a temporary injury like an ankle sprain grounds to demand a cart the rest of the way while your playing partners slog it over the hills and down the fairways?

The purists and self-styled guardians of the game can harrumph that nobody let Ben Hogan use a cart when he returned from that horrific car accident and lost because his legs weren't strong enough to carry his heart around. Who the hell is this Casey Martin, anyway, and why are the courts screwing around with our traditions?

But the judges got it right.

This was never about giving Casey Martin an advantage, it was about giving him a chance. In three and a half years of court battles, that's all he ever asked.

The odds are still stacked against him.

No court can alter the fact that the circulatory condition known as Klippel-Trenaunay-Weber Syndrome is worsening, or that some day down the road his right leg may have to be amputated.

No ruling by any judge this side of his Maker can wipe away the fact that Casey Martin undergoes more pain, more fatigue, hobbling from the cart path to the green than any of his fellow professionals will feel over the entire 18 holes.

He's not getting any mulligans. If he rims one, nobody has to say "Close enough." Put one in the trees or the water and it's still his job to get to it and make the shot.

It's been my good fortune to know a lot of disabled athletes—kids, men and women who'd sneer at a suggestion that their disabilities should give them any sort of edge. "A disabled athlete is not a disabled person who happens to be an athlete," Rick Hansen told me once, "he's an athlete who happens to be disabled. Write that. People need to understand."

Some of golf's greatest names, Arnold Palmer and Jack Nicklaus among them, have fallen all over each other to say what a great guy Casey Martin is, how much they respect the way he's overcome his disability and admire what he's been able to accomplish. No one questions their sincerity. But every tribute ends with a mostly unspoken "but . . ."

Ask them what's wrong with letting this man they so admire use a golf cart in PGA events so that he'll have something closer to a level playing field in his pursuit of a career in the sport he loves and they huff, hem and haw about the traditions and how the ability to walk 18 holes on four consecutive days is a fundamental part of the game.

They are worried, these wealthy, pampered nomads who wander

the nation as America's guests, that using a golf cart will give hobbling, pain-ridden Casey Martin an advantage.

Try it, gentlemen. Cut off the blood supply to your right legs. Down that caffeine. Force your heart to stutter and labour and pound. Ride that cart for one round of golf.

Then tell us how much fun it was, playing with Casey Martin's edge.

The Wunderkinder
Calgary Sun, June 2, 2001

FIRST, THE DISCLAIMER:
The following rant against a 12-year-old girl and an eight-months-pregnant woman playing in the US women's open golf tournament is not sexist. The author would feel the same way if it was a 12-year-old boy playing in the US Open. (Presumably, the pregnancy issue would be moot.)

Morgan Pressel is in the seventh grade, a time of life when her biggest concerns should be the incoming teens and the honking pimple that surfaces on her nose just when Billy Johnson, who is way cool and has the locker next to hers, looks like he might actually talk to her.

Instead, she was breaking down in the media tent after an opening-round 77, saying that she could have done better.

Then there were the Wongluekiet twins, Aree Song and Naree, the Thai sisters who've already played in three majors but failed to qualify here.

"We still have time," Naree said bravely.

You'd like to think so. They're 15.

Kid phenoms rushed into the pro ranks, and by definition into adulthood, have always troubled me. And today the tennis and golf factories are spewing them off the production line like SUVs.

Adjust the swing here, remodel the stance, road-test it in a tournament workload that would make a galley slave wince—Presto: the new 2001 Phenom, coming soon to a court or course near you.

Most models come equipped with at least one parent to swear up and down that it's all being done for little Mary or Susan who just *loves* to practise six hours a day when she could be hitting the malls with her friends. Why, they wouldn't *think* of doing it if the child hadn't insisted. Well, yes, they did sell their house and Dad gave up his job so they could move to another state where the coaching is better, but it was all for the *child!*

We heard it in 1976, when Nadia Comaneci came out of Romania and posted all those 10s at the '76 Olympics. Her coaches said she'd been taken out of regular school to concentrate on gymnastics, and that she had been taught, among other things, how to smile, because it could mean another tenth of a point. She was 14, and had to be taught how to smile.

Jennifer Capriati was a kid tennis prodigy until the pressures became too great and she launched a rebellion from which she has only recently returned. Todd Marinovich was raised from birth to be a quarterback—special food, special training. His own rebellion killed his pro career and left him battling drug dependency. You see it in hockey, baseball, basketball, football, golf, gymnastics, any sport where the monetary rewards are so staggering for the tiny infinitesimal percentage who do make it.

You talk to the parents about those odds and they'll tell you that their kid is special, that he or she has what it takes. All the sacrifices being made now will pay off in the end, you'll see, because their kid is going to be right up there. If Tiger can do it . . .

Mostly, their intentions are good. Hook them to a lie detector and ask them if they're doing it because the kids want it, they'll ace it. They'll tell you, too, that competition is good for the kid. The tougher the better. Prepare him or her for the real world when they grow up.

Few have asked themselves the real question: How fair is the price of adulthood when it's cost you the years when you had no time to be a kid?

Letter To The Kids

Calgary Sun, August 11, 2001

DEAR KIDS,

Thirteen years ago I wrote your older brothers and sisters a letter.

The Big People were worried that the Ben Johnson doping scandal might warp their children's minds or something, that they could get the idea that cheating was the way to go.

Their kids loved Ben Johnson, worshipped him when he won the gold in Seoul—and then found out he'd cheated. He was their hero, and he'd let them down.

The Big People fretted.

They discussed it at work, at PTA meetings, even in the halls of government. They discussed it at home, swirling their martinis as they pondered the evils of substance abuse, and mostly how Ben's conduct would affect their kids.

What would this do to them? What could they say to ease their disillusionment?

Forgive the Big People, I wrote. They're silly, but their intentions are good. Try to look sad when they bring up the subject. You could score an extra dessert, or a therapeutic trip to McDonald's.

Thirteen years later, it's your turn.

Another Canadian sprinter has blown the drug test, a woman named Venolyn Clarke, and because she's a teaching assistant and deals with kids, there's this idea that the message she has sent through her actions will corrupt your minds and warp your judgment.

Me, I have more faith than that.

If you're over 10 years old you know about drugs, you've been warned about drugs, you've been offered drugs, and some of you have been stupid enough to try drugs. By now, most of you have it figured that trying drugs even once is dumber than jumping off a building to see how high you'll bounce.

Nobody has to tell you about steroids and performance-enhancers.

But I want you to understand about heroes.

Heroes are people who did what had to be done on the day, or tried to. Victory is great, but it's not just the winning that makes heroes, it's the striving.

We've had lots in Canada, and we'll have more. Only some of them are athletes. Astronauts, doctors, scientists, inventors—we've had them all and will again. We live in a great country where we're free to chase dreams and make them come true.

Heroes aren't perfect. They make mistakes and poor choices just like the rest of us. There are temptations all around them, opportunities to go for the shortcut, to think "well, everybody else is doing it," and cheat.

You're not dumb. You can read and listen. You know it happens, as it did with Ben and as it has now with Venolyn Clarke. What's important is that when one of them does let you down, you don't let it make you think any less of the rest.

I have travelled the world with sports heroes, seen them in their finest hours, been there when they cried because they were happy and cried when they were sad. Either way, they never failed to make me proud.

The world is changing, and sport is changing with it. There's too much money in it now, too much importance placed on victory, too many temptations to take the easy road.

The Big People worry that you'll become hardened to the cheating and be tempted, in your games and in your lives, to take that road yourselves.

Don't give them cause to fret.

Cherish your heroes of today and the ones you'll have tomorrow. You can even feel a little bit sorry for the ones who took that easy road.

Every day of the rest of their lives, when they look in the mirror, they'll see a cheater looking back.

Excuse Me—Is This Part of Your Brain?
The Province, April 12, 1991

HE WAS LARGE AND LOUTISH, standing safely on the concourse behind the LA Kings bench bravely hurling insults at a bunch of hockey players he knew could not strike back.

Oh, but he was a bold one, jerking away from PNE ushers 30 years and more his senior, jabbing his finger at the Kings, putting on a show for the handful of mental midgets there to urge him on.

"I must write to that man," I thought. "I must attempt to discover why he would do something like that, and tell him what he looked like from up in the press box and to the 16,000 or so others in Pacific Coliseum."

Dear Jerk,
This is a letter to you from me. It is also to the other people like you who threw golf balls and other things at the Kings to show what great hockey fans you are. I will try to keep the words short so you can understand them.

I would like to know how you get ready to go to a hockey game.

Do you stand in front of the mirror practising your swear words and your scary looks?

Do you check your pockets before you go to make sure you have your golf balls or your whiffle ball with the tape on it so it will fly better and hurt more if it hits someone?

Do you giggle a lot about how mad you're gonna make the hockey players?

Do you get all excited, thinking about how the big people in the stands are going to be watching *you*, and how maybe you'll even get on TV?

Boy, that would be neat, wouldn't it? Right there on TV where your friends at home can see you! And maybe, if you time it just right, you could even *wave*. You'd really be a big man then, wouldn't you? People would *notice* you.

Do you have any idea what you *really* look like? You look like you're either coming from or going to your lobotomy.

Oh, I'm sorry. I used a long word. I know what a strain that is on your lips. A lobotomy is like a brain operation where they cut away the parts that aren't working right. But I guess you couldn't have one. The doctor wouldn't know where to stop.

Besides, you're just having fun, right? Hey, you're a Canuck fan, supporting your team! So you swear at the other team! So you throw things on the ice where guys might trip over them! You're just having a little *fun.*

I'll tell you a story that will really make you laugh.

Years ago at a junior lacrosse game, someone just like you threw some pennies out onto the floor. One of the players slipped on one and went head-first into the boards. Isn't that funny?

I wrote a story about him. He'd broken his spine and was paralyzed from the neck down for the rest of his life. He was 15. When he cried, his parents had to wipe away the tears.

But you're different, right? Never happen with you. You're just a Canuck fan having a few laughs.

Of course, they don't want you there. I guess the PNE people feel sorry for you, because the police never come. But no one wants you there. Not the Canucks, not the Kings, not any of the 16,000 people who came out to watch the game.

You know what's really funny? You think doing these things makes you part of the crowd, when all it does is show everyone how much you're really alone. I guess the real joke's on you.

Life with Fred and Martha

SO I'M SITTING IN THE NEWSROOM one day mocking Don Cherry's *Coach's Corner*, in which he talks like your average guy sittin' around the pub watchin' the game wit da rest of da workin' stiffs. "Guy in the pub, my ass!" I snort. "He *owns* the pub and a bunch of others. He makes big bucks from *Hockey Night in Canada* and more on the banquet circuit. How does *he* know what the average guy with the mortgage and car payments and kids in school is thinking?"

Then it hit me: Who was I to talk?

I wrote a sports column that took me all over the world to the big events, expenses paid. When I went to a game, I sat in the press box after pulling into my reserved media parking spot. Coffee and sandwiches were waiting in the media lounge. Not for me, the snow and rain and overpriced drinks and hotdogs and freezing my butt in the stadium stands or jostling through the arena mob to my seat to watch a hockey game at which some dufus would no doubt spill beer in my lap or stand up at the crucial moment to block my view. That stuff was for . . .

Omigod! The average guy.

Something had to be done. With all my perks I couldn't be the average sports fan. I knew a lot of them, spent hours in front of TV sets or on the phone listening to them tell me what a horsebleep column I'd written that morning. But quoting them wouldn't do it. For one thing, I couldn't use a lot of their words. I needed one fan—better yet, one *family*—to be my Average Guys, offer *their* opinions on what was going on in the wunnerful worlda sports.

So, in the finest traditions of journalism, I invented one: Fred Shwartz, who lived with his wife, Martha, in suburban Coquitlam and earned his wages running a jackhammer for Public Works. (In one Fred and Martha column, I called him Fred Smedley for some reason. I briefly considered a column explaining that his name had to be changed when he entered the Witness Protection Program after testifying that he saw Cherry in a limo with Xaviera Hollander, who'd written *The Happy Hooker* a few years earlier, but Don might have taken it seriously.)

Through Fred and Martha I could voice—and, of course, exaggerate—the opinions I got from readers and callers and people who stopped me on the street to agree with a column or to call me an idiot. One or two columns, I figured, then let Fred hang up his jackhammer.

As it turned out, Fred had other ideas . . .

Dead in the Water

The Province, May 20, 1982

> *Canada's America's Cup yachting challenge seeks*
> *funds as most of its $2 million "seed money"*
> *exhausted.*
> —*The Province*, May 18, 1982

"Good afternoon, madam. Is your husband in?"

"Whadya mean, in? It's 10:30 in the morning. He's working. Does street repairs for the city. Jackhammer, y'know? Seven hours a day and what it does to his kidneys you wouldn't believe."

"I see. Well, I'm here to solicit your help in launching Canada's America's Cup challenge, and . . ."

"If it's America's Cup, let America pay for it."

"Uh, no, you don't quite understand. The America's Cup is a race. A yacht race. You take these enormously expensive 12-metre yachts to Rhode Island, and four or five countries race for the right to see who races against the Americans for the Cup. We've got 38 men in Florida, and . . ."

"Can't get jobs here, eh? I know the feeling. If my Fred doesn't have a cousin in Public Works he maybe doesn't get the shot at the jackhammer and—RALPHIE! Stay out of the cupboard!—That's Ralphie, the baby. The other three kids are in school. Now, whadya need—50 cents or a buck for a raffle ticket or something? I guess maybe I can spare it. Live a little, I always say."

"Well, no. Actually, we need, oh, maybe three million dollars minimum."

"Sorry, I'm a little short this week. I went crazy at the supermarket and bought meat. Say! What kind of a boat is this, anyway? Got a john and everything?"

"Uh, it's two yachts, actually. We're practising with the *Clipper* and the *Intrepid.* Only until the one we're having built is delivered, of course."

"Of course. Sorta like Fred and me, living out here in the boonies and driving the one car until someone gives us the money to drive to the British Properties in our twin Porsches."

"You don't understand, madam. This is the most prestigious yacht race in the world! With a good showing, we can put this country near the forefront of world yachting!"

"They must be pretty excited about that in Saskatchewan."

"Madam, we have already raised two million dollars to launch this project, and it's all but gone. What if . . . ?"

"You spent two million dollars to launch a *boat?* You never heard of a car top or a trailer? You back the car down to the launch, take a few friends with you, and all it costs is a couple six-packs. Fred and me did it once. Got invited on this guy's 12-footer. Fished all day. 'Course, we had to pay a sitter to stay with the kids, and what with our share for the beer and sandwiches it came to a few bucks, but once in a while you gotta go first cabin, right?"

"*Yacht,* madam! *Yacht!* And what I'm trying to point out is that if we don't get the rest of the money those 38 men who've sacrificed and devoted two years of their lives to this project may not be able to . . ."

"To spend the time sailing in Florida and Rhode Island. I know. Well, times are hard. Listen, who started this thing, anyway?"

"A dedicated group of Calgary businessmen who . . ."

"So how come you're looking for money in Coquitlam, BC? All the oil wells hit water or something?"

"We have to be based in BC, madam. Those are the *rules!* We have to base in an area where there's an arm of the sea. That's why we formed the Secret Cove Yacht Club. We're going to put Secret Cove on the map. Some of the Calgary men have condominiums up there, I believe, and there are plans to build a marina . . ."

"Oh, good. And I guess if Fred and me give you some money to help you race in Rhode Island, when you get the marina built we can come up and ride in your boats."

"Well, no . . ."

"Free fishing trip once a month to stock up the old freezer and beat the grocery bill?"

"Madam, we can't just . . . Look, perhaps I should come back when your husband's home . . ."

"Good idea, mister. You come around about seven tonight after his kidneys stop hurting and the kids stop howling and you explain to him like you did to me. I may even keep the kids up."

"Why?"

"They've never seen a guy with a jackhammer up his nose."

Big Day at Manpower
The Province, August 19, 1982

FOR FRED SMEDLEY and his wife, Martha, who own a two-bedroom home in Coquitlam and live off Fred's job operating a jackhammer, the recession came sharply into perspective this week.

"Martha," Fred called, looking up from his paper. "Stop scrubbin' the floors and come look at this. Those yacht guys have run out of money."

"Really? You mean we're not gonna have a Canada I to challenge for the America's Cup and give the country a patriotic focal point like those nice Calgary rich guys said? Jeez! I'm so upset I could cry."

"Yeah, it's tough, all right. Probably shake up the whole damned country. It was the kinda project that sorta touched your heart, y'know: 25 crew members gallantly givin' up their jobs to go sail for six months or so in Florida; the Calgary guys tryin' to raise $5 million to throw into a boat so we could prove to the Australians and the French and the Americans that Canadians can sail yachts just as well as they can. Oh, I can see where it would have unified the nation, all right. Those Saskatchewan wheat farmers find out this country's fallin' behind in yacht racing they're likely to break out in black armbands."

"But Fred, what went wrong?"

"The guy building the yacht says he wants his money."

"You mean like our grocer and the people at the shoe store and the dentist and . . ."

"Yeah, sorta. Only bigger. This guy claims they owe him $400,000. But it may not be that bad, because the Calgary guy says it's only $53,000."

"*Only* $53,000! Fred, that's the size of our *mortgage*! What happens if they can't raise it?"

"The guy's gonna sell the boat."

"Gosh, they are ordinary people just like us. The grocer says we don't give him the $120 we owe him by Monday he cuts off our credit. So what are they going to do?"

"Struggle on, I guess. They've had a lot of problems, though. Like, they say there was a delay in gettin' the project registered as a tax-deductible charity."

"But that's not fair! What more charitable cause could there be than yacht-building?"

"Beats me, Martha. But they're not quittin'. They know how much this project means to the entire country. I heard some guys talkin' about it in front of Manpower just this morning. They were thinkin' of maybe pooling their UIC cheques and sending the money along. Then later when they get jobs they could send more."

"Fred, what a marvellous idea! They could do it, you know that? They could save Canada I. They could keep this country from losing ground in the yachting race!"

"Whadya mean? They've got families, most of 'em, and UIC doesn't go all that far. Oh, I know they'd try, but . . ."

"Be quiet, Fred, and listen. We're either a country worthy of holding our head up in the yacht clubs of the world or we're not. Could you sleep at night, knowing that somewhere out there we have yachting caps and blazers going to waste? We can't knuckle under to a recession, Fred. We've got to *fight!*"

"But . . . how?"

"Look at the paper in your hand, Fred. What does it say right there under the strike threat stories?"

"Uh, it says that 1.4 million Canadians are unemployed. So what?"

"But Fred, don't you see? If each of those 1.4 million people took just $4 from their unemployment or welfare or family allowance cheques and sent it to the Canada I people, why, they'd have the whole $5 million with $600,000 left for extras like champagne to break over the bow and drink if they win. We'd have our chance to be a yachting power! We could send our boys back to Florida!"

"By gosh, Martha, you're right. We gotta get that yacht in the water. I'll start down at Manpower. We'll organize. I'll put up signs. We'll get ourselves a slogan: 'Give What You've Got to Launch Our Yacht'. But, 1.4 million people—do you really think they'll do it?"

"Why not, Fred? They've got nothing else to do. It's not like they've got jobs!"

Marathon Revisited
The Province, December 9, 1982

> *Alberto Salazar and Bill Rodgers to run original marathon route wearing the kind of armour Greek soldiers may have worn in 490 BC.*
> —*The Province*, December 8, 1982

News that the great marathon argument is about to be settled triggered a certain amount of dissension between Fred and Martha Schwartz, who pride themselves on keeping abreast of world events.

"Makes a man feel proud," Fred said, "knowing that while most of us are wasting our time making a living there are still folks willing to sacrifice to expand the limits of human knowledge, to seek the answers to questions that have plagued mankind for centuries."

"Like what, dear?" Martha asked.

"Like, was the original marathon fixed? Did that guy Pheidippides run the whole route the first time, or did he take a shortcut? We gotta know these things, Martha, or a whole bunch of scholars are gonna go to their graves wondering, and we'll be responsible."

"Pheidippides? I didn't notice his name in the Vancouver Marathon. Is he one of the new boys?"

"Jeez, Martha, haven't you ever read any of your classicals? Pheidippides was the first guy ever to run the marathon. He was a soldier fighting for this hotshot Greek general, and when they beat the crap out of the Persians at Marathon, the general sent Pheidippides running off to Athens to tell the politicians so he could maybe parlay it into a job in the Senate. Pheidippides ran like hell, all 26 miles, 385 yards, delivered the message, and dropped dead.

"But some people say he didn't run the whole route, that maybe he cut through the hills, in which case his time would be phony and the International Track and Field Association would have to take away his medals."

"But, Fred, if he was running to deliver a message, what difference does it make how he got there? That's what I could never understand about all those people being angry at that Rosie Ruiz person. She wanted to get somewhere, she took a shortcut or maybe a subway. Seems entirely sensible to me."

"You don't understand! These two hotshot runners, Salazar and Rodgers, have decided to run the original route wearing armour like the kind Pheidippides wore, and . . ."

"Pheidippides. My, that *is* a long name, isn't it? Good thing they put numbers on their backs instead of names. Otherwise, he'd have to be continued on the next runner."

"Martha, will you *listen?* It wasn't a race! This one won't be, either. They're running to settle the argument, to prove once and for all whether a guy in armour could run that far or whether he got exhausted and died because he left the road and ran through the hills, or . . ."

"Uh, Fred, settle *whose* argument? I never hear about it at bridge club. Do the boys on the Public Works crews argue about it much?"

"Well, no, but . . ."

"Until you read the paper had you ever heard of *anybody* arguing about it?"

"Not exactly, but . . . Look! What they're trying to do is recreate the original run under the original conditions. Armour and everything, except of course they'll be wearing proper runners, likely so the shoe people will pick up the tab."

"Why? Did Nike provide shoes for Pheidippides? Did Adidas have a model with those thongs that wrapped up around the leg like you see the soldiers wearing in all those religious movies? Richard Burton looks lovely in them. Mind you, he has marvellous legs and I've never met Mr. Pheidippides, so . . ."

"It was in 490 BC! Running shoes weren't *invented* yet!"

"Well, then I certainly think Mr. Salazar and Mr. Rodgers should wear thongs. Either that, or dress sensibly in one of those toga things that look like a woman's nightdress. They're cool, comfortable . . . but no, I guess they wouldn't dare do that. Bad for their image and all."

"Okay, I'll bite. Why not?"

"Well, you know what they say, Fred: 'Beware of Greeks wearing shifts.'"

Go Back to Him, Martha!
The Province, December 12, 1982

ONE NIGHT IN 1982 Vancouver sports entrepreneur Nelson Skalbania—former owner of two pro hockey franchises, one pro soccer franchise and, briefly, the playing rights to a 17-year-old hockey player named Wayne Gretzky—rose at an intimate dinner for 150 to announce his bankruptcy and plead with his wife, Elena, to come back to him. The Vancouver media went nuts.

Radio and TV people hounded him for interviews. One columnist wrote a tear-stained open letter pleading for a reconciliation. Me? I found myself wondering how much fuss there'd have been if they hadn't been jet-setters . . .

Friends and fellow workers sat in stunned silence Friday night as Fred Schwartz, video sports-game whiz and high-stakes Monopoly magnate, tearfully confessed that his empire had crumbled and his wife had left him.

The admission—made at the weekly beer-and-bunfeed in the Legion Hall—completely upstaged feature speaker Melvin Fry, whose long-awaited speech entitled "How We Gonna Raise Dough for the New Bumper Pool Table?" received only token applause.

"I'm tapped," Fred announced. "But that ain't important. What's important is, Martha's left me. As soon as I realized she was gone, I knew what a big hole had been ripped in my life. So Martha, wherever you are, I'd really appreciate it if you'd come back. And bring the car keys."

The meteoric rise and fall of Fred Schwartz, first revealed in a hard-hitting *Province* series after an anonymous caller submitted his name as a candidate for help from the Empty Stocking Fund, is classic Canadiana.

Fred Schwartz didn't always have the big job pushing the jackhammer for Public Works. He and Martha didn't always live in the famous two-bedroom Coquitlam bungalow, or drive the Nash Metropolitan, or spend two or three hours a month fishing off the ten-foot rental with outboard. The luxuries didn't start rolling in until the night Fred hit big at Bingo and won a hand-held electronic football game.

It opened up a whole new world.

Suddenly, people were fighting to sit next to him at lunch, offering to share their peanut butter and banana sandwiches—important people like Sam from Hydro, who's in charge of water pressure. If Sam throws a switch, not a john in Vancouver flushes. That's power. And he wanted to play football with Fred Schwartz.

"Games!" Fred thought. "Sports games! A man who's a bigshot sports-games type can call his own shots!"

He sold his car for $200 and bought electronic baseball, hockey and soccer. Overnight, he became one of the Beautiful People. There wasn't a Legion where he could buy his own beer. He was king of the video games. He could have relaxed and lived comfortably forever. A nine-to-five job and nights at the Legion—what more could a guy ask?

But the bug had bitten deeply. He wanted more. One fateful Monday night he gathered all the hand-held games, went to a video shop and flipped them in a package for an Intelevision, an Atari and a Coleco. For collateral he put up the house.

He began to gamble. After all, they were playing on his home machines. A quarter, then 50 cents, then a buck—why not? His credit was good. Every Legion branch knew that. They all had his markers.

When he wasn't gambling electronically he was moving equally vast sums of money in lightning real estate deals.

"That's what did me in," he told the crowd Friday. "The economy and Monopoly. They cost me everything, and now they've cost me Martha."

Close friends call his downfall a tale of three houses: one on Baltic, one on Marvin Gardens and one on Boardwalk. "He kept flipping small properties for big ones," they sighed. "Every time he got $200 for passing Go he'd throw it into another mortgage, borrow from the bank, grab another property. And houses weren't good enough. Not for Fred. Oh, no. He had to have hotels. And one day, everything just started to crumble."

It started, they claim, with a custody fight.

Martha, weary of staying home while Fred hit the Legions, began making the trips with him and joining in the game. Soon she owned Boardwalk. The crunch came when she insisted it was her turn to use the Milk Bottle token. Fred refused.

"You had it last time," he snarled.

Martha leaped up, snatched her hotel off Boardwalk, warned him to keep his Milk Bottle off her property, and fled.

Right then, the life seemed to go out of Fred Schwartz. All the fun things—the foreclosures, the squeezing out the player next to him, the sheer joy of watching an opponent languishing in Jail while you refuse to lend him the $50 to get out—suddenly seemed so *meaningless* without Martha there to share them.

He began making mistakes. Three hotels on Mediterranean, one house on Baltic. Chance and Community Chest hit him for Income Tax. People weren't buying him beer anymore. The Atari, the Intelevision, the Coleco all went to pay his pub tabs. In a matter of weekends his empire crumbled. Friday night at the Legion it all spilled out.

His friends hailed his courage. ("Out to here," the bartender said, holding his hands a foot out below his belt. "He's got 'em out to here.") The Saturday afternoon newspaper carried a fervent editorial plea: "Go Back to Him, Martha! It's Your Roll!"

Saturday night, he and Martha were seen together in the living room of the Coquitlam home. Fifty television cameras and six reporters surrounded the house, demanding a picture and a statement.

Martha came out on the porch. "I'll give you a statement," she said. "This is private property. Get the (bleep) off my lawn or I'll call the cops."

Departing reporters heard Fred's voice from within.

"Honey, you rolled a six. Shall I move the Milk Bottle for you?"

Life, it's assumed, went on.

The Old Five-Hole
The Province, April 20, 1983

FRED SCHWARTZ, breadwinner of the Coquitlam Schwartzes, put aside his sports page and wiped the sweat from his brow, "Thank God!" he said fervently. "They finally did it."

"Did what, dear?" Martha Schwartz asked, somewhat surprised that he'd spoken aloud. In an average hockey season, Fred said one word to her between April 5 and mid-May, that word being "Shuddup!"

"The Calgary Flames," he replied, snapping another cap and flicking traces of foam from his undershirt. "It says so right here in the *Province.* When they beat Edmonton Oilers Monday night they really came to play."

"That's nice, dear," she said. "But isn't that what they're supposed to do? I mean, they're professional hockey players and it's their work and they get paid for it so . . ."

"No, no, no, Martha! You don't unnerstan'! See, they lost the first three games to the Oilers and if they lose this one they're out. So they dug down deep for that little something extra and *really came to play.*"

"But . . . does that mean in the first three games they didn't come to play? Sounds sort of a waste of time to me, Fred, flying up to Edmonton, spending all that money on hotels and meals and such if they weren't going to play once they got there. My goodness, think of all the people sitting in the rink waiting for the game to start and not only do the Calgarys not show up, they don't even have the common courtesy to phone and let the people know so they can go home and save money on the baby-sitter."

"Martha," Fred said kindly, "you gotta stop drinkin' that prune juice. I think it's going up instead of down and flushing out your head."

"But, Fred, you said . . ."

"I said it says here they came to play. It's a sports expression, like when a guy says they were really up for the game."

"Well, I should think so. I mean, if they're making all that money and don't even have enough pride and gumption to get out of bed in time for a game that starts at five o'clock at night . . . .You know, Fred, sometimes I think young people today . . ."

"MARTHA! Drop it, okay? Just drop it. If you can't say nothin' intelligent or ask nothin' but dumb questions I don't want we should talk about it no more."

There was a long and painful silence, broken only by the occasional belch and muttered complaint about light beer being for pansies. Then:

"Fred? I do have one question about hockey. Where, exactly, is the old five hole?"

"What?"

"The old five hole, Fred. That squeaky chap—you know, the one who tells you what you just saw?—keeps talking about it. Somebody shoots the puck into the net and he yells 'Right through the old five hole.' I'm not sure that's a nice thing to say, Fred. A lot of children watch hockey games, and . . ."

Fred patted her on the head with just enough force to make her eyes water.

"The old five hole means between the legs," he explained. "It means the guy shot the puck through the goalie's legs. Unnerstan'?"

"Certainly, darling, and thank you. Uh, Fred?"

"What now?"

"Fred, where's the old four hole?"

"The what?"

"The old four hole. I was thinking, if the five hole is between the legs, would the old four hole be on the outside of the left leg, or do they go counter-clockwise, in which case that would be the old six hole and the space on the outside of the *right* leg would be the old four hole, which would probably put the old three hole under the right armpit. Or, naturally, under the *left* armpit if they were going clockwise the way I figured they were in the first place. And that would put the old two hole over the shoulder, I suppose, although *which* shoulder . . ."

"MARTHA!"

"Yes, Fred?"

"I don't want you should watch the Stanley Cup no more, okay? It's a game for men, on accounta broads aren't bright enough."

"All right, Fred. If you say so. But can I ask one non-hockey question?"

"Non-hockey? Okay."

"Well, that squeaky man said Edmonton had Kenny the rat on the ice, and while I've always felt naming pets is cute, do you think it's wise to let them run loose on the ice with all those skates out there? Even if the Calgarys did come to play and its nice of the Oilers to share their pets, I'm not sure it's sanitary and . . . Fred? Where are you going, Fred? The game's starting. You'll miss seeing the rat. Fred? . . . Fred . . . ?"

The Accord According to Fred

The Province, May 25, 1990

WORD THAT THE COUNTRY might be splitting in two has not gone unnoticed in the Coquitlam home of Fred and Martha Schwartz.

"Fred," Martha said over breakfast, "I'm afraid we could lose the Accord."

The sports pages rustled impatiently.

"It ain't an Accord," Fred said. "It's a Nash Metropolitan. And it ain't lost. It's in the garage."

"Not the car, Fred. I'm talking about the country. Meech Lake! Constitutional reform! We're teetering on the edge of disaster. Mr. Mulroney says so."

"Who'd he ever beat?" Fred asked.

"Pardon?"

"Who'd he ever beat?" Fred repeated impatiently. "Joe Clark in the semi-main when Clark's fighting miles out of his weight class. Then John Turner. Big deal, John Turner."

"But . . ."

"But nothin'! I should get excited because some Irishman with his feet in Ontario and his heart in Quebec tells me BC's gotta do what he says or we're all going to hell in a bucket? You wanna talk problems, I'll tell you the problem: I took the Bruins in six."

"But, Fred, every day the paper is full of stories saying we have to pass Meech Lake or Quebec will pull out of the country. And then what will we have?"

Fred gave it some thought, counting on his fingers.

"A 19-team NHL," he said triumphantly. "But it's no big deal. San Jose's coming' in next season, and maybe Seattle and Milwaukee after that. Lose two, gain three. Where's the problem?"

"But, Meech Lake . . ."

"Will you knock it off about Meech Lake? Eighteen months ago, who heard of it? I don't see it in any fishing guides. Name me one team from Meech Lake. You can't! Nobody can! You could watch network sports all year and never hear one damned thing about how the Meech Lake Whatevers are doin' . . ."

Fred was shifting into high.

" . . . but a bunch of guys we pay to run the country got a problem and what do they do? They go to the lake for the weekend, probably drawing overtime, and they come away without one damned thing settled! You think I could get away with that at Public Works? I should maybe go tell the foreman that sewer line is blocked so I'm goin' to the lake for the weekend to figure out how to unplug it? He'd kick my butt off the truck!"

"But, Fred, what if we lose Quebec, we lose . . ."

"What?" Fred roared. "A lousy hockey team in Quebec City. A baseball team TV keeps telling us is Canadian and we all should pull for it. Hell, *Montreal* ignores it! Montreal ignores everything. It ignored Canadian football. Now it's got a team in some dumb NFL farm league that's gonna play in the spring and go head-to-head with the Stanley Cup playoffs. Whoopee!"

"But your hockey team, the one you always pull for. You'd lose them, too . . ."

"We lost them years ago. The Flying Frenchmen, my butt. The Flying United Nations is more like it. Used to be they had all those great French-Canadian players. Richard . . . Béliveau . . . Cournoyer . . . Geoffrion. Now a guy's gotta have four languages just to read the line-up."

"But surely, Fred . . . surely there must be *something* in Quebec worth saving."

He thought for a long time.

"Danny Gallivan," he said finally. "I wouldn't wanna lose Danny Gallivan. To the rest I would say what my old coach used to say to guys who got big-headed."

"What was that, Fred?"

"'Hey, I'd love you to stay. But get on the team or get off the bus.'"

The Suite Life
The Province, February 25, 1983

AT APPROXIMATELY 11:55 P.M., after much soul-searching and minimal destruction of crockery, Fred and Martha Schwartz of suburban Coquitlam selected the style of Pacific Rim suite they wanted at BC Place stadium.

The argument had raged since shortly after noon, when Fred threw his apple core and peanut butter sandwich crusts into his lunch kit, booked off early at Public Works, and drove the Nash Metropolitan home to pick up Martha and head to the stadium to look at a model suite.

As they drove, he recalled the excitement of the night before when they read the stories detailing the 101 suites soon to be available for lease.

"Air conditioning, Fred!" Martha exclaimed. "Room for 12! Telephone, wet bar with refrigerator! Upholstered furniture! My goodness, that's more than we've got here at home, and it's right downtown!"

Fred attempted to calm her down in much the same manner as he'd done through 25 years of marriage.

"Cool it, stupid!" he said. "We gotta think this out."

They sat down at the kitchen table and began to list the advantages and disadvantages.

"On the minus side, we got no en-suite john," Fred said. "On the other hand, there's 1,200 of 'em right there in the building. Even you ain't got enough panty-hose to drape over that many sinks. And just once I'd like to get up in the morning without standing at the bathroom door with my legs crossed, screaming at the kids to get the hell out of there!"

"A big back yard," Martha enthused. "Just think—150,000 square feet and no lawn to mow because it's artificial turf!"

She paused as a thought struck her.

"But, Fred, there is the crowd factor: 60,000 people outside our door. What if they all drop in for coffee? And the noise from the rock concerts—Fred, who are the Grateful Dead?"

"I dunno, Martha. Probably people who kicked off and don't hafta listen to the music. But forget that—lookit here in the paper. It says the suites will be scooped up by the movers and shakers. That's us, Martha. We move every time there's a rent increase, and sometimes after a day on the jackhammer I don't stop shakin' for hours."

So they drove out for a look, and the fight started. From the moment she saw the brochure, Martha wanted the International Suite.

"Look here what it says, Fred: 'For the urban lifestyle, a New York kind of sophistication is created with mirrors and marble, velvet and plush carpet.' Let's go for it, Fred. You got the six-percent raise."

Fred was having none of it.

"Plush carpets," he sneered. "You know what the dog will do to plush carpet? As for your New York sophistication, I been in New York for the Elks' convention, and sophistication can run you $50 an hour.

"Nah! What we want, Martha, is your West Coast Suite: 'Wicker and light colours provide a pleasingly airy, laid-back setting for those who enjoy casual comfort.'"

"Oh, sure! You can't sit in a wicker chair without picking at it till it falls apart. As for laid-back, you do that every Friday at the Legion. Sometimes it would be easier to take you home in a sponge."

They went home, argued, and settled on the Canadiana Suite, 'a cozy, cabin-style environment where the occupants will feel comfortable with feet up on the furniture.' Immediately, Martha began making plans to change it.

"I want the windows on the outside wall," she said. "Who needs a view of 60,000 seats when you can look at the Cambie Street bridge?"

They returned the next day to close the deal.

"Here's my 150 bucks, like it says in the brochure," he said. "When do we move in?"

"Ah, the $150 doesn't get you a suite," the agent said. "That buys you a kit that tells you how to bid. The suites will lease for a minimum $35,000 a year."

Fred stared in utter disbelief, whirled, and grabbed his wife by the arm.

"C'mon, Martha, we're going' home," he snapped. "It ain't much, but at least it's got its own john."

The Sweet Science

BEFORE MIXED MARTIAL ARTS made boxing irrelevant, the fight game was a gold mine for the working columnist, full of hustlers, con artists and promoters so ambidextrous they could pat you on the back with one hand and pick your pocket with the other, assuming the back-patting paw didn't hold a shiv so they could separate you from your dough at their leisure.

I saw the Muhammad Ali of the magnificent body, the thorough-bred's legs and the scalpel left hand, and Mike Tyson when he was a malevolent fighting machine instead of a tattoo-faced caricature and convicted rapist. I listened to Don King before the bombast grew tire-some and saw the ancient George Foreman con the world with his comeback before settling full time into barbecue grill sales. I saw the pre-A-Team Mr. T when he was a bodyguard and the tough guys part-ed like the Red Sea as he passed. I saw the hangers-on fawn, the hus-tlers pitch deals and the small-town girls named Mary who thought it was all so romantic to be part of a fighter's entourage, and saw some of them again later when the party ended, wiping away the tears as someone younger took their place.

I met a short, bent-nosed story machine named Mouse Strauss, manager of Canadian flyweight Scotty Olson, who bragged that he'd fought 245 times and lost most of them. "Once I fought twice on the same card," quoth the Mouse. "I'd just been kayoed in one fight, and when I woke up in the locker room I was listening to the main-event fighter coming up cold feet and duckin' out on his fight. I put on a different set of trunks and fought that one as my twin brother. Got knocked out in that one, too—but I got paid twice."

Or, the Mouse on his world record: "I had the world's shortest fight. Eleven seconds. I was gettin' some last-second instructions in my corner, turned around, and woke up in the dressing room. Getting the record was easy enough. The tough part was getting paid for it."

Boxing was a seamy, dirty, glitzy circus back then when pay-TV produced paydays so huge it didn't matter how many fighters were overmatched or how many paid with concussions or were driven into the shadowy world where the phone never stops ringing.

You want a look? Come with me for a week back in 1997, when the *Calgary Sun* sent me to Las Vegas to cover the Tyson–Holyfield fight. And when one of the girls on the strip asks you if you'd like a good time, trust me—you don't!

Summit Meeting
Calgary Sun, June 25, 1997

LAS VEGAS—JIMMY "THE WEASEL" FRATRIANO, a former hit man who grew so loquacious in custody that the FBI had to hide him in maximum security lest his Mafia brethren purchase his silence with an ice pick, was always puzzled by one aspect of this city of gambling and glitz.

"I dunno why nuttin' grows there," he said. "We planted enough stiffs to fertilize anything."

The Weasel was right about the vegetation but dead wrong about the cash crops.

Hotels grow here, each generation bigger and tackier and more ersatz-opulent than the yesterday wonders demolished to make room. Casinos flourish under artificial light in stadium-sized caverns devoid of fresh air and clocks, where slot machines have moved from pull handles to push-buttons lest the tourists' elbows give out as they pump in coin after coin.

And, once or twice a year, when the fight mob gathers for a

heavyweight title bout, hype grows here—hype based on speculation and odds and the anticipation of watching two multi-millionaire warriors try to pound each other to jelly, all overlaid with the faint, sweet smell of con.

On the parking lot next to the 16,331-seat arena that sits like a pimple on one side of the MGM Grand has risen a huge white tent. It is here that the sporting media gather daily, awaiting Saturday's Evander Holyfield–Mike Tyson rematch, the fight that is supposed to settle the burning question of whether Holyfield's stunning 11th-round win here November 9 was a dazzling display by a man who started as a 25–1 underdog, or a case of Tyson believing the tales of his own invincibility after demolishing sacrificial lambs like Peter McNeeley as part of his post-prison rehabilitation.

Tyson has trained in secret, emerging briefly Monday night for a press conference in the home of promoter Don King at which he claimed the fighter with whom he most identified was Sonny Liston, who also had his troubles with the law and died in a hotel room in what police delicately called "suspicious circumstances."

Holyfield has chosen a different road, training in private but coming daily to the tent to spar and answer questions while gospel music blares incessantly in the background with tent-revival fervour and the decibel level of rap. The real work is already done, but the media ritual must be observed.

It's pretty tame stuff. Holyfield puts his faith in the Lord and His plan for him, whatever it may be. Tyson has eased up on the me-and-Allah-and-Chairman Mao theme that has been woven through his post-prison tune-ups, speaking more of his family and his faith that the real Mike Tyson will show up on Saturday and scrub away the blot of November 9.

Neither man can or would answer the question that has generated a $35-million payday for Holyfield and $30 million for Tyson, the question that has sold every seat—from a top of $1,500 to a bleacher at $200—and created a pay-TV climate the promoters say could be the biggest of them all: Can Tyson find a way under or around that darting, daunting left jab that prevented him from getting inside where he likes to work?

In an effort to find an answer he has made his peace with Richie Giachetti, his trainer when he was mugging the heavyweight division at will. Giachetti, it is hoped, will re-hone the tools he needs to get under and inside, and to avoid some of the cumulative punishment dealt by Holyfield in the first fight.

If he can do it well enough to win, the inevitable rubber match will make this one seem like the payoff on a nickel slot. Which is why some insist that's the way it will be. The Weasel was wrong about nothing growing here. Cynicism grows just fine.

Only in America
Calgary Sun, June 26, 1997

LAS VEGAS—DON KING IS STILL BULLISH on America, accent on the bull.

Okay, America put him in jail for four years in 1966 on a manslaughter rap after that unfortunate incident when he was in the numbers racket in Cleveland and killed one of his runners in a fistfight later described as a stomping. But hey—America let him out. And has he not become the Barnum of Boxing, the Sultan of Shtick, the Falstaff of Fistiana? Is this a great country, or what?

But he is approaching 66, this man who has put together some of the biggest fights in the history of boxing and may well top them all, in dollars at least, when Evander Holyfield battles Mike Tyson here Saturday night. And there are signs that he is growing weary.

The famous wet-toe-in-a-hot-socket haircut no longer points skyward with the old arrogance. There's a forced quality to the bombast, the sound you hear from nightclub comedians telling the same joke for the thousandth time.

Once he could argue the cause of Black America with lines like "George Gershwin wrote *Rhapsody in Blue*, but he couldn't have done it without the black keys," and describe a fighter on the undercard of the Tyson-Peter McNeeley fiasco as "a young man who rose from the bowels of the ghetto seeking fame, fortune and effluence." Once he could castigate the rumour mongers with words like "trickeration" and "insinuendo."

Media types laughed with and at him. He was always colourful, always good copy. For the post-prison Tyson, who despises the media anyway, King has been the perfect fit. As long as Don was talking, he could sit back and glower, a Samson using King as the jawbone of an ass.

But it was bafflegab with a reason: Tyson was fighting people who could barely fog up a mirror.

McNeeley was a joke. Buster Mathis Jr. couldn't beat Buster Mathis Sr.. Frank Bruno shook like he was waiting for a call from the governor. Bruce Seldon did everything but put his hands behind his head and ask for terms. King knew the fights were ridiculous and knew that the media knew it, too. So he gave it the old soft shoe, not to showcase the product but to disguise it.

He kept it up even for the first Holyfield–Tyson fight last November. Remember? That one was supposed to be another laugher. At the beginning of fight week, Holyfield was a 25–1 underdog. By fight time the smart money still had Tyson at 4–1. More jokes, Don. Mispronounce a few words for us, Don. Either that, or we write about the fight.

But now a truly funny thing has happened: Suddenly, there's a title fight that can stand on its own. The Sound and the Fury may well be better than the Thrilla in Manila, the Rumble in the Jungle and the Barrage at the Taj rolled into one. The experts—perhaps unwisely, given the dismal record of title rematches—are viewing it as a potential classic.

And there was Don King, doing the old thing, throwing Rosie O'Donnell, Henry David Thoreau, Ernest Hemingway and William Faulkner into a mélange of malapropisms, praising the fighters, promoters, managers, television producers, working a crowd that had seen the act too many times. He bombed, and he knew it, but still he pressed on, a weary old vaudevillian refusing to believe that the talkies were here to stay.

There are those who say that Don King has never really changed, that beneath the geniality the old numbers guy from Cleveland is still alive and well, and that now that he's in boxing's Hall of Fame they'd better nail down all the other busts. Maybe. But he was up there at the podium Wednesday, doing the old, tired act and dying with it. Love him or hate him, it was a little bit sad.

The Powers That Be
Calgary Sun, June 27, 1997

LAS VEGAS—FIGHT WEEK IN VEGAS, and the shills are alive with the sound of music.

In the camp of Iron Mike Tyson, who now marches on the path of Islam and opens every interview with a soft-spoken commitment to Allah, it is the bap-bap-bap, don't-gimme-no-crap of Black America rap. But when Evander Holyfield works, he toils to the pounding beat of Gospel—revival meeting stuff with the key-thumping fervour of backwoods church piano, long on inspirational chorus, heavy on the Hallelujahs, and laced with the shouts of the preacher man promising better days to come.

Saturday night in a basement arena of a bread-and-circuses casino in a city built on gambling, drinking and the scenic wonders of semi-naked flesh, these two servants of a Greater Power will try to pound each other into road kill . . .

In a sporting world where too many athletes tend to find God shortly after the cops find them ("Ah did it! Yes! I stole them things, your honour! That shoebox full of cocaine was MINE! But I seen the light, judge! Honest!"), it is difficult not to view these shenanigans with a certain cynicism.

It is particularly difficult in the land of Evander Holyfield and his wife of eight months, Dr. Janice Itson.

Without even looking at the records, says Ms. Itson, a medical internist, she knew that the medics had misdiagnosed Holyfield's alleged heart condition in 1994, the one that was supposed to keep him from fighting ever again.

"I knew in prayer," she said. "And it turned out it WAS (a misdiagnosis)."

She knew when it was time for Holyfield to begin training for this second Tyson bout because God told her "during a walk to the store."

She knew when the fight date was set for March that it wasn't going to happen. She even phoned Holyfield and told him to quit training and come home—which he did—because the fight wouldn't happen in March, it would happen in June.

When Don King set it for May, she didn't waver. It would be in June.

And, after Tyson suffered a cut eyebrow in training and it was, indeed, set for June 28.

"He (God) wanted him to fight in June," she says. "We just try to live by the Lord in everything we do, even the timing of the fight. Because God has a purpose for the timing and everything else."

That purpose, she says, is for her husband to successfully defend his heavyweight crown. God has told her. "You hear God, and God promises you victory. And I think that when you've got that assurance . . . the outcome (is settled)."

A query about the possibility of a Tyson victory throws her for a second. Then: "No, no. I can't answer that because that's not going to happen. He will win . . . he WILL win!"

Holyfield, while totally committed to his beliefs, has what seems a more rational approach: that the Lord has given him the talent and the ability to work and to learn. "The only time bad things happen," he says "is when I don't do the work."

But Tyson is working, too, his Islamic convictions apparently every bit as firm. The bookies, a bottom-line lot, have him at 2–1 now and figure he'll still be favoured, although at lower odds, come fight time. If the Greater Power factor has a place in their equation it is in the old story of the two boxers of equal religious fervour, crossing themselves just before the bell.

An old Irish-Catholic priest was sitting at ringside.

"Does that help?" a man asked.

"Only if he can fight, my son," he answered. "Only if he can fight."

Lost Vegas
Calgary Sun, June 29, 1997

LAS VEGAS—FORTUNATELY the no glass in the bars on fight weekend rule at the MGM Grand didn't kick in until Friday night. The guy who peeled $700 off a roll that would choke a T-Rex for a single bottle of champagne on Thursday might not have appreciated having it served in a plastic glass. He did not look like the type of guy you'd be wise to offend.

The flash-a-roll game, a monetary version of the old mine's-bigger-than-yours gambit, is one of many played here this week as the fight crowd gathered to watch Evander Holyfield and Mike Tyson pound the snot out of each other.

The gold chain contest is another—the heavier and flashier the better. And the cut-down-to-there, slit-up-to-here, thank-God-for-spandex dressathon of dozens of staggeringly gorgeous, frighteningly young women who apparently have their own definition of the main event.

In truth, only a small percentage of the people packing the hotels were here for the fight.

Tourists here to cram as many shows and as many hours at the slots as holiday time allows had no time to worry about a fight they couldn't afford to see anyway and couldn't find a ticket if they could.

For the Oriental gentleman who purchased $70,000 worth of chips in the casino and took the money out of a plastic shopping bag, the fight probably wasn't a priority. "Money laundering, most likely," a bored blackjack dealer shrugged. "Buy the chips with dough you want to ditch, walk around the casino, then cash them in and get clean dough back. We get a lot of that."

Or maybe he just didn't like traveller's cheques. Nobody cares. In a city born of the mob and raised on avarice, it takes a lot to raise an eyebrow.

But the fight mob was here in numbers, drawn like lemmings to the place where the two baddest dudes in boxing would settle who's the boss of the heavies.

They did not come to see an exhibition of skill and science. Make headgear mandatory and see who shows up. As they filed into the Grand Arena or parked in front of closed-circuit TV they weren't talking about the Christie Martin–Andrea Deshong catfight. For all they cared, the undercard could feature Beavis and Butthead.

This was a primal urge thing, a desire to watch two big men whale on each other, to see the noses flatten and the sweat fly and the blood flow. In a perfect world, they could turn thumbs down and do in the loser.

There's no explaining pro boxing. It is a sport without logic, a sport in which men have died from blows to the head and others have been driven into the shadow world where the thought processes don't function and the bells never stop ringing.

This is the sport where a Bundini Brown can lean over the ropes and shout at Muhammad Ali as he stalks a bleeding and battered George Chuvalo: "Work the eye! Work the eye! Squeeze out that beet juice!" Because a damaged eye full of blood can bring victory. Blindness, perhaps, but victory, certainly.

Strip away the trappings and the millions and boxing is indefensible, the only sport in which the objective is to hurt, to damage, if necessary to destroy.

But men have always fought. Take away the pay-TV and the millions in purses, make the sport illegal, and they would fight in barns, on barges, by lantern light in clearings in the woods. And as long as they fight there will be people who'll flock to see it.

The Romans built a great civilization of poetry, art and music, but at the height of it they filled the Coliseum to watch the gladiators.

And one day, the Huns came over the walls.

The Real Meal Deal
Calgary Sun, June 29, 1997

LAS VEGAS—AND SO, AFTER ALL THE HYPE, it will go down as the first heavyweight title fight in history where one of the shots should have been tetanus and the champion won by an ear.

And maybe, in the end, it did answer the week-long question about the psyche of Iron Mike Tyson. Maybe the guy IS nuts. Or maybe he was just hungry. If that's the case, it may turn out to be a $30-million snack—$15 million for biting the right ear of Evander "The Real Meal" Holyfield, $15 million for coming back for seconds on the left.

When a man is disqualified for biting his opponent on both ears, as referee Mills Lane disqualified Tyson at the end of the third round, he surely must forfeit his purse. It also raises some question as to whether he will ever fight again.

I hope they have great videotape. I hope they were close enough with those new jillion-dollar cameras to chronicle it fang by fang. For without the evidence of their own eyes, who will ever believe what happened here at the MGM Grand last night?

Title fights are settled with fists, not teeth. They do not end with the champion standing in the corner having his ear power-washed and the challenger raging in the other corner like a pit bull who's slipped his collar. This was supposed to be a fight for the ages, not the comic pages.

Take it bite-by-bite.

They're clinching, as they've done through the first two rounds. Suddenly, Holyfield rocks back and jumps into the air in rage. A line of blood shows under his right ear.

Lane signals time out while he considers the possibility that one of his fighters has been bitten.

Tyson, tired of waiting, rushes over and shoves Holyfield from behind into the ropes.

Lane restores order. They pound away at each other. It is shaping up as a fight they should move out into the alley where they can use garbage cans and lead pipes. Maybe it's going to be a classic after all.

And then—another clinch, and another bite, this time on the other ear.

The bell goes. The round is over. Confusion reigns.

Lane goes to Holyfield's corner, takes a look, and signals disqualification. The Sound and the Fury has become the Fanged and the Famished. Fights break out in the ring. Tyson wants everybody—anybody.

Tyson's entourage leaves. Somebody in the stands spits. Somebody else throws water. All hell breaks loose. Security troops land on the guy and haul him away. The crowd of 16,333 is stunned to near silence. And millions of Pay-TV customers are left thinking that if they were going to watch someone eat they should have used the $29.95 to order pizza.

And now the whole mess falls in the hands of the Nevada State Athletic Commission, the World Boxing Association and possibly the Campaign Against Hunger.

One thing you can take to the bank: There'll be no rubber meal. Evander Holyfield is a religious and forgiving man, but he has but two ears to give to his profession, and he gave them both last night.

Where does this leave boxing? Looking for another contender—Michael Moorer, perhaps, or Andrew Golota, who was ahead of Riddick Bowe in two fights before losing for hitting him down where Nellie wore the beads.

A better question might be where it leaves Mike Tyson. When he promised all week that the old Iron Mike would return, we thought he meant the fighter. We didn't expect him to reach further back and resurrect the thug.

Get a Grip, Mike
Calgary Sun, January 22, 1998

VANCOUVER—THREE DECADES BACK, an old sports editor took me aside and said he wanted me to do a weekly column interviewing professional wrestlers.

Since the same guy allowed a local bookie to come in early Saturday morning to check our racing wire, I suspected his motives might not be entirely journalistic in nature. Besides, everybody knew the bouts were as fixed as a squealer's shoes in concrete.

"Trust me," I said. "You don't."

But he did, and I did it, building along the way a wrestling resumé I'd assumed covered just about everything:

- Interviewed Whipper Billy Watson as he held me upside down over his head.
- Compared hairlines with Mr. Kleen ("It's my real name," he assured me. "My fadder was a Russian and my mudder was a Gypsy. I've wrestled all the big guys: the Bat, the Bolo, all of 'em.").
- Learned the secret of crushing an apple in one hand from the Fabulous Kangaroos, who crowed that they were big all over the world and especially Australia. "One night we're buckin' the opera and we outdrew Joan Sutherland," said Kangaroo Roy Heffernan, "And she was singin' the semi-main!"
- Watched on TV as a Japanese wrestler named Antonio Inoke, in an exhibition wrestlebox with Muhammad Ali, earned $4 million for basically lying on his back for 45 minutes. Barring a claim from Xaviera Hollander, it was deemed a world record.
- Listened enraptured as Gene Kiniski told me about the time he thought he was using Chapstick and smeared his lips with Preparation H.

But Mike Tyson, pretending to get into an argument with Steve Austin in the televised hype for his scheduled appearance as guest referee at Wrestlemania in Boston March 29? Promoters saying they really hate each other and suggesting (nudge-nudge, wink-wink) that Iron

Mike might actually WRESTLE Austin as part of the show, because he WANTS Austin?

Let's see, now . . .

Wrestlemania is on pay-per-view. Tyson is getting $3 million for appearing, which will barely keep him in dental floss as he awaits the inevitable third meeting with Evander Holyfield. You don't suppose, do you, that the Tyson-Austin argument was a SET-UP, a scam to hype Wrestlemania pay-per-view sales, and Tyson has no intention of doing anything in the ring but referee and perhaps bare his fangs each time an earlobe comes into camera range?

Nah! Wrestling—rehearsed? Not a chance.

What probably happened was, Tyson heard the name Steve Austin and thought it was that guy who played the Six Million Dollar Man, who'd be about 60 now. "Kick his ass," he'd think. "Mutha comes at me, I rip his plug outa the wall."

Expect further bulletins on Tyson's possible wrestling career over the next few weeks. Expect all sorts of chest pounding from both sides, and much intellectual discussion over the relative merits of the two sports.

"One punch, I drive your teeth so far down you can re-chew the food in your stomach!"

"Oh, yeah! Just get within reach, prison boy. I got holds you never seen!"

"Holds? Yo momma got better holds! She showed me las' night!"

Expect all this and more. But do not expect Mike Tyson to wrestle anybody.

Unless the money is right.

The Las Vegas columns, for all their sordidness and cynicism, occurred at the glamour end of the business where, with the right promoter to gull the public yet again, a fighter could become a millionaire in 45 ring minutes or less, even if the odds were that he'd lose it and die broke. But only a few get that chance. At the other end, the kids dream big dreams and the plodders who've watched their own dreams die wander from town to town, purse to purse, taking their lumps for pin money.

A Day at the Office
The Province, March 5, 1982

NANAIMO—His name is Arnold Sam. It's stitched in white across the back of the bomber jacket he strips off for the weigh-in: Arnold Sam, Indian Heavyweight.

He's from California or Reno, Nevada. No one seems to know or care which. When he steps on the scales his obsidian eyes gaze through the weights and the people out of a flat moon face that seems as old as time. In a few hours he will give away 46 pounds to a large-bellied, droop-chested 274-pound ex-linebacker named Harold Rice, spend about 17 minutes absorbing what punishment Harold can dispense, then plod wearily out of the ring, loser by a technical knockout, to collect payment on his pound of flesh.

It will come to about $800—more than he's received on other nights on other cards in other forgotten towns, because this time he's on the undercard of a championship fight. He's fought in a lot of towns, has Arnold Sam, and he'll fight in more until the offers or the body run dry. He's a fighter, and this is Nanaimo, and it's Friday . . .

His name is Francisco Roche—"The Cuban" Roche, it says on the fight card—a junior welterweight thrown in against Sanford Ricks, a Halifax kid said to be of some promise. Roche is from Carson City by way of Seattle, where he's training in matchmaker Dick McDonald's gym. Ricks beats him unimpressively, but for Francisco Roche, who dreams big and perhaps futile dreams, it means a minor payday and perhaps a more comfortable bed.

"You know where he's been sleeping the past few weeks?" McDonald asks. "In the back of an abandoned car . . ."

Gord Racette was there for the weigh-in. He saw the impassivity of an Arnold Sam headed down a too-familiar road to nowhere. One look at Harold Rice's hulking form ("For God's sake, Harold," a fan would plead during his pawing match with Sam, "wear a brassiere!") should have told him this is no profession for anyone not totally prepared and utterly committed. Francisco Roche's housing arrangements offer mute testimony that even preparation and commitment carry no guarantee.

Today, as the soreness eases in a face pounded hamburger red and the swelling leaves a battered right eye and the aches and stiffness make sudden movement risky, he should be thinking about all those things and checking his hole card. Because it may be time for Gord Racette to put his dreams in a box and store them unfulfilled.

He dreams of being a champion. So do thousands of fighters all over North America who had 15 years' experience before he ever laced on a glove. Sanford Ricks has been fighting since he was eight years old. Laurie Mann, his professional career just starting, is a six-time Canadian amateur champion at 21. Racette is 27, and barely underway.

It isn't that he lacks potential, it's that he lacks time to achieve it. He has fought two men who have been at or around the upper echelons of the trade. An out-of-shape Jimmy Young stopped him and Friday night Trevor Berbick chased and battered and pounded him for 11 rounds and looked capable of ending it any time after four.

He should at least read the warning signs implied. Then he must decide: stay on a crash course of an education where fees are paid in blood and battered tissue, or grab a couple of fast minor paydays in Europe against men of his own skill level, then tell manager Tony Dowling it's all over.

He is a nice, big, carefree and handsome kid, but the nose is bent now and there are spidery white lines around the eyebrows. How many more are waiting down the road?

His backers take a more optimistic view.

"Gordie showed me something," Dowling says. "He's never been hit. Let's face it, he's been brought along so he wouldn't be. But he took it, and he showed me a heart as big as outdoors."

He said it as though heart were all that mattered. Racette should get a second opinion from Arnold Sam.

"The Times, My Friend, The Times . . ."
The Province, September 5, 1982

MOSTLY THEY ARE KIDS in their 20s, out of work and willing to risk a beating for a shot at a few bucks. Some of them don't have the bus fare to get to the doctor for their medicals, so Jack McLaughlin leaves his temporary office in the back room of the video movie store on East

Hastings Street, picks them up and delivers them personally. That way, he gets to see for himself if a kid has let his desperation get in the way of his common sense and steer him in another direction if he has.

"It's the times, my friend," the old fight promoter says. "It's the times. When you can't get a job and your UIC's run out and you're not the type to mug a guy and take his wallet, it's always been the same: First you hit the pool rooms, and then you hit the gym."

The times are the reason McLaughlin has changed the name and scaled down the house for his latest *So You Wanna Fight?* card Thursday night at Queens Park Arena. Now it's called *Hard Times Promotions*, tickets down to $12 and $8 from the old $15 and $10. "You've got to let the people know that you know the times are hard," he says. "So far, they're going like a hot damn."

Not that everyone on the card will be a hungry kid desperate for money. As usual, it will be laced with street types who figure they might as well check their chains at the door and do in the ring for money what they do in the pubs for free. But some will be throwbacks to Depression days when some men pounded one another in the ring and others roamed the continent in box cars, stopping wherever there was a town with a tough guy, squeezing out a living on the side bets.

They, too, had "managers," guys who'd open the scam in the bars with "You people got a guy who thinks he can fight? Fifty bucks says my man here can take him." And off they'd go to back alley or barn to battle bare-knuckled and fully clothed. Win or lose they were on the next train out, nursing their cuts and bruises en route to the next town, the next fight for the next meal.

Times like those produce good fighters. ("Some of them were lucky," McLaughlin says. "Jimmy McLarnin had a great manager named Pop Foster who not only knew the game, he could also make a great stew. When him and Jimmy went to California to fight, Pop would make a big pot of stew and they'd live on it for a week.") In 1979 the *So You Wanna Fight?* fad in Vancouver spawned Gordie Racette and Jerry Reddick, the one they called Mack Truck.

"Oh, the Truck," McLaughlin recalls, "he could bang. He could bang like hell. He had a lot of raw ability—more than Racette, lots more. I had it set up with Angelo Dundee for him to go to Angie's camp for a couple of weeks so he could win the Canadian. But he got headstrong. He could think, the Truck could. He thought himself right out of the ring."

McLaughlin, lifelong fight fan, 26-year owner of logging camps, 63 come October and not long on gold himself, is hoping another Reddick or Racette will surface Thursday, but it isn't necessary. "Some people come out looking for good fighters," he concedes, "but let's face it, a lot more just want to see a bunch of guys knock the crap out of each other."

Come Thursday they'll crawl into the ring two by two for three two-minute rounds or less, winners to fight again later, twice if they reach the final. For some it will be a lot tougher than they figured. "I been hit with clubs, bats, chains, guns, you name it," a biker named Schnoz said last year. "But I never been hit that hard. This guy hits me once, I think I'm gonna have a cardiac. So I think 'To hell with this', and I leave."

For him it wasn't important. For some it will be. The $1,000 top prize may be out of reach. They may get badly whipped. But bruises heal, and for just getting into the ring you get $50. In hard times, it beats having no job at all.

Boxing Day
Calgary Sun, December 26, 2000

ON THE BOXING DAY that matters, Paul Ingle lies in a Sheffield hospital, where the best Christmas present was that his eyes were open, he could move one hand, and no longer required a machine to breathe.

On the Boxing Day that matters, Michael Watson is home from London, where he sat in his wheelchair as the governing body of British boxing lost its appeal of a ruling holding it liable for the massive brain damage he suffered in a world title fight nine years ago.

On the Boxing Day that matters, medical associations all over the world have renewed their pleas for a ban on the only sport this side of hunting in which the objective is to do bodily damage to an opponent and, on a really great night, render him temporarily senseless.

On the Boxing Day that matters, knowing the chances of outlawing the sport are minuscule, a British labour lawmaker is proposing legislation that would allow the sport to continue, but prohibit blows to the head.

It is not, of course, the real Boxing Day.

The real Boxing Day we celebrate today is about sales and Christmas present returns and an extra day off work. It is the day we visit friends or they visit us, when the conversation is about who got what from whom and how distended the stomachs were after the Christmas turkey.

Boxing Day, the holiday, has nothing to do with boxing, the sport, in which men—and lately even some women—are paid big money to do unto each other acts of violence in the ring that would be considered assault in the parking lot.

It is not a day to discuss dead boxers, or traumatized boxers, or boxers doomed to wander forever in shadowed worlds existent only in their broken minds.

Lost in the rush for door-opening specials featuring prices the stores could have put on the items before Christmas and still made a tidy profit, not many will recall that Boxing Day got its name from the day the English gentry would give "Christmas boxes," generally money, to servants, trades people and others of humble life.

It is a day to exchange gifts you didn't want for things you did, a day to get the sizes right, a day to clean up the post-Christmas chaos, a day when the only boxers that matter are undershorts.

So maybe what we need is a second Boxing Day, where we pause a moment to consider real boxers.

Not the champions, the millionaires or the thugs. The damaged ones, and those who one day will be.

Because boxing is not going to be banned. Not ever.

It is not going to be amended, at least not at the professional level where most of the injuries occur, to a fight where blows to the head are outlawed.

We will never see the day when the pros wear helmets like the amateurs, because the people who buy the tickets or shell out for the pay-TV telecasts want to see noses flatten and cheeks compress and mouthpieces fly from the force of a blow that might have destroyed 10,000 brain cells.

Maybe, the human genome now fully mapped, scientists will one day be able to find the gene that triggers the boxing lust and turn it off.

Until then, man will always fight. Outlaw it and he will fight in barns on deserted farms, or on barges outside the legal limits. And there will always be those who'll pay to watch, because there is an electricity surrounding a heavyweight title fight unmatched anywhere in sport.

It says something about us—perhaps that, surrounded by gifts and possessions and electronic marvels that expand and enhance the senses, we are not as far from the jungle as we choose to believe.

Sex and the (Semi-) Single Jock

IF PROSTITUTION IS, INDEED, THE OLDEST PROFESSION, then sex surely must be the oldest participation sport—or do we really believe that all Adam got for giving in to Eve was a mouthful of apple?

There was a time, of course, when such things could not be discussed in the public prints, especially on the sports pages, where every baseball writer knew that Babe Ruth was a beer-guzzling womanizer and heavyweight champion Gene Tunney was hailed as an intellectual when an enterprising photographer snapped a shot of him reading a book. Back then, pre-television, the public preferred its heroes wore haloes as well as jockstraps.

The pendulum has swung the other way. Mass communication has seen to that. Public dismay has given way to public snigger. When Tiger Woods fell from grace the only sound heard from anywhere but in the offices of his sponsors and the top floor window ledges at television networks was a worldwide giggle—for which sports reporters and gossip-mongers in every form of the communications media would like to say a heartfelt "Thank you!" To the working columnist or commentator, all is grist.

Personally, I've spent 30 years and more wondering what all the fuss is about. Infidelity aside, what we have here is male and female athletes in the prime of youth and health and the most competitive folks on the planet. Were I the father of a healthy and probably rich and famous young single athlete, I'd worry if he *wasn't* spending a good portion of his off hours in pursuit of the feminine form divine.

My prime emotion re the whole sex thing and public reaction to it is gratitude. If laughter truly is the best medicine, I've had at least one daily dose, and tried to pass it on . . .

Holy Epidermis!
Calgary Sun, February 25, 2001

THE *SPORTS ILLUSTRATED* SWIMSUIT EDITION landed on my porch this week. The big surprise was that it didn't bounce.

It was shocking, of course. You wouldn't believe the price of those swim suits. The one on pages 68 and 69 sells for $350 US, and it didn't even come with a top.

Now, you may wonder what a man with grown, adult children is doing, poring pore-by-pore over the annual monument to depilatory creams, air-brushing and lust.

We all know what happens when you do that. If we don't, the letters to the editor pages of the next two issues are there to remind us:

"SI: How dare you waste valuable space publishing this smutty, evil, degrading attempt to seduce the young men of our nation and make them go blind, or at least need glasses? Don't you know the Leafs didn't get Lindros? TICKED IN TORONTO."

"SI: Cancel our subscription. I bought one of those suits, waved both pieces in front of my husband and asked him if it gave him any ideas. He used the bottom to blow his nose. OUTRAGED IN OMAHA."

"SI: Those supermodels think they're so smart! Well, gravity will get them. It gets us all! And what'll they use those skimpy little outfits for then—their new jobs at the car wash? FLOPPY IN FARGO."

"SI: You have two days to replace the bathroom door lock we had to kick in to get Freddie out of the bathroom. FREDDIE'S MOM."

"SI: When the Almighty in His wrath sends the grasshoppers and the asteroid hits, and the tidal waves sweep humanity back to the primordial ooze, THEN perhaps you will understand the depths of your depravity. Until then, keep up the good work. GRATEFUL IN GREENWICH."

"SI: Thank you for the swimsuit issue. Halfway through, all my zits popped. FIFTEEN IN 'FRISCO."

Why do I do all this eye-glazing research? The answer is simple: Duty.

SI is a sports magazine, I am a sports columnist. Keeping a finger on the sporting pulse, no matter how distasteful it may be, staring at page after page of beautiful, semi-naked women with their acres and acres of epidermal excess and their bedroom "Hi-big-boy-what's-your-bank-balance?" eyes and . . .

But I digress.

People say the swimsuit issue has nothing to do with any sport but the oldest. Not true.

You want sport? The girl on the cover is Elsa Benitez, and she's married to Ron Seikaly, who used to play in the NBA. And Carol Alt, who used to be married to Ron Greschner, is Alexei Yashin's main squeeze even though she's 40 and he's only 27. If that isn't an ad for keeping fit, what is?

So, because this is clearly a sporting issue, a few professional, sporting observations:

1. Putting aside what Woody Allen used to call "the chestal area," most of the models look about half a happy meal this side of anorexia.
2. Anybody who tries to swim in one of those suits will be naked in three strokes. Discuss among yourselves.
3. On Page 80, a model named Aurelie Claudel (Yeah, right. "I've got an idea, honey! Let's call her Aurelie!") is wearing a bottoms-only suit by Frivole that sells for $28 US. We used to get the same thing at Eaton's, three for six bucks. It was underwear by Stanfield's.
4. Cheryl Tiegs (who was once briefly in my motel room in Brantford, Ont., and gave me the picture now hanging above my desk, signed "To Jim, with warm thoughts of Jamaica. Lots of love. XXX Cheryl Tiegs") makes them all look like bench-warmers.

But honestly, we're just friends.

Making the Top Two
Calgary Sun, March 16, 2000

ANNA KOURNIKOVA says that there'll be topless tennis within a decade. Titillating thought, to say the least.

The toothsome Anna K., who has yet to win a tournament on the women's tour, has something that money can't buy except possibly in certain Swedish clinics. In the words of country troubadour Tom T. Hall, she is developed to a fault. On a topless tennis tour she would be an even bigger attraction than today.

But she had to be kidding.

Topless tennis? In a world where female volleyball players are in full protest over the mandatory skimpiness of their outfits? A world where women athletes rightly demand to be respected as athletes who happen to be women?

Not likely.

And yet . . .

A decade ago, who'd have dreamed there'd be an audience for people who roam the world inventing sports like street luge and parasurfing and push-the-envelope stunts where a mistake can put you in traction or the morgue? But the Extreme Games are fully sponsored and draw huge TV ratings.

A decade ago, who knew from snow-boarding, whose mushrooming popularity is based at least in part on the inherent dangers in striving for the newest, even-more daring trick. In BC at least, the incidence of spinal cord or head injuries is four times that of skiing, but the sport's growth is exponential.

A decade ago, who'd have dared to suggest that ballroom dancing would become an Olympic event.

A decade ago, when professional wrestling was just beginning to flex its TV muscles, who'd have predicted that the candied ham of Gorgeous George and Gene Kiniski and Whipper Billy Watson would be supplanted by the trash-talking, scripted goons of Vince McMahon?

A decade ago, could there have been an XFL pro football league in the works, a TV contract already in place and sponsors lining up?

A decade ago, technology hadn't expanded the TV grid into channels by the hundreds, each with a 24-hour appetite demanding to be fed and using sports as a diet staple.

What television demands, the market will create.

Not everyone can have or afford the NFL, NBA or major league baseball, but for relatively few bucks a network can take a niche sport with a strong 25-and-under following, splash it onscreen and be reasonably assured of success.

No, the NHL hasn't managed it and won't until the sticks come down to attract the moderates or their use as shish-kebabs is legalized to attract the teen-to-20s masses. Right now the league is at the awkward stage, pretending to abhor the violence on one hand that it markets on the other.

So, as the marketplace grows steadily more jaded, who's to say that Anna K., even if she was speaking in jest (which seems likely), doesn't turn out to be a prophetess?

In early radio days, Bob Hope was briefly off the air for a skit in which a man pounding upstairs yelled "I'm laying linoleum!" and Hope yelled back "Has she got a sister?" Today's TV has freed the four-letter expletive.

How big a step then, from Gussie Moran's shocking glimpse of lace underpants at centre court to Anna and her sisters baring all above the belt? All television would worry about would be how and where to stick the logos.

Light in the Window
The Province, July 29, 1994

ONCE IN A WHILE a guy has to exit the toy department and become involved in something more meaningful. This is the day, and I have chosen the objects of my involvement.

Hookers.

Not in the physical sense, you understand. No, indeed. Not in the move-'em-here, move-'em-there game of musical beds that has passed for Doing Something About Them for generations. As a member of the second-oldest profession, I simply feel a duty to assist practitioners and proponents of the first.

In that context—average citizen just trying to help—I offer today a simple, cost-effective way to handle a complex situation to the betterment of all concerned. To wit, a perfect site for the controversial "safe-stroll zone," where favours can be offered and purchased in an atmosphere of cleanliness, comfort and safety, free from the harassment of police, pimps or outraged residents.

I nominate GM Place.

Okay, it takes a little getting used to. But think about it. Here we have this beautiful, big, 20,000-seat luxury sports palace now under construction as a playpen for the NHL Canucks and the NBA Yomommas. Even allowing for playoffs, you're talking a maximum 120 game nights. That leaves 245 nights that Arthur Griffiths and friends must fill to make the operation fully viable—246 of them in Leap Year when, under my plan, February 29 would be designated Leap Night with specially reduced rates and truly amazing gifts.

Consider the advantages to turning those nights over to the ladies of the evening:

- Two red lights are already in place, one at each end.
- Arthur and partners could rent the building to the city (which would write off the costs against money saved by cutting patrols on Richards and Seymour), take a flat fee from the occupants or, in the same entrepreneurial spirit with which he launched the NBA franchise, gamble on a percentage of the take.
- The celebrity boxes would give the place that touch of old Amsterdam, with the ladies sitting back-lit in the windows in fetching outfits that would say "Come hither" and dare a john to yawn.
- With 20,000 comfortable seats—not a bad view in the house, it promises in the brochure—even the nights when demand overwhelmed supply could turn into a plus as hot dog and beer vendors worked their way through the crowd peddling wares of their own at prices only slightly less staggering.
- GM Place designers, rightfully proud of their creation, have said from the beginning that the communication system will be state of the art. How tough would it be for a john to dial the number listed on the front of the celebrity box in which lounges the lady of his pro-tem dreams, whisper sweet figures in her ear and arrange a tryst? For an extra $10, management could even offer her enlarged photo on the big screen scoreboard.
- With the celebrity boxes equipped with TV, washroom and food

and beverage service, the ladies could even rent one for the evening, thus eliminating those awful and unsightly late-night traffic jams as johns try to drive away from the current curb-side negotiations with one hand on the wheel and the other holding their hats over their faces.

- The rink is not in a residential area. There's plenty of parking. Keeping the ladies safe from harassment would be as simple as stationing an usher at the stairs leading to the celebrity-box floor. One policeman could handle the whole night.

Give it a go, Arthur. If it works, you might even consider expanding to include game nights. You might not win the Stanley Cup, but you'd lead the league in post-game shows.

Enter Jogger, Exit Sex
The Province, April 20, 1982

THE RUNNER, acknowledged bible of the sweat set, has published the results of a survey claiming that 26.5% of the 3,140 runners polled said they'd rather give up sex than running. Good-bye, Participaction.

The survey also claims that:

(a) 47.5% of those surveyed spent more time thinking about running than about sex;

(b) 82.2% think about sex while running;

(c) 18.9% think about running during sex;

(d) 62.7% say a perfect Sunday afternoon consists of a run, a shower with one's mate, a bottle of wine and soft music;

(e) 11.1% figure a great Sunday schedule starts with a run and a shower followed by a few beer and an afternoon in front of the TV watching a track meet.

It is a depressing picture, even for those of us who've long viewed runners with suspicion. (Did you ever wonder why Earl Cameron wears a trench coat in those walk-a-block-a-day commercials? Or what he's got on under it?) Anyone with such single- or simple-minded dedication must be running from something. Now *The Runner* implies that the pursuer could be a sex-starved mate.

"Well, darling, we've had the run, and the nice warm shower. The wine is at room temperature, which is more than I can say for me. The music is soft and low. I've sent the kids on a marathon. In Greece. How about . . ."

"Not now, dear. I've got a shin splint."

Examine the survey's figures closely and you come to some inescapable conclusions about the sex life of a runner. For instance:

If 82.2% think about sex while running and 26.5% would rather give up sex than running, it means that even without duplications 8.7% of the people running are jogging along thinking that what they're doing on the road is a lot better than what they could be doing at home.

Not that it doesn't make sense to think about sex as you pound mindlessly across the landscape. When you run, you need rhythm. It's also helpful to have a song or jingle running through the mind. We've all seen the rowing commercial on TV. Why not the same tune for runners, with slightly altered lyrics:

> Another one sights the bust;
> Another one sights the bust.
> And it won't be long 'til her chaperone's gone,
> Another one sights the bust . . .

On the other hand, the trained scientific mind boggles at the ambiguity of the news of the 18.9% who say they think about running during sex. Do they mean that during sex they think about running—or that they think about what it might be like to be running during sex? If the latter, the word marathon could take on a whole new dimension.

That 47.5% of those surveyed would confess to giving more thought to running than to sex is not surprising. There are similarities—both activities tend to be sweaty—but running should require more thought. It takes longer and requires more equipment.

A runner is constantly on the prowl for the latest in shoes, sweat suits, stopwatches and invigorating drinks. A sexer, if one may use the term, leans more toward depleting his wardrobe than adding to it. Shoes of any kind are considered more hindrance than help, and at the very least bad form. The sexer bringing a stopwatch to bed may never get a chance to click it. A partner expecting brandy and a cigarette may not view with love a proffered salt tablet and Gatorade.

Naturally, there is the possibility that the survey is a crock. A 3,140-runner sampling may not be statistically relevant. Some of those surveyed could have reacted to the infringement on their private lives by pulling the leg of the surveyor. Certainly, runners as a group will deny most of the findings.

There is, however, that famous story of the runner who asked his doctor how to improve his sex life and was told to run five miles a day.

Three days later he phoned.

"It ain't workin', doc," he complained. "I'm 15 miles from home and I ain't had a proposition yet."

Gunilla Makes the Cut
The Province, December 16, 1987

GUNILLA AXEN, 22, a member of the Swedish national women's soccer team, says she had her breasts surgically reduced to improve her athletic performance. I trust she was not in her cups at the time.

Ms. Axen says the decision had nothing to do with her looks. She was simply too well endowed to give her all in the games, so she gave part of herself on the operating table. *Sic transit gloria booby.*

Naturally, the world will be watching her performance with more than a passing interest. The implications of her re-definition of the term "giving a little bit extra" are potentially staggering, and not just among women athletes in other sports who feel pressured into following her example.

What about the husbands and boyfriends who admire their lover's figure, and face the prospect of watching it deflate like a soccer ball with a slow leak?

What about male athletes? Did she ever think of what it could cost them?

No longer can a baseball player take a week off because he has a bwister on his wittle fingy. "Pop it, drain it and tape it, you wimp!" his coach will snap. "You call that a bump? That Axen dame gave up ten times that much before the doctor even got to the other side of the table."

No more will a Refrigerator Perry be able to come to camp weighing more than the dressing room, and protest that weight loss is too great a task. "Uh, William, just lie down here on this table. This is Gunilla Axen's physician. Go ahead, doc. Trim the drumsticks, flatten the butt, and if he gives you any trouble, nip off the jockstrap, contents included."

And yet, we cannot blame Ms. Axen for the chaos she hath wrought. Hers was a decision based on pure logic. If weightlifters and others in sports requiring strength are stupid enough to use steroids to bulk up, what's wrong with a woman who feels the weight of two worlds on her chest being wise enough to pare down?

Besides, it's a decision that could prolong the competitive life of women athletes, and one that should have been made long ago. For was it not Shane Gould's swimming coach, back in the 1970s, who watched his young water sprite blossom as her freestyle times declined and sighed, "Once they develop like that you've got two choices: Retire 'em, or turn 'em over and make 'em backstrokers."

Not all sports would require such radical trimming. Surely a sprinter straining to breast the tape is better off with the maximum in natural equipment to get the job done. And I'm not certain how the cutback will improve Ms. Axen's performance in soccer, where the rules allow women to chest a ball down with the arms crossed over said chest for the same reason male players are seen with hands covering their nether regions while forming the wall defending a free kick.

The lady obviously feels she'll play better a size smaller—but her solution to the problem does not mean that other athletically inclined young women should follow suit. Only time and performance will give us the true picture. Until then, ladies, please do not adjust your sets.

Bubby Takes the Buss
The Province, January 8, 1991

SEVERAL ALERT READERS phoned on the weekend to discuss the latest NFL sexual harassment case. You could hear the shock and outrage in their voices.

It was pretty horrible—worse in a way than the overblown Lisa Olson case in the New England Patriots' dressing room. Ms. Olson, a

Boston reporter, was subjected only to lewd gestures and suggestions by naked players as she attempted to conduct an interview. In this latest shocker, something Actually Happened.

That's right. A sexual advance was made without so much as a by-your-leave, a what's-your-sign? or even a your-place-or-mine? In the month that has passed since the incident, not a finger has been raised in protest.

It seems that Ms. Shari Warren, a reporter for KSLA-TV in Shreveport, Louisiana, had just finished interviewing Pittsburgh quarterback Bubby Brister in the Steelers' locker room. Brister, it should be added, was fully clothed and co-operative.

As another reporter asked Brister a question, Ms. Warren said "Bye!", leaned over and *kissed* him. Just flat laid one on him right out there before God and the rest of the Steelers. Worse yet, she has made no attempt to deny the assault. Instead, she has attempted to write it off as a harmless joke.

"I've known him since he was in high school," she said. "We were teasing around. That's what we've always done. I hugged him like I would an old friend."

Oh, sure. A man trying to do his job as an athlete and co-operate with the media has no protection even in the privacy of his own locker room. Instead, he is left at the mercy of any pair of hungry lips that happens by.

Perhaps it was the speed of the attack and the hurried departure. I like to think that's it—that given a second's warning the Steelers would have rallied behind their quarterback, perhaps scaring off his assailant with outraged screams:

"Hey, over here!"

"Second!"

"Thirdsies! I get thirdsies!"

"You got a sister?"

But no. Ms. Warren was able to kiss and bolt. And today, a month later, not one story has been written, not one investigation launched, to help Brister repair his life and make certain such a thing will never happen again.

The TV station has not suspended her. She has not been required to obtain counselling. NFL commissioner Paul Tagliabu has not stepped forward as he did so quickly in defence of Ms. Olson.

When Ms. Olson suffered the verbal assault by some of the Patriots, women's groups organized a boycott of products produced by team owner Victor Kiam. Sales of Lady Remington razors dropped dramatically over Christmas.

But Bubby Brister was actually kissed! Did you hear of any protests in Pittsburgh? Did the women of Shreveport turn their TV dials from KSLA-TV? Did sponsors look elsewhere?

No. Bubby Brister was left to suffer alone.

He'll be back on the field next season, quarterbacking the Steelers and trying to forget. Whether he'll be able to return to the locker room, only time will tell. Sometimes, the scars are too deeply burned.

Warm-Up is Everything
The Province, February 21, 1992

I HAVE AN IDEA. Let's make a rule that on the opening day of every Olympic Games, winter and summer, every covering newspaper must run the following front page story under a headline in the biggest type that will fit:

OLYMPIC ATHLETES LIKE SEX!

According to a survey conducted by the International Olympic Committee, every athlete in the current Olympiad says he/she has the same interest in sex as non-competitors.

While opinions varied on whether or not the act of love-making should take place (a) in the hours before the event, (b) immediately after the event or (c) all of the above and as often as possible, the unanimous opinion was that boys will be boys, girls will be girls, and since the activity is (a) enjoyable, (b) physiologically stimulating and (c) better than sitting in your room reading *The Wit and Wisdom of Juan Antonio Samaranch*, they plan to follow their natural instincts on every possible occasion.

Given this overwhelming support of sex as a participant sport, the IOC should submit a motion at its next Congress that the motto of the Olympic Games be changed from "Swifter, Higher, Stronger" to "Faster, Harder, Yes! Yes! Yes! More! More! Oooooh!"

You see all the trouble it would save?

With the sex question out of the way early we wouldn't be biting our nails today wondering whether Kerrin Lee-Gartner did or did not get a 120-second jump-start from husband Max on the morning of the day she won the women's downhill at Meribel.

A Swiss paper ran what it claimed were quotes from Lee-Gartner: "Beside me [in bed] my husband Max opened my eyes with a warm-up under the covers. We made good vibrations for the race. That was enough to be in good shape." The paper then added "One hundred and 20 seconds later, the quickie was over. A quickie is very good. Longer sex is bad for condition."

Upon her arrival in Canada, Lee-Gartner said she was embarrassed by the story and had never spoken to the Swiss reporter who wrote it. But since she didn't actually deny the event itself, we are left to mind-boggling speculation.

Had we run my Games-opening sex story, the Lee-Gartner story wouldn't have caused a ripple. We might even have been mature enough to think that a married couple in a romantic chalet in the mountains of France might have awakened on medal morning with a Really Good Idea. And that either way, it was nobody's business but theirs.

As to the advisability of sex before competition, it is a question that has plagued scholars for centuries.

Believers trust in the words of the Bible to the flock ("The bridegroom coming out of his chamber . . . rejoiceth as a strong man to run a race") and Babe Ruth to the desk clerk ("Tell her to come right on up"). Doubters lean to Casey Stengel's warning to his New York Yankees: "You gotta learn that if you don't get it by midnight, chances are you ain't gonna get it; and if you do, it ain't worth it."

Every athlete has his or her own ideas on the subject. But because they are athletes, they're not silly enough to ignore the possibility that they might be wrong. Actually, they probably hope they never will find out for certain. In this case, the result isn't nearly as interesting as the research.

Condom
The Province, October 28, 1993

NO DOUBT you are as relieved as I at word that the 1994 Victoria Commonwealth Games now have their own official condom.

Ortho Pharmaceutical recently began distributing its Ortho Shields—"Official Condom, Victoria 94"—complete with a Games Logo on the package. Okay, so the Games don't open until August, but you know what the coaches say: "Practise, practise, practise. You'll never get anywhere unless you do your reps."

Until now, this may have presented a problem to a generation raised on the theory that if Nike isn't giving it away it ain't worth having. The shoe people who tell us to "Just Do It" have never bothered to add that, in matters of the heart or libido, it is wise to enter the event wearing something besides really spiffy shoes.

Now Ortho has provided the answer as part of its $25,000-to-$200,000 payment in cash and product—the range set by the Games Society to qualify for "Proud Sponsor" status. (Slogans leap to mind: "Be Proud. Wear Ortho.") Ortho's offerings include condoms and muscle relaxants (now that's what you call covering both ends of the market) plus, for those who may have been caught short of one or the other, pregnancy-test kits.

Given that boys will be boys, girls will be girls, and we are throwing a few hundred of the world's healthiest and most competitive young people together in one big, happy village, the approach makes nothing but sense. There is, however, one teensy potential problem.

Games bylaws state that the host country must provide a complete pharmacy in the village. Again, common sense. Trainers, doctors and athletes have more important things to do than go searching for local drug stores, and prescriptions filled out by foreign doctors may not be worth squat. Therefore, the Games provides doctors with prescription pads for the village pharmacy, and the process is so closely monitored that, in the words of Games spokesperson Amy Hart, "if an athlete wants an aspirin tablet, he'll have to get a prescription."

So what happens if boy meets girl, the windows steam up, the guy is trying to play it like Omar Sharif, and ...

"Uh, excuse me a minute, okay? Got to go see the Doc for a

prescription. I need a . . . a . . . *Aspirin!* That's it: an *aspirin!*" That's not Omar; that's Gomer.

Word of the condom caper has drawn one irate call to Ms. Hart, pointing out that nothing was mentioned in the release about abstinence. No doubt there will be more. The problem with abstinence is that, given the marketplace, it's such a tough sell. How do you package nothing?

Face it: We live in a world where you market or die. That's why there is an official Games potato chip, an official Games drink, and an official Games clothing line soon to be announced. Our athletes are the cream of our physical crop. It's only logical that Ortho would want to tie its condom to a star. Particularly one that's proud.

The Stilt Comes to Play
The Province, November 14, 1991

WILT CHAMBERLAIN says he has slept with almost 20,000 women, which works out to about 1.2 per day since he was 15 and doesn't even allow for the nights he had a headache. No wonder they called him The Stilt.

Mind you, he never liked that nickname. He preferred the one he gave himself, The Big Dipper, which until now I'd always assumed was based on his ability to stuff a basketball into a hoop. But The Stilt was the one that stuck, it being difficult to campaign for a change from a prone position.

I don't know about you, but I find the information on Wilt's sexual prowess—in Chapter 11 of his autobiography, *A View From Above*, which he wouldn't be terribly upset if you rushed out and bought a copy of to find out if he goes into (slobber, pant, pant) *details*—absolutely fascinating. Not for the sex, for the logistics.

Think about it.

Here's a guy about 7'2" tall, travelling from city to city through the National Basketball Association, seldom spending more than one night—two, maximum—in one place. One of those nights he's not free until the game ends about 10 p.m. Then he has to shower—no quick task, given the area to be covered—and that's not even considering the cost of body cologne, which he'd have to buy by the vat.

So let's say he's in the bar or disco by 11 p.m. Allowing time for ice-breaking ("No, I don't play basketball, I work at the zoo washing giraffes") and foreplay ("You got a room, babe?", "My car or yours?"), he's probably not in Operational Mode until midnight.

Now, then: If The Dipper's mathematics are sound, in order to achieve that average 1.2 conquests per day he would have to make love to *two* women one day out of every five. (I have checked with the rules committee on this: Making love to the same woman twice in the same evening does not count.)

This would necessitate a whole new approach to foreplay ("You two babes got a room?") and all but eliminate the car gambit. (I have a picture in my mind of the teenage Wilt, a lad of 6'10", trying to make out at a drive-in movie. It ends with a chiropractor and the Jaws of Life.)

Assuming Wilt, the dedicated professional, overcomes all these hurdles, ignores the headaches, maintains his average and still manages to get up, morning after morning, to make the plane for the next town, the next game, the next bar and the next 1.2, we are left with the real burning question of the whole issue:

How does he live with the pressure?

What about those nights when the team has won a big game and the boys want to kick back with a few brew and play a few hands of poker? The rest of them can do it, no problem. But not Wilt. As they're dealing he's thinking:

"Jeez! It's Saturday night! It's 11:30! Thirty minutes from the start of a new week and I haven't had my 1.2! I skip tonight, that means sometime between now and next Saturday I've got to 1.2 twice or 2.4 once just to break even! Damn, those doubleheaders catch up with a guy late in the season. First thing you know it's Christmas and you've got nothing left to give."

It must have been awful for him, all those years. No doubt it's all explained in his book, which I certainly plan to read if they ever send me a free review copy. He must have had phenomenal endurance. Only a dedicated professional and superbly conditioned athlete could have survived.

Then again, he may be lying in his teeth.

Some Folks Along the Way

THERE ARE PICTURES I carry with me, forever filed away in my heart and soul.

Some are snapshots of key moments in games I've been blessed to witness: Paul Henderson's winning goal in the '72 Canada-Russia hockey series that forever changed the sport

Larry Holmes pleading with Muhammad Ali ("Go down, man! Just go *down!*") as he pounded the fading Ali in a title bout in Las Vegas, and the bloodied Ali mumbling a defiant "Fight, sucka!"

Andrés Escobar, the Colombian whose toe had been the last to touch a ball that went into his own net to help the US to a 2–1 victory in a 1994 World Cup soccer game, the fear plain in his eyes as he said, "I don't want to go home." He was right. He flew home and a Colombian fan stuck a gun into a taxi, shouted "Thanks for the goal!" and killed him.

Standing alone in Walter Gretzky's hospital room in Brantford hours after the surgery following his brain aneurism, looking down at my friend and thinking how small and frail he looked as he slept, wondering if he'd ever awaken and how much of him was gone.

Mario Lemieux, snapping home the Wayne Gretzky pass that beat the Russians in the 1987 Canada Cup with the shot that made the eternal highlight reel. Lui Passaglia, kicking the field goal that gave the BC Lions a Grey Cup win over the Baltimore Stallions in 1994....

So many more...

But, more than any of the action shots there are the faces of people who made me laugh and others who told me stories of courage and determination and a kind of bravery almost beyond comprehension.

Let me leave you with these . . .

Willie Gets a Haircut

Calgary Sun, January 17, 1998

VANCOUVER—HE SQUARED HIS SHOULDERS and walked through the front door of the barber shop—15 years old, scared, and black. It was 1951, and Willie O'Ree was about to test the limits of a curious friendship.

He'd grown up in Fredericton, N.B., youngest child of 12 in the only black family in the city, so he knew the unwritten rules as well as he knew the ones set down in print in the games he'd always been able to play. One of them was that the barbers in the shops did not cut black people's hair.

There were no signs. There didn't have to be. It just was.

But there was a barber, Joe McQuade, who lived down Willie's street. He knew the kid was an athlete, had watched him play baseball. One day he took him aside and said, "Willie, you ever want your hair cut, come down to my house and I'll cut it for you."

For two years, Willie trudged down the street to Joe McQuade's house to get the haircut he couldn't get in the shop. Finally, he asked his friend a question.

"Mr. McQuade," he said, "What would you do if I came into your barber shop? Would you cut my hair?"

The white barber paused for a second. "Yes," he said, "I'd probably get a lot of grief for it, but I'd cut your hair."

Two weeks later, Willie O'Ree walked into the barber shop where several Caucasian barbers were clipping Caucasian hair. Even today he can remember the way the snipping stopped. "You could hear the silence," he says.

"Good morning, Mr. McQuade," he said.

The barber nodded. The two men awaiting their turns shifted uncomfortably, stiffly aware of the boy who shouldn't be there.

The boy sat there silently until a chair became available.

It wasn't Mr. McQuade's chair. The barber dusted off the customer, shook the hair to the floor, whisked off the seat—all without looking at the black boy sitting patient and still.

Willie could see his face in the mirror. "He didn't say 'Next!' or anything. He just fussed."

But the chair was empty. There were other customers waiting. Finally, he turned. "Are you next?" he asked.

Willie looked at him for a moment.

"No, thank you," he said politely. "I'll wait for Mr. McQuade."

There is no relish in Willie O'Ree's voice as he tells that story, no sense of did-I-fix-him. Someone had asked him what it was like, growing up the only black kid on white teams, a kid whose ancestors had arrived with the Loyalists, whose parents had been born in Gagetown, just outside Fredericton, a kid growing up with the realization that his colour made him from but not of. The story was his way of answering.

There were other brief references—the many minor hockey battles with those who wanted to try the black kid, the fight with Eric Nesterenko, the endured epithets, the two trips into the stands when the slurs became too hurtful to bear.

But when he'd finished—this man who 40 years ago Sunday became the first Negro ever to play in the National Hockey League by suiting up for the Boston Bruins—the image that stuck was of a 15-year-old boy, head up and heart pounding, pushing open the barber shop door and stepping across an invisible line into he knew not what.

Last November, Willie O'Ree went back to Fredericton. The house at 245 Charlotte Street where he'd been born was gone, replaced by an apartment block, but the house they'd moved into across the street at 212 was still there.

He sat down in front of it for a few minutes, and remembered the times that were.

Down, but not Out
Calgary Sun, July 27, 1998

SHE WILL HEAR OR READ OF SANG LAN, the 17-year-old vaulter who's been told she'll never walk again. A stumble landing a simple vault done a thousand times, and a life shattered in a millisecond.

Shattered, but not destroyed, she'll think. Not if the inside Sang Lan is the fighter she seems to be. She will follow the story, and sometimes she may cry. She knows the road ahead for Sang Lan. She has travelled every mile . . .

Her name was . . . well, never mind. Long ago I used it in telling this story, and she asked me not to do it again. She wasn't angry, but she neither wanted nor needed anyone's pity, and she didn't think her story was all that big a deal.

No names, then. But the story—forgive me, kiddo, but it still belongs in the light.

She was 19, a gymnast who'd missed her plane east for tryouts for the '76 Olympic Games. No problem. She'd catch the same flight next day. Meanwhile, she had another night with her friends.

Four of them were in the car, parked at a stoplight, when a drunk hit them from behind at 85 mph. The other three died. She was left quadriplegic.

We got to know each other in hospital. My daughter was in the bed next to hers, lost in a coma that would last three months. Maybe, for the long-haired girl in the hateful neck brace, the talking briefly pushed the nightmares away, as it did for me. One day a nurse mistook me for her father, and from then on she'd laugh and call me Dad.

I watched reality wash away denial. I watched her rail at the frustrating rehab, the clumsy efforts at moulding clay, the hours spent stumbling between parallel bars, trying to force dead limbs to work.

The gymnast in her, the girl who'd hurled through routines on the uneven parallel bars, rebelled at the hopelessness, the indignity. "Dad," she cried once, "they want me to try to walk like *this???* Don't they understand—I could *fly.*"

We took my daughter home, quadriplegic and brain damaged from a ski accident, and in the battles to give her some sort of life I lost track of the girl in the next bed. We heard that the strain had split her parents, that there'd been an insurance settlement, that she had her own home, specially equipped and ramped for a motorized wheelchair she could run with limited motions in one hand. We heard there'd been some bad times.

Then one day, maybe two years later, she phoned.

"Dad," she said, "can you get football tickets?"

"You mean on the wheelchair ramp?"

"No," she scoffed. "I mean seat tickets."

And she told me the rest of the story.

She'd gone back to school and was getting her degree. Yes, in the chair. No, there'd been no physical improvement. But she had help to, from and in class, and she was fine. And, oh yes, she'd met a boy.

He'd met her after the accident. He kept asking her out. She, fearing pity, kept saying no and putting up excuses. The heavy, motorized chair was the handiest. It was too awkward, too difficult to move. Out of the question.

One day he rang her doorbell and told her to look in the driveway. She did, and saw a truck. He'd bought it, he said, to carry the chair when they went out. Now, did they have a date, or didn't they?

"What could I say?" she giggled over the phone. "He'd bought a truck."

They went to football games. He'd drive the truck to the entrance, carry her to the seat, then go back and park the truck. They had good times and later, when the relationship had run its course, good memories.

It's been too many years since I've seen her. She got her degree, she has a successful career. Life has taken us different ways. But I thought of her Sunday, reading the report on Sang Lan, thinking of the times that face her, and taking heart from the words of the doctor who visited her. "Her spirit was uplifting," he said. "You had to be encouraged in her presence."

As was I, by another girl starting down the same road, 22 years ago.

The Chicken Pecks his Spots
The Province, August 7, 1979

THE GIANT ORANGE CHICKEN with the purple, yellow and orange head and the spindly yellow legs and griddle-sized yellow flat feet flopped seductively back on the hotel room bed. "Where do you want the girl?" the manager asked.

The chicken opened one wing. The delectable little honey recruited from the willing dozens in the hall crawled obligingly into his embrace.

Flashbulbs popped as they cuddled beak to cheek. For Ted Giannoulas, it was the end of another hard day at the office.

Friday night he was at a baseball game in Tacoma. This was Saturday afternoon, spent poolside entertaining the mob at Superflop V, the bellyflop diving salute to cholesterol. In three hours he would catch a plane to Chicago to open a supermarket. He didn't have a day off in July, won't likely have one in August. It's why he makes $100,000 a year jumping around in a chicken suit.

"Five or six more years like this," he says, "then I see The Chicken picking his spots. Like Sinatra, y'know? He doesn't play Caesars Palace every night, right?"

For those who've dropped in from another planet, The Chicken— *née* The KGB Chicken—is the mascot-for-hire who plays pro football, baseball and basketball games, turns up on national TV a lot, and has turned cheerleading into an art form.

He is the feathered fowl who runs the bases backwards and ends with a Pete Rose bellyflop slide; the barnyard badgerer who follows umpires around with a noose and puts the whammy on opposing pitchers; the Pulitzer pullet who sticks his beak into basketball huddles when there are seconds left in the game and somehow emerges unfried.

He was born in March of 1974 when San Diego radio station KGB hired a journalism and communications major named Ted Giannoulas for two dollars an hour to climb into a chicken suit as a promotion and hand out Easter eggs to kids.

It was supposed to last two weeks. Four and one-half years later he was still laying 'em in the aisles and turning down a $100,000-a-year offer from Ted Turner to bring his act to Atlanta. Eight months after that he was being sued for $200,000 by KGB and within a month—in a brand new suit—"I became a born-again chicken." Not bad for a kid from London, Ontario . . .

Ted Giannoulas pulls off the chicken head and wearily tosses it on the bed. The publicity photos are finished. The suit feels like a furnace. But he is still hyped by his performance—or, rather, The Chicken's.

"I don't see The Chicken as a mascot hanging around banging a drum and going 'Hi, kids!'," he says. "The Chicken is a comedian in the Harpo Marx sense. He gets away with things others might not because everybody knows The Chicken is his friend. He doesn't intrude. They can see he means no harm. His biggest fans are the referees and coaches—his biggest fans!"

When Giannoulas speaks of The Chicken it is in the third person. You can hear the capital letters. "How long can The Chicken go on? Well, Mickey Mouse just turned 50." It is Dr. Jekyll and Mr. Chicken. "I view The Chicken," he says, "as my son."

In many ways he is correct. There is Chaplin timing in some of his routines that makes him far more than a man in a chicken suit. When KGB and The Chicken parted company in May after a lawsuit over who owned the rights to the suit (the station won the decision but not the money), it put another guy in the suit and sent him out at a baseball game. He lasted 15 seconds. The crowd booed him off the field.

Giannoulas has his own explanation of the differences.

"The Chicken has an inbred sense of comedy, a high energy level and a thorough knowledge of sport. I know the games. I know when to get in, when to get out, when to improvise. I'm not a Chaplin freak, although I love some of his stuff. I appreciate the Three Stooges more now than I did as a kid. And Popeye, and vintage Bugs Bunny cartoons. See, *nobody* ever beat old Bugs. And nobody beats The Chicken."

Nobody beats him, nobody hates him, and nobody sees him. Like Batman, Spiderman and the four guys in the Kiss rock group, he changes to Ted Giannoulas, 5'4", 24 years old, from San Diego by way of Windsor, in the privacy of his room. The Chicken had to battle his way down the hall, averaging about two bikinied popsies per door. Ted Giannoulas can make the walk back unscathed and unnoticed.

"Movie stars would give millions for what I've got," he says. "Stardom and privacy at one time."

The act brought him recognition. The split with KGB and the resulting lawsuit gave him national impact.

"It was a philosophical difference," he shrugs. "The station saw The Chicken as a commercial tool, I saw him as a career. They'd taken the suit off a shelf in a costume shop. After The Chicken caught on they had a guy in Salt Lake City design the real Chicken suit, but they didn't copyright it. So in 1978 I flew up there and got the rights."

When KGB wouldn't let him freelance, he took the station call letters off the suit and worked anyway. The station sued and won. The

Chicken went underground for a month, only to emerge in an outfit virtually identical except for the colour—orange instead of red.

He stayed in San Diego, where he was given the keys to the city, where the mayor phoned and asked him to come out in support of his campaign, and where his autobiography, *From Scratch*, has sold 15,000 copies in the city alone.

"The Chicken was born out of their laughter and support," he says. "He couldn't leave them."

He is a phenomenon of his time. Women want to hold him, to cart him off to their rooms and take him to bed like a Teddy bear. "I'm like the guy at the party who puts on a lampshade and makes people laugh," he says. "There's nothing like the feeling. It's the greatest thing in the world."

And when the party is over he can take off his Chicken suit and walk away. Just like Batman.

Still Workin' His Side of the Street
The Province, April 28, 1981

AT NINE he was a ridge-runner, roaming the Appalachian Mountains of Virginia trapping fox, coon, possum, mountain hawk and, on a good day, skunk.

Skunks were best, says Sam Snead, "cause you trap one of them, you weren't goin' to school that day. No way!"

There wasn't much money—but then, there didn't have to be. The table in the house in Hot Springs, Virginia, was covered with wild game, "turkey, chickens, two or three kinds of preserves," and the five Snead boys and the sister would sit on the long bench next to it and there was always plenty for everybody, even if you were mostly barefoot.

"On skunk days," says Snead, sitting in his hotel suite sipping on a brandy, "my momma would meet me at the door and yell 'Don't you go bringin' them clothes in here! Take 'em outside and bury 'em.' That was how they'd get clean, you see. In the dirt.

"My mother," he said. "Lord, but she was strong. She could lift a barrel of flour up onto the wagon. You know what a barrel of flour weighed? 192 pounds.

"Happy days, y'know?" he sighed. "Really happy days."

Samuel Jackson Snead has come down the road a fair piece from Hot Springs, but he's carried the soul of it with him. He will be 69 come May 27, a living, breathing legend who plays the seniors golf tour and could still shoot the lights out if the putter would hold still. But he's at his best when he speaks of the tour that was, as opposed to the tour that is. Speak of Jack Nicklaus and there will be respect and admiration. Speak of Ky Laffoon or Lefty Stackhouse and the lights go on in his eyes.

"Laffoon was a tobacco chewer," he said. "He was always spittin.' Hit a gnat at 20 paces. Play behind him and you had the stuff all over you and your ball. Stackhouse, he'd get so mad he'd bite his own hand. One time I saw him throw his clubs in the lake. 'For five cents I'd jump in with 'em,' he says. And some guy says 'I'll give you five bucks.' 'Put it up,' says Lefty, and jumps in. He came out wetter'n a duck, took the money and said 'At least I beat this sumbich game for five dollars!'"

Those were different days, of course. The pro tour was just getting started when Sam Snead joined in 1937. In the early years you put up your own prize money—$50 a head—and played 36 holes in three days. You stayed alive as best you could, hustling when you had to, and California and Florida stops were best because you could pick oranges from the groves and hide them in the rough to save on meal money later. The professional golfer had not yet become America's guest when the kid from Hot Springs ambled onto the scene.

He was to win 135 tournaments and earn $620,000 in a career that's been reborn with the seniors tour and the Legends of Golf tournaments like the one he'll play June 8–14 at Capilano. But back then he was just Sam Snead, who'd swung his first sticks at rattlers and copperheads at home, then graduated to rocks and finally to golf balls, by accident.

He was a good high school halfback, a baseball pitcher and basketball player. He could run a ten-second 100, and got his start at play-for-pay in tennis earning 50 cents each time he whipped a spoiled brat, paid by the kid's father.

When he broke his hand playing football he began swinging a golf club because he thought it would knit better that way. Fuel for the legend was there almost from the start.

His first job was at the Homestead course in Hot Springs, as a clubmaker. It lasted, he says, two weeks and four days, until he was offered a job as pro at the nearby Cascades course. "No salary, just what you could hustle plus a sandwich and a glass of milk at lunch. I didn't make enough to pay for my laundry that first year, but boy, did I beat on them golf balls!"

He almost shot the job out from under himself. One day Alva Bradley, owner of the Cleveland Indians, was bending over on the fifth green when a ball delivered by Snead bounced once and hit him on the rear. He was going to have the kid fired for hitting his second shot while the foursome ahead was still on the green. "It wasn't his second shot," Snead's partner explained. "It was his drive." The hole was 335 yards long. "I really caught that one," he says with relish.

He has caught a few with that honeyed, rippling swing. He has over-driven a green 360 yards away. In 1959, at the Sam Snead Festival, he shot an outrageous 59. "For pure animal grace," wrote the late Grantland Rice, "the sight of Sam Snead murdering a tee shot is the acme of tigerish reflex in human form."

In 1945, on a bet, he shot successive rounds of 83, 82 and 81—playing with one hand. His left. Nine years later, recalling his boyhood days, he trimmed a piece of swamp maple with a bulge on one end, had the head balanced, and used it and a wedge to shoot a 76.

He is a horn player (1960 scouting report: "Can't improvise much, but he'll be in there blowing his brains out on the melody"), a man who made the coconut straw hat famous, a man whose earnings in today's dollars would be $8,500,000. But mostly, he is a legend with memories.

Dutch Harrison, whose biggest purses came from the wallets of club members who thought they could play, recalls the day he met the pre-legend Snead. He talked the kid into playing for money, shot his usual solid round—and got taken to the cleaners.

"Say, sure do thank you folks," the kid twanged to Harrison and his partner as he collected his money. "What time tomorrow you folks gonna be out here?"

"Son," Harrison said, "you work your side of the road and we'll work ours."

He's been working it almost half a century now. He fishes a little and golfs a lot and spends his home time on a farm tucked against the forest in Virginia. And when he closes his eyes and inhales, he can smell his momma's preserves.

One Push at a Time
The Province, March 22, 1985

HUNCHED DOWN in the wheelchair, the useless legs tucked almost to his chin, he suddenly looked so *frail*.

The muscles on the arms were still clearly defined under the striped T-shirt. The bulk of shoulder still showed promise of the strength he would need so desperately in the 18 months to come. But he was down there at waist level to the hundreds pressing around him to say good-bye, and as he ran his grease-encrusted racing gloves over the tires and blinked the moisture from his eyes, Rick Hansen didn't look like a hero at all. He looked like a small boy screwing up his courage to ride a pony or take a dare.

All at once, people in the parking lot at the Oakridge shopping mall were whispering the numbers:

"Twenty-five thousand miles! . . ."

"In 18 months! Seventy miles a day, three days a week. For 25,000 miles! . . ."

"Around the world! Hell, I couldn't wheel that thing around the block . . ."

If the figures had come to overwhelm Rick Hansen on this overcast Thursday morning it would be a temporary thing. Fourteen hours earlier, wheeling into the chaos of his West End apartment to find five people waiting to interview him or give him something or bring up another last-minute hitch in plans, he'd retreated briefly to the apartment block lounge, where there was a chance of some privacy.

"Tomorrow," he confided to a friend. "Tomorrow the easy part starts. Tomorrow, all I have to do is wheel . . ."

But yesterday, just for a second, he looked as though every one of those miles to come was a stone around his neck. It was an understandable reaction. The path that's brought him this far has been laced with minor miracles and major disappointments, each in its own way adding to his self-imposed obligation to succeed. They offer interesting contrasts.

A motor home was needed and there was no money. Suddenly, it was there, provided by Vanguard Trailers Ltd., and specially modified, right down to a hole in a panel so Hansen can slide off the end of his bunk and be in the bathroom. Expo 86, under whose banner Hansen will wheel as he tours the world, has provided some 200 Expo pins.

School kids sold oranges and washed cars to raise a few bucks for the fund. Prime Minister Brian Mulroney sent a congratulatory telegram—thus far in lieu of a cheque.

But the people were there. Hundreds of them, picking up the fund-raising appeal carried yesterday morning on virtually every radio station, and re-routing to Oakridge to be briefly a part of something they sensed could be great.

Some came in wheelchairs they could move themselves, some in motorized models steered by joysticks designed to accommodate limited hand movement. Some—the silent ones trapped by fate or circumstance inside their minds—came with parents or friends, seeking a glimpse of the young man who wants to raise ten million dollars for spinal-cord research that may some day set others free.

For Rick Hansen it all added up to an emotional overload. He was excited, inspired, overwhelmed—and I think, a little bit scared.

By now, as he pumps down the road toward San Francisco, that will have worn off. He's free now—free to focus muscle and mind and heart on a single goal, knowing that every turn of the wheels brings him that much closer to achieving it. But there was a moment there yesterday I will never forget.

The reception was held indoors. As he headed for the open doorway of the reception hall, the wheels of his chair hit the aluminum strip across the floor that stops the door as it shuts. The chair stopped dead.

Without a pause, Rick Hansen reversed the chair half a roll, threw it forward again, and rolled out to challenge the world.

The Kids in the Hall
Calgary Sun, March 12, 1998

VANCOUVER—WHEN DANNY WESLEY was 13 years old he tried to hitchhike on a train and lost both legs when he slipped under the wheels. A year later he was racing his walker down the hospital corridors with a kid named Rick Hansen.

They laughed a lot—Danny with his new artificial legs, Hansen with the braces he'd rigged out of plaster casts because the doctors said it would be months before he'd be ready to try real ones and he damned well wasn't going to wait.

But they competed. They were athletes and they had these problems, but athletes compete. So they went at it with what they had.

"Danny had a four-point walker and I had a two, so he was usually a bit slower," Hansen recalled later. "One time I got through a door before he did, reached behind me, and closed it.

"In rehab," he explained, "You learn to take your humour where you can."

They were in the initial stages then, each finding his own path through the disbelief, the fear, the self-pity where it would be so easy to quit. "We were kids," Hansen says. "And you can't always be brave. Sometimes, you have to cry."

The crying was private, the rehab a relentless push to who knew where.

If someone had suggested the day would come when they'd both make their living as motivational speakers, that they'd both become great athletes despite their disabilities, that Hansen would go round the world in a wheelchair, that Wesley would make his own world tour as a skier, tennis player, sprinter and marathoner, they'd have pointed the guy to the psych ward down the hall.

They were just two kids, competing as kids have always done, in the moments that put their fears on hold.

But the good things happened, all of them in their time, all of them earned. And they are still happening.

Dan Wesley's picture hit the front page here this week. He and Calgary's Stacey Kohut had finished one-two in the super-ski event for sit-skiers at the Paralympics in Nagano. A day earlier, Wesley had won the bronze in the downhill.

In the aftermath of the Winter Olympics it is not a major story, this wonderful thing that is happening this week in Nagano. Just 34 events in sports altered to fit the disabilities of those who can't play them as originally designed. But think about it.

Think about wanting to ski so badly that you strap your legless body into a seat attached to one ski, and hurl yourself down the mountain.

Think about crawling into a sled and pushing with your arms to race or play your own form of hockey.

Think about the courage to say "I will not let what happened control my life. I'm an athlete, damnit!"

This is Dan Wesley's story, and peripherally Rick Hansen's, only because they are two disabled athletes I happen to know. They are out there by the dozens, by the hundreds, pushing their chairs over tennis and basketball and volleyball courts in summer, hitting the hills and the rinks in winter, competing at the highest level they can.

Ten years ago during the Man in Motion tour, I watched a bunch of reporters climb into sleds in a rink in Quebec to try their hand at sledge racing. One by one, they barrelled into the end boards, unable to stop.

An eight-year-old in a cast that forced his legs apart and supported his degenerating spine reclaimed his sled and consoled the big person who'd borrowed it.

"Don't worry," he said. "You just gotta practise."

The Kid Next Door
Calgary Sun, November 5, 1999

MAPLE RIDGE, BC—They began to line up two and a half hours before the service—the very old to the very young, in suits and ties, coats and jeans, team jackets with the logos on the back, coming to say goodbye to one of theirs.

The formal memorial service for Greg Moore had been held the day before in Vancouver, a service for family and close friends and drivers and officials from the racing circuit that had been his life and ended it.

But this service wasn't about Greg Moore the race car driver, who died Sunday in that obliterating crash into the wall in California. This was about the kid they'd watched grow up, or shot pool with, or shared a pizza and a laugh with and basked in that megawatt smile.

This was about Maple Ridge, gathering to share a loss and relive the good times with the kid who never flew too fast or too high to remember the place that would always be home.

And so they came to the Maple Ridge Baptist Church, the only place in town big enough to hold them. They filled the 1,500 seats, spilled out into the tent that was supposed to hold 500 but probably held more, and into the church foyer, where there was room for 100 or so more as the fire marshal turned the other way.

Ric Moore was there, the man so close to the son he lost that they almost shared a soul. Greg's sister, Annie, and stepbrother James came up to receive the checkered flag, neatly folded, from the Vancouver Indy, because Greg Moore always wanted to see it go down as he flashed across the finish line, the winner in his own province.

CART publicist Rena Shanaman was there, recalling the time they had to haul Greg off the podium in Portland to get him back to Maple Ridge for his graduation, this kid next door who got his race driving licence three days after his 16th birthday and was on the podium after his first race five days later.

Neil Micklewright of the Player's Forsythe racing team was there, speaking eloquently without notes about his friend and employee because he'd tried to jot something down until he realized that Greg would get a great kick out of him standing there like an idiot not knowing what to say.

There were some tears, yes, but not many. It's said at too many such services that it is "a celebration of life," but in this case it fit.

Ric Moore told the crowd a story they probably all knew, about the day his Chevrolet dealership took a battered little go-kart as a trade-in, and how his little boy looked at it and fell in love. "He knocked down every drainpipe on our building at least once," he said, then choked a little as he added that he still had one of them, twisted and beaten up.

Alan Robbie, Greg's best friend, told of the endless times of growing up together, and the pool sessions with Greg and Ric, and how the last game every night would be for the Emperor of the Universe title.

One by one, the speakers stood amid the floral tributes that began to appear in front of the car dealership last Sunday when word of Greg Moore's death flashed through the town, and told stories not of Greg Moore the driver, but of Greg Moore the kid, the friend, the one who woke up every day smiling and knowing that good things were going to happen, and somehow made you feel the same way.

There was no talk of the evils of the sport that took their friend away, no laments that in another line of work he might be alive today.

In Maple Ridge, they know how much he wanted it, how hard he worked to get it. They know his last words on earth as he sped around that track in the instant before the crash were "Man! This is fun!"

He was one of theirs, knowing the dangers and respecting them, but doing what he was born to do. You can't ask an eagle to clip his wings.

New Link, Old Chain
The Province, January 24, 1988

HE SAT THERE at ringside in Atlantic City, heavy dark glasses covering his eyes, his puffy face frozen into immobility.

All around him the Beautiful People gossiped and chirped and waved at the TV camera—Kirk Douglas, Cheryl Tiegs, John McEnroe and Tatum O'Neal, billionaire Donald Trump, Don Johnson with a proprietary arm around Barbra Streisand, all there to see and to be seen. But Muhammad Ali, with them yet curiously alone, stared straight ahead in silence.

Once he would have stolen their spotlight and matched them quip for quip. Once he would have bounced around the ring during pre-fight introductions, giving it the Ali Shuffle or the Rope-a-Dope. Nobody ever played a crowd like Ali.

This man, this stranger, looked out into the blackness above them as he briefly touched his fingers to his lips and allowed himself to be led first to Larry Holmes' corner, then to Mike Tyson's. Only there did those lips move ever so slightly.

Holmes ignored him. Tyson nodded briefly, a man with other things on his mind. Then they cut to commercial, and Muhammad Ali was gone.

Did he know where he was? Did he understand that these men were about to fight for the heavyweight boxing title he'd held three times? Was there life in the eyes behind those glasses? Doctors have suggested that the cumulative years and the punches took their toll on his brain as they'd coarsened and slowed his speech. Did it cross his mind, I wonder, that he'd become another link in the chain . . . ?

October 1, 1980, Las Vegas. Ali is there to fight Holmes. But now he is leaning over the wheelchair of Joe Louis. He's refused to have his picture taken with this stroke-ridden caricature of the former great champion—not out of arrogance but out of respect for the champion that was. Now he whispers into Joe's ear:

"Does it hurt, champ?" he asks softly. "Does it hurt bad?"

Louis croaks an indecipherable reply. The following night, sitting in his chair at ringside, he stares fixedly at a spot off in one corner of the Caesars Palace parking lot as the fight begins. An attendant leans over and gently turns his head toward the ring.

"How did it happen?" Ali asks reporters, staring at the withered wreck in the chair. "Why did he come back that time? How did they let it happen?"

"Make you wonder if maybe you shouldn't be trying *this* come-back?" a guy asks.

Muhammad Ali, age 37, slips into the shuffle. "You're gonna see a miracle!" he chants. "A miracle . . . !"

October 2, 1980. Larry Holmes is discussing the Ali that was, as opposed to the man he would face that night.

"No chance," he says. "The man's got no chance. He's 37! His brain is making appointments his legs can't keep. Why's he wanna come back? Why?"

January 22, 1988. Larry Holmes, 38, is clubbed to the canvas three times in the fourth round before it's mercifully over.

"He's the greatest fighter in history," says 22-year-old Mike Tyson. "If he'd been like he was I would never have stood a chance."

At ringside, Muhammad Ali stares fixedly into nothingness as another link is forged in the chain.

Mongoose Memories
Calgary Sun, December 10, 1998

> *Archie Moore, who knocked out more opponents than anyone in the history of boxing, died Wednesday at a San Diego hospice. He was 85.*
>
> —News item

IN 1940, seven years a pro, Archie Moore was the world's fifth-ranked middleweight, and washing dishes at $4 a day on a train between Oakland and Ogden, Utah. Even then, nobody wanted a piece of the Ol' Mongoose.

He talked about that and other things on an afternoon in Edmonton eight years ago, an old black man in a blue pillbox hat sitting motionless in a hotel lobby, thinking perhaps of the many years when just sitting in a hotel lobby was denied him.

"The last time I fought?" he said. "Well, now, I guess that would have been about 1963. I stopped in Dallas on my way home to San Diego after fighting somebody in the east, and there was a wrestling card that night.

"Well, there was this truck I wanted, but it cost $4,000, which I didn't happen to have. So I phoned the promoter and said 'This is Archie Moore. Can you use me on the card?' He said sure, I could fight the main event. So I boxed this wrestler fellow and got the $4,000 and bought the truck."

A sly grin crept across his face.

"Course, I was in trouble then because I couldn't drive the truck, one of those big 16-wheeler things. So I had to have a boy come out by night coach from San Diego and drive it back for me."

Archie Moore was 72 that afternoon in Edmonton, or 74, or more likely 77 because his mother always insisted he was born in 1913, not four years later as he claimed when he bothered with approximations. He was there as George Foreman's "assistant trainer" for a bout with Ken Lakusta.

It was mostly an honorary thing, a gesture from a man trying to cheat time to another who'd long since put it down for the count. But there was a moment during training sessions when he gently moved a prelim kid away from the heavy bag, stepped into it, and in a brief flurry showed him how it should be done.

But now he was just sitting, hauling back the memories and musing on how it might have gone were he just starting out. "I don't fret over it," he said softly, "but sometimes I wonder . . ."

Archie Moore fought 228 times in 29 years, and about the only mistake he made was being too damned good. By the time the big names were ready to fight him, he was getting by on guile and memories and the art of making do. "Give him a ball of steel wool," it was written, "and he'll knit you a stove."

He was 39 when he finally won the light-heavyweight crown from Joey Maxim (and held it for nearly a decade), 42 when he dropped Rocky Marciano early but lost in the ninth, 45 when he climbed off the canvas four times to beat Canada's Yvon Durrell, 49 when he fought an up-and-comer named Cassius Clay. "He laid a trap for a tiger," he chuckled, "and all he caught was a mangy old fox. He stopped me in four and danced around my ancient carcass."

We talked for an hour. Then he excused himself briefly and came back with a scrapbook, 10 pages or so of old fight clippings and pictures laboriously assembled and pasted, taped or stapled to the pages, the cover a pencil sketch of the master in his late prime, sitting on a stool in the corner, towel draped over his shoulders.

"I make these for charities, auctions and such," he said. "Would you like this one?"

It's in front of me now, his signature in the top corner, as the magical afternoon comes flooding back with the news that he's gone.

He spoke of his poetry, of the boys club he ran in San Diego in his personal war against drugs, of the boy he'd met at the training session that day who wanted to be a fighter and had no place to sleep.

"Oh, my wife is going to give me heck," he chuckled. "Looks like I'm takin' another one home."

He rose then, shook hands, and thanked me for my time. Two steps toward the elevator, he turned back.

"You know that fight with the wrestler?" he said. "It may not have been *exactly* my last fight, because it seems to me I had a couple when I got home . . ."

Rest easily, champ. And thanks for the memories.

Rest In Peace, Percy
Calgary Sun, August 8, 2001

IN THE WAKE of Donovan Bailey's farewell lap, the words "greatest Canadian sprinter ever" were thrown about with great abandon. They may even be correct.

But I'll take Percy Williams.

No Canadian sprinter posted a better time than Donovan Bailey. At least not running stock instead of modified. The world saw him blaze to gold in Atlanta. It's there on tape for the ages, in blazing colour: Donovan Bailey running a 9.84 100 metres.

But I'll still take Percy Williams.

There is no tape on Percy, who went to Amsterdam in 1928, just some grainy black-and-white photos of this unknown 20-year-old Canadian, 125 pounds on a good day—"as frail as a frightened fawn," it was written then.

He was there as Canadian champion, which meant so much in those days that a year earlier he hadn't even been allowed to run in the Canadian championships. The Amateur Athletic Union man was sure Percy was no good, so he used the train ticket to Hamilton himself.

Percy got there because an old friend bought his ticket. His coach, Bob Granger, made it by waiting tables on a CPR diner, as he would do again a year later to come back for the Olympic trials, after which he got to Amsterdam by working on a cattle boat.

At the Canadians it was discovered that the Hamilton track had only five lanes instead of the then-regular six. So they flipped a coin to see which of two Western Canada runners would compete in the final. Percy lost, and went home.

The medical records on Percy Williams said he had a damaged heart, the result of rheumatic fever as a child. But Amsterdam saw his heart in the 100-metre final, where he pulled away from the field for gold, and again the next day when he did the same in the 200.

The times were not great, but respectable for the new track whose softness his American rivals blamed for his victories. When he went on tour in the US later that year and won 21 of 22 indoor races, a Vancouver columnist wryly reported that "the tracks must have been made of soft wood."

In 1930, Williams set the then-world 100 metres record at 10.3 seconds. It stood for 11 years, the same time Jesse Owens posted in winning at the '36 Olympics in Munich.

Percy's career ended early. Forty yards from the tape in the first British Empire Games in '31, he tore a thigh muscle, but kept going and won anyway. The damage might have been corrected, but Canada didn't have a team doctor.

It soured him. Still Canada's best sprinter, he could no longer run with the world. He competed in the '32 Olympics in Los Angeles, and never attended another track meet, either as athlete or spectator.

And in 1982, when the pain of his arthritic knees became unbearable, Percy Williams, named Canada's greatest Olympic athlete, climbed into his bathtub with his shotgun, and ended his star-crossed life.

It is no slight to Donovan Bailey, this personal choice of Percy Williams and, perhaps, Harry Jerome in second place—Harry Jerome, who co-held both the world 100-metre record in 10 seconds flat and the 100 yards in 9.1 seconds, also beat near-impossible physical odds, and died of a brain seizure at age 42.

Comparing eras is a chancy game. Conditions change, training methods improve, there is funding available to smooth some of the rough spots.

Percy Williams had no A-card funding, no recognition, no chance for endorsements. He was just a skinny little kid who ran his damaged heart out in circumstances that I suspect would drive today's best into snit-filled retirement. We have never been better represented.

God, Fleet Feet—and The Giz
The Province, November 27, 1987

COUNTING HIS PARENTS, there were 11 people in the three-room house in the Memphis ghetto where Henry "Gizmo" Williams was born and spent the first 15 years of his life. All but four are now dead.

Multiple sclerosis took his mother first, but not without a fight. It dragged her down slowly and moved on to claim his brother Milton and sister Barbara. Two years ago it took Edgar, the eldest, the one who'd become a father to the rest of the family when the parents divorced. In the years between, sister Charlene died of a drug overdose, brother Ross was shot and killed by a stray bullet from a robbery across the street, and his father died in a fire.

"I used to think about it," admits the Giz. "You know, wondering whether I had it [MS], whether it was going to get me, too. But I quit that. Now I just let the Lord guide me."

He says it matter-of-factly, minus the me-and-God overtones of post-game jockdom. "When I was 15 I moved from Memphis to live with Aunt Urshalean Dorsey in Tunica, Mississippi. She was a strong, church-going lady. When I didn't want to go, she made me. And every time I came out, I felt better. I don't know why, I just did."

The house was bigger than the one in Memphis. It had to be. Urshalean had her own kids and family. "About 21 of us in three or four bedrooms," he recalls. He spent four years there—happy years, because while there might not have been much, there always seemed to be enough.

But then, happiness always did come easily to the Gizmo.

"In Memphis it wasn't the best house, but I had a place, and food and clothes. If somebody else had something better, well, that was them. I remember I wanted Converse running shoes, but they cost $16. My friend had them and I was running around in three-dollar shoes. But I just told myself his were new and mine were, too."

He knew about money and the things it could buy. ("My brother Otis and me were the youngest, so we were really tight. We shared everything, and it had to be even. If he had 25 cents we'd split it, ten cents each, and throw the nickel away so nobody had more.") But only once was he tempted to take the easy way that was a way of life in the mean streets of the ghetto.

"About five of us decided we'd steal a bicycle. We did it, and we got caught, and they took us home in a police car. I was sitting there in the back seat like in a steel cage. I told myself 'I'll never do this again.' I wanted my freedom."

Drugs were also something for someone else if that was their choice.

"What I learned was, find out who you are. I know how to adjust to people. I started to learn in high school. If you're my best friend and do drugs, that's you. I'll still be your friend. I'll have a beer, but if my friends see me with one they might come and take it from me and say 'Man, that's not you!'"

Given the conditions, it was an attitude that had to be built on a rock of pure stubbornness. And that the Gizmo had in spades.

Football had grabbed him in elementary school, where he played only because the coach paid the $30 registration fee. It never let go. Coming out of high school as a track specialist with world-class speed, he was 5'4" tall, weighed 155 pounds, and resented anyone who suggested he was too small to play.

The football coach at the University of Mississippi tried it and Gizmo went home and tore up the four-year track scholarship the school had given him. His lady gym teacher did it, and when he turned pro with the Memphis Showboats after two years at Northwest Mississippi Junior College and two years at East Carolina University leading the nation in kickoff returns, he rushed back to the school to tell her.

He chose the Showboats for the same reason. "I always said if there was a pro team in Memphis that was where I'd be," he said. "Just to show them."

There were NFL clubs interested when the Showboats folded, but by that time he'd talked to the Edmonton Eskimos' personnel man, Frankie Morris. He didn't know where Edmonton was—"Take a map," Morris advised him, "and look on top of Montana"—but he agreed to come anyway and now he's in the Grey Cup game Sunday against the Toronto Argonauts.

He is a pleasant picture, sitting in an easy crouch against the wall at BC Place stadium. He smiles a lot, tells his story matter-of-factly, and talks of Otis and Larry, the brothers still alive, and of his five-year-old daughter from junior college days, Paris Nicole, who lives with her mother.

He says he will teach his children that life is a gamble, that things don't come easily, and that the best things won't be there just because Daddy is a pro football player. Life, he says, is for living and trying and remembering all that is good.

The Gizmo: bigger now than in college days—two inches taller and 26 pounds heavier—muscular, but still without the look of a pro football player, a fireplug who's been clocked at 4.1 to 4.9 seconds over 40 yards and says he doesn't believe there's a man in football anywhere who's faster.

Some day, in a year, perhaps, when his contract is up, he may go to the NFL to find out. All it will take is someone to say he can't.

Teresa Fantillo: The Real Numbers Game
Calgary Sun, March 30, 1996

SHE STOOD AT THE PODIUM, slender and big-eyed under one of those chic slashes of colour that are the badge of the breast-cancer fighters— the hats and scarves and caps and tams that cover the shorn heads and bravely try to cover the fear.

Teresa Fantillo, age 32. Wife of Dino, mother of Gillian, seven, and Sophie, four. Teresa Fantillo, breast-cancer victim, trying to get across a message no one wanted to hear.

She knew she was in tough. This was a Vancouver Grizzlies' luncheon, and while the Canadian Breast Cancer Foundation (BC Chapter) was to benefit from the team's charitable enterprises, she was there only as a representative, given two minutes at the end, after the Grizzlies' shoe raffle, to catch a restless, mostly male audience peering at wrist watches and anxious to be gone.

"GM Place," she said, "has a seating capacity of over 17,000. Imagine, if you will, 17,000 female fans at tomorrow's game against Sacramento. That is the number of women diagnosed with breast cancer last year, and the number that will be diagnosed again this year. That is 17,000 mothers and daughters, grandmothers, sisters, wives and friends.

"I hazard a guess that there are approximately 5,400 professional athletes in North America—hockey players, skaters, golfers, tennis players, race car drivers, soccer players, basketball players. Now, imagine if this entire membership of professional athletes was wiped out *every year.*

"This represents the number of women who died of breast cancer in Canada last year. That number has not changed in years."

No one was looking at a wrist watch now, or inching toward an exit. The Grizzlies, the dignitaries, the crowd, the media—every eye was pinned on the young woman in the bold, brave hat, putting a face on the unspeakable.

"As ugly as the disease is," she said, "the treatment is even uglier. Losing a breast is usually followed by highly toxic chemotherapy that leaves even the strongest of us feeling like we would rather die than have another treatment. Living without hair has been a big challenge for me. I look forward to burning all my caps when my hair grows back. All but my Grizzlies' one, of course . . ."

Teresa Fantillo sits in her Burnaby living room, serving tea and cookies. The hair has grown back into an attractive, close-cropped look, showcasing eyes that sparkle and roll with the joy of laughter as she hears the stereo shift into the Eagles doing *Get Over It.*

"Don't I wish," she says.

Her chemo and radiation treatments are over, but the battle is not and never will be. For breast-cancer survivors there is no magical test, no finish line. Every three months, or six, or whatever, she'll live with the knot in her stomach waiting for the test results that will stretch the happiness until the next one, or tell her that the enemy is back and the fight begins anew.

That speech to the Grizzlies' luncheon has left her much in demand as a face, speaker and message carrier in the other fight, the one to raise public awareness and with it the funds for the research that might some day slay the loathsome dragon. She does them all and looks for more, and only she knows at what cost.

"You know what cancer is?" she asks. "It's something someone else gets. Not someone I know, or someone in my family, not me. Maybe, because I'm 32, I can help get the message across that the threat is there for everybody and it's got to be fought."

"Do you ever get tired of being brave?" she's asked.

"Not yet," she says. "Not yet."

In August, 1998, I had to write a post script.

I phoned Teresa. "How you doing?" I asked.

"Well," she sighed, "I'm wearing caps again."

The cancer had returned, worse than ever. This time, there was no hope. "But don't worry," she said. "It's going to be okay."

She had a new goal, you see. She wanted to stay alive to see her kids for one more Christmas. She kept that in front of her through the chemo and the pain and the numbing weariness, refusing to give up hope.

She didn't make it. In late November, the monster won. Teresa Fantillo died at 35.

She'd be happy to know the Grizzlies are back, young and rich and healthy, playing their children's game. Some of them might even remember her, the big-eyed, beautiful girl who came to their luncheon one day to speak of the unspeakable, and shone with an inner light.

She asked them that day, asked all of us, to help slay the monster. It's still out there. She would not want us to forget.

The Pride of Billy Gauld
The Province, July 7, 1989

HE FIRST CAUGHT THEIR EYE on their early-morning jog, a boy in his late teens or early 20s delivering *The Province* at as fast a clip as his dragging left leg would allow. He never stopped, they said. He jogged in and out of the yards, he jogged down the street, always smiling, always upbeat. There was obvious physical impairment: the leg, a left arm that wasn't functioning quite right, a slur to the voice. But whenever they talked to him, they went away feeling good.

"His name is Billy—Gould, Guard, something like that," they said. "We think he's a great story, but we can't get anybody interested. They say it's no big deal. And we thought maybe you . . ."

I did, and I owe them. This, then, is the story of an athlete named Billy Gauld . . .

Billy Gauld is 24 years old. He has cerebral palsy, some mental retardation, and three jobs.

He delivers *The Province* in the morning, *The Sun* in the afternoon, near his home in the Kerrisdale area. In between he was working four days a week, 11 a.m. to 3 p.m., walking a sandwich board advertising a shaver shop. He's cut that back to two days a week now, because he's about to start job training as an assistant stock boy at a 7-Eleven store in Richmond. If that works out, he says he'll quit one paper route. One, not both.

But there'll be no work this weekend.

Today, Billy Gauld is in Campbell River, competing as a soccer player in the BC Special Olympics Summer Games 1989. He'll be one of 570 athletes and 150 coaches billeted in two schools, sleeping in the classrooms and the gym according to sport: soccer, power-lifting, track and field, bowling, rhythmic gymnastics and swimming. He could have entered the track and field or power lifting events, but it's one competition per athlete, and he opted for soccer on the "B" team, where he plays forward.

It is a major event, and he went in confident that all that jogging would pay off. He'd be strong. He could run all day. He was ready—and if the team won, there'd be a spot in the national championships.

But before he left, he took care of business: He checked with both newspapers for permission to take the weekend off. When they asked who'd do the route, he broke into a big grin.

"M-O-M," he said.

Mom is Janet Gauld and yes, she admits, she does the route sometimes. But not often. John Ko of *The Province* circulation department gave Billy his route eight years ago. "When the weather was bad and we had kids phoning in sick, Billy would be out there doing his job," he says. "Billy didn't just have the route. Billy had pride."

He's kept that route without a break. Five years ago he decided he could handle an afternoon route, too. They, and the Special Olympics, have been a major force in his life.

"Special O brought him friends," Janet Gauld says. "They do things together. The paper routes—we go to the Arbutus Mall and people know him. We walk in Kerrisdale and they stop to talk to him. He's accepted."

Special O . . .

Janet Gauld is secretary for the Vancouver chapter now. They get a small government grant and some private donations, but mostly they hold car washes and garage sales, sell raffle tickets and work to carry their own weight. And they see the results every day in the eyes of athletes like Billy Gauld, who set Olympian goals and learn faster than any of us that the reward is in the pursuit as much as in the capture.

No, it's not a big story. There are hundreds out there like it. The sadness of Special O is that it never runs short of competitors. But when you're up to here with steroids and gambling and tales of sulky millionaire jocks, give yourselves a break. Close your eyes, and think of Billy Gauld.

Index

Akiyama, Leilani, 197–198
Akiyama, Mariko, 197–198
Ali, Muhammad, 224, 232, 258, 273–274
America's Cup, 76, 209–210, 211
Anaheim Ducks, 154
Ardan, Van, 178, 179
Ashton, Brent, 94–96
Ashton, Susan, 94–96
Axen, Gunilla, 250–251

Bailey, Donovan, 276, 278
ballroom dancing, 157–159
Barrett, Danny, 137
baseball, 14, 164, 263
BC Lions, 16, 126–127, 133
BC Place, 166
Becker, Boris, 190
Bellegarrigue, Stephanie, 178, 179
Bettman, Gary, 81–82, 87
Bias, Lennie, 179
Bishop, Eric, 60–61
Borland, Bruce, 178, 179
Boston Bruins, 99
boxing, 224–225, 231–232, 239–240
bridge, 21–22
Brister, Bubby, 252
Buchan, John, 33, 34
Buffalo Sabres, 99
Butler, Tom, 31

Calgary Flames, 98
Campbell, Hugh, 138
Casey, Tom "Citation", 55–56
Cats (musical), 67–68
Chamberlain, Wilt, 256–257
Champion, Jim, 40, 57
Cherry, Don, 86, 208
Chicago Blackhawks, 98, 101

Clarke, Venolyn, 204
Cobb, Ty, 164–165
Coleman, Jim, 101–102
Comaneci, Nadia, 180–182, 203
cricket, 155–157
curling, 19–21

Davidson, Tiger Al, 53–54
Detroit Red Wings, 96, 98
diving, 31
Dobson, Ken "the Dobber," 56–58

Eaton's, 81–82, 171
Eckhardt, Shawn, 188
Edmonton Oilers, 98, 158
Edmonton, 17–19
Escobar, Andrés, 258
Evanshen, Terry, 128–130

Fantillo, Teresa, 280–282
FIFA World Cup, 78, 113, 114–116, 199–200, 258
fishing, 14–15
Flutie, Doug, 140–142
football, 63–65, 112–114, 117–118, 122–123
Fraley, Robert, 178, 179
Fratriano, Jimmy "The Weasel," 225

Gaudaur, Jake, 119
Gauld, Billy, 282–284
Giachetti, Richie, 226–227
Giannoulas, Ted, 263–264
Gillooly, Jeff, 188–189
Giraud, Butts, 31–32
GM Place, 247
Graf, Steffi, 190
Greene, Sammy, 130–133
Gretzky, Mary, 48–50

Gretzky, Walter, 102–103, 104–105
Gretzky, Wayne
    and Mary Gretzky, 48–50
    retirement, 102–105
    trading cards, 71, 163
    and Walter Gretzky, 102–105
Grey Cup, 55, 56, 117–119, 143–145

Hansen, Rick, 268–271
Harrison, Dutch, 267
Hartford Whalers, 98
Hawkshaw, R. Crichton, 38–40
Henderson, Paul, 258
Hewitt, Foster, 99–100
Hilterson, Butch, 31
hockey
    and Eaton's, 81–82, 171
    fans, 205–206
    government subsidies of,
        193–194
    and National Hockey League, 28,
        98–99, 147, 192
    and Olympics, 89
    pools, 83–84
    and religion, 191–193
Hockey Night in Canada, 86, 99, 208
Hodler, Marc, 21
Holmes, Larry, 108, 258, 274
Holyfield, Evander, 226, 229–230,
    232–233
Homer, Lawrence "Sonny," 142–143
horse racing, 152–154

Ingle, Paul, 239

Johnson, Ben, 203–204
Johnson, Joe, 47–48

Kearney, Jim, 38, 39
Kelly, Brian, 122–123
Kepley, Danny Ray, 138–140
Kerrigan, Nancy, 186–187, 190
King, Don, 227–228
Korbut, Olga, 181

Kournikova, Anna, 245
Kreig, Michael, 178, 179
Kusserow, Lou, 55–56

Lan, Sang, 260–261
Lemieux, Mario, 50, 258
Lindburgh, Pelle, 179
Los Angeles Kings, 98, 205

Manley, John, 195–196
marathons, 213–215
Martin, Casey, 200–201
Matthews, Don, 127, 131
McLaughlin, Jack, 101, 237–239
Minnesota North Stars, 99
Montreal Canadiens, 98
Moore, Archie, 274–276
Moore, Greg, 271–273
Murray, Dave, 51–53
Murray, Jim, 18
Musso, Johnny, 124

National Basketball Association
    (NBA), 159–160
National Football League (NFL),
    169–170
National Hockey League (NHL), 28,
    98–99, 147, 192, 193
NBA. See National Basketball
    Association
New York Islanders, 98
New York Rangers, 98
NFL. See National Football League
NHL. See National Hockey League

O'Ree, Willie, 259–260
Olson, Lisa, 72, 73
Olympic Games, 106–108, 253
    1980 boycott of, 182–184
    inclusion of new sports, 21–22,
        157–159
    security of, 187, 190
Orser, Brian, 177
Ottawa Senators, 90, 92–93